Chicken Soup for the Soul.

Thanks to My Mom

D1056280

Chicken Soup for the Soul: Thanks to My Mom
101 Stories of Gratitude, Love, and Lessons
Amy Newmark, Jo Dee Messina

Published by Chicken Soup for the Soul Publishing, LLC www.chickensoup.com
Copyright © 2015 by Chicken Soup for the Soul Publishing, LLC. All Rights Reserved.

The publisher gratefully acknowledges the many publishers and individuals who
granted Chicken Soup for the Soul permission to reprint the cited material.

Photo of floral arrangement on front cover—Teleflora's Sunny Day Pitcher of Daisies—
courtesy of telefora.com.
Back cover photo of Jo Dee Messina courtesy of Krista Lee of Krista Lee Photography.
Interior photo courtesy of iStockPhoto.com/anamed (©anamed).
Interior photo of Amy Newmark courtesy of Susan Morrow at SwickPix.
Interior photo of Jo Dee Messina courtesy of John Zocco.

Cover and Interior Design & Layout by Brian Taylor, Pneuma Books, LLC

Distributed to the booktrade by Simon & Schuster. SAN: 200-2442

Publisher's Cataloging-In-Publication Data
(Prepared by The Donohue Group, Inc.)

Chicken soup for the soul : thanks to my mom : 101 stories of gratitude,
 love, and lessons / [compiled by] Amy Newmark [and] Jo Dee Messina.

  pages ; cm

 ISBN: 978-1-61159-945-9

  1. Mothers--Literary collections. 2. Mothers--Anecdotes. 3. Mother and child--Literary
collections. 4. Mother and child--Anecdotes. 5. Anecdotes. I. Newmark, Amy. II.
Messina, Jo Dee, 1969- III. Title: Thanks to my mom : 101 stories of gratitude, love,
and lessons

HQ759 .C45 2015
306.874/3   2015930163

PRINTED IN THE UNITED STATES OF AMERICA
on acid∞free paper

25 24 23 22 21 20 19 18 17 16 15   01 02 03 04 05 06 07 08 09 10 11

Chicken Soup for the Soul.

Thanks to My Mom

101 Stories of Gratitude, Love, and Lessons

Amy Newmark
Jo Dee Messina

Chicken Soup for the Soul Publishing, LLC
Cos Cob, CT

Chicken Soup for the Soul

Changing lives one story at a time™

www.chickensoup.com

Contents

❸

~Maternal Mischief~

❹

~Love and Acceptance~

❺
~The Best Cheerleaders~

❻
~The Wisdom of Mothers~

7

~Mom Was Right~

8

~My Mother the Teacher~

9

~The Other Moms in Our Lives~

Introduction

Gratitude makes sense of our past, brings peace for today,
and creates a vision for tomorrow.
~Melody Beattie

There is a fifteen-year age difference between my oldest sibling and myself. If you asked the four of us kids to describe our mother, who she was, and what she was like, I bet you would get four totally different answers. My mother was twenty-five and a newlywed when she had my eldest sister. By the time I came along she was forty with three other children. Her marriage was not that new and exciting by then, and in fact she would be divorced within five years. She also didn't have the energy that she did as a twenty-five-year-old when her first child was born.

So I had a very different mother than any of my siblings. She made her mark on each of us in a very positive way, but for each of us it was a different experience. And that's what I got from this collection of great stories as well—101 different experiences. There are many different kinds of Moms, many different ways to be a mom and still be the perfect mom for your children.

Many of us have a preconceived notion of just what it is a "mom" should be: a teacher, a caregiver, a shoulder to cry on, a font of all wisdom? Is a mom a Clair Huxtable or a Carol Brady? A Lorelai Gilmore or a Claire Dunphy? They all have it going on. I think what we look for in a mother is defined by our own experiences. And that is what made putting this volume together so fascinating... and fun. My coauthor Amy Newmark and I got to choose from thousands of stories that were submitted for this book. We left a lot of great stories by the wayside, but we are confident that the ones we chose represent all the different types of mothers out there. The unifying factors that we saw in these stories about terrific moms were their selfless love, their passionate interest in their children's dreams and lives, and their lifelong commitment to their kids, even if they were juggling other children, jobs, volunteer work, husbands, and housework.

Being a mom myself, I put massive pressure on myself to be "perfect" with my children. Is that even possible? These stories opened my eyes to the reality that what is important to each of us is different. But whatever our priorities, our kids appreciate what we choose to do for them. As a mother of very young children, looking ahead to many more years of hard work, I found it encouraging to read about how much children appreciate the sacrifices their mothers made for them.

You need appreciation when you are a mother! And that's the key here. This book is a gigantic "Thank You" to all the moms out there. It's your way to say thank you to your own special mother who poured her heart and all her effort into making you who are today. To all the moms out there who are reading this, who have "been there, done that," you are appreciated. You'll get that when you read these stories and you see the outpouring of love and thanks from our writers.

In Chapter 1—"Great Role Models"—you'll read about my mom and what she taught me, and you'll also read about the great examples that other moms set for their children. Donna Finlay Savage, for example, describes how her mom bravely taught her kids to live without prejudice in the South during the early days of the civil rights movement. And Alisa Edwards Smith tells us how her mom taught her to "fake it till you make it," something we all sometimes need to do when we are not feeling quite confident enough about a new challenge or opportunity.

Moms can be incredibly strong, and in Chapter 2—"Rising to the Challenge"—you'll meet some very impressive moms who handle all kinds of situations with great aplomb. Amy talks about her mom's stroke and how she bravely and diligently recovered from it, returning to her normal active life. And Connie Pombo used her mom's own example fighting cancer to handle her own breast cancer when she was diagnosed.

Amy and I decided to look at the lighter side of life in Chapter 3 — "Maternal Mischief." After all, our mothers can be a hoot! You'll read about how Jody Lebel's mom crept into a tattoo parlor to see if they could get Sharpie cat whiskers off her face, and how Eva Schlesinger and her mom inadvertently snuck contraband fruit into the U.S. and then had to scarf down the evidence right in front of a Customs agent.

We all want our moms to be proud of us, even when we're adults. In Chapter 4 — "Love and Acceptance" — you'll meet moms who surprised their own kids by being more open-minded and loving than they ever imagined, whether their kids were coming out to them, being obnoxious teenagers, or just being unappreciative. And you'll read Joe Ricker's story about how he never understood how much his teen mother loved him until she showed him her cache of artwork and letters after he rebelliously eloped.

Chapter 5 — "The Best Cheerleaders" — reminds us who's really there for us at all times no matter what. It's our moms, who are always willing to share our dreams and help us make them come true. Larry Miller, a successful journalist, tells us how his mother steered him on the right course to his writing success by telling him to write about what he knew. And Maril Crabtree ends up finishing every project she ever starts, including a thesis and a law degree, because of her mom's wise motivational words.

Harriet Beecher Stowe, a New England girl like myself, said, "Most mothers are instinctive philosophers." And that's why we made Chapter 6 — "The Wisdom of Mothers" — to pass on some great advice and sage thinking. Mark Leiren-Young talks about how his mom did nothing wrong and everything right when she raised him as a latchkey kid. He learned all about responsibility, discipline, and even how to cook. Since my mom raised me the same way, I loved Mark's story.

Did your mom ever fiercely defend you or stand up for your rights? Amy and I both have stories about our moms doing that, so we loved the stories in Chapter 7 — "Mom Was Right." Even when Kathy Lynn Harris's mother embarrassed her by not letting her go on a sports team trip when the roads were icy, she knew she was right. And how about all those things that your mom insisted on when you were a kid that you swore you would never do to your own kids… except that now you are! You'll love Carol Commons-Brosowske's story about having the "meanest mother in town," one she emulates now that she is a mother herself!

Teaching our kids is one of the most important things that we do, and various grown children thank their mothers for that in Chapter 8 — "My Mother the Teacher." Bill Jager tells a fascinating story about how his mom was his kindergarten teacher in his rural town, where school didn't start till the first grade. And we loved Elizabeth Greenhill's story about how her mom made the family go back to the bank to return money the teller had given her in error. It was a great lesson for Elizabeth and her siblings.

As I read through these stories, I realized "mom" is defined in myriad ways. Some people consider their "mom" to be a person who isn't even biologically or adoptively connected to them, but who still served the "mother" role. Johnny Tan talks about the nine mothers he has had throughout his life — yes, nine — in Chapter 9, "The Other Moms in Our Lives." And Chris Rainer talks about how she came to love and rely on her stepmother, regretting how she had not embraced her when she first came into her life.

You know, we women tend to be self-deprecating. We wonder if we are "enough." I wrote a song about this a couple of years ago. It's called "Me." My sons look at me and they see the world. I look at them and see the same! But sometimes, when you are a mom, and your kids are relying on you, or they are grown and you wonder how you did, you can feel a bit like an imposter. You might think, "Hey, it's just little old me. Who am I to think that I can do this mothering thing?" That's what my song is about. One of the lines — "When I look in the mirror all I see is me" — pretty much sums it up. But it's clear from reading these stories that it will all work out. We moms rock! And we are "enough." So I say "thanks to my mom" and thanks to all you moms reading this special volume. I hope it will make you smile, laugh out loud, and even tear up a few times. And overall, I hope it makes you feel loved and appreciated, because you clearly are!

~Jo Dee Messina

ME

I'M SOMEBODY'S DAUGHTER
SOMEBODY'S FRIEND
A SHOULDER TO LEAN ON
NO MATTER WHEN

I'M SOMEBODY'S TEACHER
WHEN THEY DON'T UNDERSTAND
GOT A SEAT IN THE BLEACHERS
I'M THE WORLD'S BIGGEST FAN
OH WELL

I WISH I WAS HALF THE WOMAN I'VE GOT TO BE
I WISH I HAD ALL THE ANSWERS RIGHT IN FRONT OF ME
I'M EVERYTHING TO EVERYONE AND I'M SCARED AS I CAN BE
BECAUSE WHEN I LOOK INTO THE MIRROR ALL I SEE IS ME

I'M SOMEBODY'S SWEETHEART
SOMEBODY'S GIRL
SOMEONE'S DIRECTION TO FIND THEIR WAY IN THIS WORLD

I'VE GOT TO BE PERFECT
EVEN WHEN I FEEL BAD
I'VE GOT TO KEEP GIVING
WHEN I'VE GAVE ALL I HAD
OH

CHORUS

WHEN I FEEL UNCERTAIN
I'M ON MY KNEES TO PRAY
I KNOW THAT IT'S ALL WORTH IT
BUT AT THE END OF THE DAY

CHORUS

IS SOMEBODY'S DAUGHTER
SOMEBODY'S GIRL
SOMEONE'S DIRECTION TO FIND THEIR WAY IN THIS WORLD

Use this link for Jo Dee's performance of "Me"
www.jodeemessina.com/chickensoup

Chapter 1

Thanks to My Mom

Great Role Models

The String that Binds Our Hearts

Even when tied in a thousand knots, the string is still but one.
~Rumi

I still remember it vividly. It was my first day of kindergarten and I didn't want to go in. My mother and I pulled up in front of the school and parked along the curb, behind the big yellow busses. No matter how my mom tried to calm my nerves, it wasn't working. I didn't want to get out of the car. I didn't want to go inside and leave her. I just wanted to go back home and spend the day around the house with my mother.

As I cried, my mother told me the magical truth that has carried me through many a challenge. "You can go into school because I will be with you," she said. I asked her how that could be. "There is this string that goes around my heart and ties around yours. No matter where you go or what you do, the string will always be there connecting us." That calmed me down, and after a bit of coaxing, I finally made it inside for my first day of school.

My mother's wisdom and advice have helped me through many a challenge. And my mother has been a great role model for me. My parents divorced when I was about five, so for much of my childhood I watched my mother do the job of two parents. My two eldest siblings were on their own by the time I was eight so my mother had to raise my brother and me on her own. When I was growing up, I remember my mother always showing the ultimate strength. She also displayed discipline and dignity in all that she did, no matter how stressed she was about time or money. "Never leave the house without lipstick on," she'd advise. Make sure you "run a brush through your hair." She would get dressed for work every day and don a scarf or big pearl necklace (fake, of course). She had quite the collection of clip-on earrings and always looked and acted like a lady.

Mom was the ultimate multitasker, too. When I was a kid, she would take me to work with her at the answering service where she was a switchboard operator. I would sit in the window of the office looking at the Brigham's ice cream shop across the street. Sometimes I sat at a board that wasn't in use and pretended to answer phones while she manned the real phone lines, taking messages for doctors, contractors, and whoever else needed an answering service. She always made sure we went across the street for ice cream at some point.

My mother always strived to be the best she could be and that meant that even as she was raising two young kids, she was bettering herself. She was over forty when she went back to school to get her psychology degree. Back then, you could leave kids on their own, so she would bring my brother and me along at times to play in the library or on the campus grounds while she was in class.

My mother didn't earn a lot but she somehow managed to save all year to take my brother and me on vacation for one whole week. It was usually a place close to home like New Hampshire so we could get there by car. She made so many sacrifices so we could have what we needed. When I was little, I never remember her buying clothes for herself—just clothes for my brother and me.

Mom gave so much of her time to us, too. When I began singing, I was too young to drive so my mother drove me to shows, staying up well past one, only to get up for work before six in the morning and drag her bones through the next day. She was always selfless, always giving everything she could to us.

When I got older, I wanted to chase my dreams of a music career. After finishing high school I decided I should go for it. I packed my car full of everything I owned and set off on the 1,100-mile drive to

Nashville, Tennessee. My mother, always the giver, handed me some money she had saved to get me started on my new career. As she saw me off, I said, "Mom, it's going to kill me being so far away from you." She responded with that magical string story again: "Remember, there is a string that goes between your heart and mine. I am always with you. Even when you think you're far away. Our hearts are joined together, always."

Fast-forward about six years and my mother had sold our family home in Massachusetts and moved to Nashville so I could take care of her. Her sister moved in with her in a little house I got for them outside Nashville. But then I signed my record deal and began touring extensively. I was rarely home. My mother was getting older and I worried about her. We were in the kitchen talking one day as I was getting ready to leave for another run, and I voiced one of my biggest fears: "Mom, what if something happens to you while I'm on the road?"

She calmly responded, "If that happens, stay out there and do your thing."

"What?!" I exclaimed.

She smiled and said, "That little string that goes between your heart and mine can't be broken by anything. By distance, time or even death. I will always be with you." As my eyes got teary she went on to say, "Besides, you can't come home. I won't be here. I'll be out there, waiting for you to go on stage." Then she giggled.

The string story has resurfaced whenever I needed it. When my mother had to undergo heart surgery in 2013, she had many complications. There were times my mother would be unconscious for days, even weeks. When she was awake, she was lost and confused. I learned more about medicine, the human body, doctors, hospitals, and medical protocol than I ever wanted to know.

I struggled with this new challenge. What could I do for her in such a helpless state? How was she feeling? Was she even aware of what she was going through? The woman who was my rock and my strength for my entire life was being kept alive by medicine and machines. My world, my soul, was rocked to the core time and time again, with every complication, every procedure, and every decision that had to be made. This went on for months. There were nights when I would stay with my mother at the hospital and climb into bed with her. I'd pretend she was simply asleep and I was a little kid cuddling up beside her just like I had as a child. At times, it seemed like that little string she always told me about had become a lifeline that kept me from losing it completely.

My children are not quite ready to learn about the string that binds our hearts. They are two and five. But, I will tell them about that magical string one day soon, so that when I have to travel for work or when they go off to camp or to college, they will know. They'll know that the string that binds my heart to their grandmother's also binds theirs to mine. I hope it will mean as much to them as it does to me. That string connects us. It can't be broken by anything. Not distance, not time away, not even death. The string has made me stronger. I will pass it on, with love, to give my sons the strength to make it through whatever life brings their way, too.

~Jo Dee Messina

Without Prejudice

When you teach your son, you teach your son's son.
~The Talmud

If my mom had followed the pattern of her mother and grandmother, she probably would have been a racist. A kind and loving racist with gracious manners and Southern hospitality, but a racist nonetheless. And I might have been a racist too.

My mom experienced the typical racial prejudice and segregated lifestyle of white families in Jackson, Mississippi long before that segregation was portrayed in the book and movie, *The Help*. She found the same culture of segregation and discrimination when she moved to Louisiana in her early teens. But at some point on the road to adulthood, my mom decided not to share that culture with her children.

Though few black families lived in our Houston neighborhood in the 1960s, my mom was determined to help her girls embrace racial equality. When Alabama's governor tried to prevent the desegregation of the state's public schools in 1963 and state troopers were called to block elementary school doorways, my mom grabbed our hands and lined us up in front of the family television to watch the grainy, black and white images. Mom cried as black children were turned away, clinging to their parents' hands. My sisters and I were young—just three, five and seven. We were far too young to understand the issues and emotions behind Mom's tears or the battle over integration. But our age didn't matter to Mom. She wanted us to share the history-making moment with her.

Mom followed the news of the civil rights movement and talked about it at the dinner table. When Dr. Martin Luther King, Jr. was jailed in Birmingham in 1963, my mom sent him a letter. She didn't know Dr. King, but she wanted to assure him of her prayers. He was changing the world her girls would live in.

On those weekends when we visited my mom's dad and step-mom, stepping back into the world of white prejudice, Mom showed us how to respect her dad's black employees. My grandfather may have called the lawn man "boy," but my mom introduced him to us as Mr. William. She took time to visit with Mr. William during each visit and ask about his family. She taught us the same respect for the women who cooked and cleaned at my grandparents' house.

Once my youngest sister started school, Mom put feet to our dinner table discussions about racial discrimination. She began volunteering once a week at a Baptist ministry center in one of Houston's poorest neighborhoods. There she talked with young black and Hispanic moms who came for sewing classes and food distributions. She cuddled their babies and joked with their children. And she encouraged us to volunteer with her during school breaks once we were old enough.

As I approached ninth grade, Houston's school district was pressured to rezone the schools to speed up integration. I wasn't excited about switching to a new school—a school four miles farther from my home—or the prospect of leaving my friends behind. For weeks after school started, I came home with stories about knifings and fights between black and white students. I worried that I might get caught in the middle of one of those fights. But my mom encouraged me to plow through fear and discomfort, keep the big goal in sight, and make new friends with students of other races.

Mom's lessons stuck. Today my husband pastors a multi-ethnic church congregation in Nevada. If you scan the crowd on a Sunday morning, you'll see people from almost a dozen ethnic heritages. Funny, but I rarely notice the diversity until a newcomer or friend comments on it.

I think my mom notices the diversity though. When she visits our church, she smiles at the rainbow of races. After the worship service is over, Mom shakes hands and greets people without any hint of prejudice. I see her joy as she talks to my wide array of friends, and I know she is pleased. This is the life Mom always had in mind for her girls.

~Donna Finlay Savage

A Last Request and a Lasting Lesson

When you are sorrowful look again in your heart,
and you shall see that in truth you are weeping for that
which has been your delight.
~Kahlil Gibran

My mom died just before dawn on a miserably cold and rainy December morning. The dark clouds and constant drizzle over her Cape Cod neighborhood fit our somber moods as my brothers and sisters and I arranged with the local funeral home for Mom's last departure from her beloved house on the edge of the tidal marsh.

All five of us were there, having been alerted earlier that week. As soon as we had gotten "The Call," we had immediately flown or driven from our homes in California, Florida, Georgia and New York to the house on the marsh. We had left behind our sympathetic spouses, needy children, pending projects and full schedules. My husband bravely took over for me to support our nine-year-old son, who was nervously anticipating his first school-wide Geography Bee that week. In spite of their shared anxiety about the upcoming Bee, both of them understood that I needed to be with my mother and my brothers and sisters. They didn't want me to worry about them, because I had more important things to worry about.

As I joined my brothers and sisters at the house on the Cape, I felt oddly peaceful. Though I dreaded losing my mother, I wasn't anxious about the process. I knew that Mom had prepared well for her death. All we had to do was be present for her and each other during this final stage. She had done everything else.

Mom was a born teacher and a natural organizer. When she had received the diagnosis of incurable cancer that September, she had planned her death as pragmatically as she had planned her busy life as wife, mother and professional. She had asked all five of us to take turns being alone with her at the Cape for one week at a time, for as long as she needed us. When it was my turn for a "week with Mom" I flew up to the Cape gladly. It was an incredibly special time together. I managed her medications in partnership with the Hospice angels who kept her pain-free. Together Mom and I admired the ever-changing view of the tidal marsh, with its flocks of starlings and visits from deer and foxes. Mom discussed her burial wardrobe, funeral invitation list, and other practical details of dying. We gave each other our undivided attention and made precious memories of intimate moments together. It was a privilege to share her final experiences of gratitude, love, and forgiveness.

During those weeks Mom wanted only her children with her. We took turns protecting her from the outside world, fielding numerous phone calls and attempted visits from friends, relatives, and neighbors who valued her friendship so dearly. On Mom's behalf, we asked them to understand her need to preserve her evaporating energy for the precious time with us. And we reassured them of her continuing love and respect, and appreciation for all their years of friendship.

Now, in the subdued gray light of the wintry morning, the funeral home station wagon rumbled slowly away with its precious burden. We wrapped ourselves in blankets and nestled close to each other in the dimly lit living room as the noise of the vehicle faded into the distance. I felt the tense energy of the morning's activity gradually drain into peaceful stillness. For the moment, we could rest. Characteristically, Mom had seen to every detail: transportation back to her New York birthplace, funeral arrangements, even the florist who would provide the graveside floral arrangements. In a day or two we would travel together to New York. For now, as we sat watching the mist roll over the marsh, in a room fragrant with flowers from the well-wishers in the neighborhood, we had nothing to do.

Well, almost nothing. As a matter of fact, there was one more task to attend to, one more errand to run for Mom.

In spite of her shrinking horizons, Mom did think fondly of her neighbors and friends. Even though she had declined to share her remaining time with them, she wanted to acknowledge their friendly overtures and express her lasting affection for them. So Mom had asked my older sister to purchase, on her behalf, a case of splits of sparkling wine. The small bottles were to be decorated with ribbons and delivered by us in person, after Mom's death, to those neighbors who had been her favorite local companions.

Accordingly, in the early afternoon, as the cold morning rain gave way to a watery blue sky, all five of us set out to walk through the neighborhood together, braving the chilly air and picking our way around the puddles. Taking turns carrying the heavy boxes, we visited every house. Together, we carried the news of her death, that final gift of beribboned bottles, and her instruction to her friends: "Please use this Champagne to toast to our friendship."

We hugged, and cried, and laughed, with neighbor after neighbor. We gave each special person Mom's last gift, a gift that reflected her unique flair for life and honored the strength of their mutual affection. And my mother the teacher taught me one more lesson. As I walked in her shoes and hugged in her place, I felt her love flow through me to each grieving friend. With it flowed my love for her and my heartbreak at her death. And, with each hug, an answering affection poured from each person. My breaking heart opened as I absorbed, through my sorrow, the joy of a life well lived and friends well loved.

As the five of us returned to the house with empty boxes and full hearts, we saw, against the backdrop of the gloomy sky, a breathtakingly beautiful rainbow. It made us all laugh. Obviously, Mom had orchestrated the whole thing from her new seat in the heavens. "Stop the rain so my children can deliver those bottles without getting wet," she probably instructed. The storm clouds had obediently dispersed, just long enough for us to fulfill Mom's last request and, in the process, learn one more lesson about whole-hearted love. Clearly, a rainbow that arched over the whole sky was the perfect way for Mom to express her approval.

~Judith Lavori Keiser

The Play's the Thing

Flaming enthusiasm, backed up by horse sense and persistence,
is the quality that most frequently makes for success.
~Dale Carnegie

I t was a cool evening during a long, wonderful summer break. I sat with my two younger sisters lamenting that while kids on TV had school plays, our school in real life did not.

Enter Mom.

Mom has never been one to sit idly by. She is a woman of action, especially when her children are involved. Her daughters wanted to be in a school play, so a school play they would have.

Mom agreed that it was a shame to not have a school play. She had always encouraged us to try new things, to challenge ourselves. Whenever we were scared or nervous, like when we had to play a solo at a recital, she would remind us that it was a good experience. So it was that Mom declared she would do her best to change the school play dilemma.

I was in fifth grade; I had learned many years ago that Mom could do anything. So, with never a doubt in my mind, I looked forward to our school play.

This was pre-Internet, so Mom read books and consulted the high school theatre director. She taught herself basic theatre terminology, the ins and outs of arranging rehearsals, the tricks of the trade for lighting and sound effects, how to obtain the rights to a script—everything.

Mom made a plan; we were to do *Peter Pan*! I had already spent many magical moments watching Mary Martin fly as Peter Pan; this was so exciting! While my sisters and I busied ourselves watching the video and dancing along with Princess Tiger Lily, Mom got down to business.

Mom contacted our school and got permission to do the school play; I can only imagine how that went. She bargained for use of the school gym, fighting with the needs of the school's various sports teams. She made it happen.

She held auditions. She got volunteers and built a stage. Mom scavenged for costumes and props at thrift stores, and created what she couldn't find. She rented lighting and sound equipment. She designed sets and drew scenery. She prepared the music accompaniment and she choreographed. Mom was the producer and the director. On top of this, she coordinated a substantial team of volunteers, which is no small feat.

During this time, Mom was also being a normal mom. She worked a full-time job, she prepared meals for our six-member family, she drove us to our various other extracurricular activities, and somehow she kept the house in one piece.

When the time came and the stage was set, Mom put her final efforts into publicity. And the seats were packed! Every night!

It was a hit, and everything went off without a hitch.

Mom went on to do *The Wizard of Oz*, *The Sound of Music*, and *Fiddler on the Roof* before handing over the torch. Each play got increasingly complex. She even went so far as to compose original songs so that more kids could have solos. She altered the scripts to give more kids lines. And crazier still—she somehow managed to have double casts, so she could double the number of starring roles (and double the workload for herself).

See, Mom was not just there for my sisters and me, she was devoted to giving as many kids as she could the opportunity to have that good experience, to get up on the stage and be brave. She was so very proud of everyone. She still talks about all the different kids who impressed her, who she noticed came out of their shells.

It continues to amaze me when I think back on my school plays.

To being a Lost Boy and watching my sister shine as Maria von Trapp. But mostly, I think about what Mom accomplished. How she made this unbelievable effort in order to give invaluable, strengthening experiences to so many. I'm inspired.

~Maggie Anderson

Fake It Till You Make It

Always act like you're wearing an invisible crown.
~Author Unknown

I watched my mom stride with purpose into a large group of men standing around a pile of concrete mixture that was going to be used to build a new water tower for the orphanage my mother helped run in Ogbomosho, Nigeria. Her shoulders were back and she used every inch of her five feet ten inches as she talked. I was tired; we had already made stops at the leprosy settlement and the blind centre. But tired or not, my siblings and I piled out to play with the children in the orphanage. We loved them and they loved us. It was 1967 and the Biafran War was raging, so the orphanage was filling up and definitely needed a new water tower. I recognized the determination on my mother's face; she was about to give someone a lecture, so I paused to watch.

"There is too much sand in this mixture," she said with absolute authority and confidence as she picked up a handful of the concrete and let it slide through her fingers. I stopped and stared. What did my mother know about concrete or construction? Medicine, mothering, managing—definitely. But concrete? The men all nodded and promised to add the correct ingredients, and my mother strode away.

As we walked down the hall of the orphanage, the children jumped into our arms for kisses and hugs. "You are a force of nature," I said to my mother, but she was too busy instructing the women who ran the orphanage to respond.

I was nearly a teenager, and it had made me a slight bit sassy. After her work was done and we sat in the car going home, I said, "Mother, I didn't know that you knew anything about concrete."

"I don't!" she said. "I just know that putting too much sand in the mixture is how they cheat you." I laughed and laughed. My mother was indeed a force of nature. She grew up in the Appalachian Mountains in a house with no heat and no plumbing, and she was the first person in her family to graduate from high school. She had dreams and hopes way beyond her family's means. But she said she would go into medicine, marry a doctor and go to Africa; and there she was striding fearlessly into a group of men, supervising the building of something she knew nothing about.

When I was frightened my first day in class at Duke University, I channeled my mother. When I was uncertain about how to be a mother after my children were born, my mother was there to show me the way. When my children had a high fever, I called my mother. But most of all, when the uncertainties of life hit and I did not know exactly how to proceed, I thought of the saying, "Fake it till you make it." And I realized… that was the lesson my mother taught me that day in Nigeria in 1967.

She was faking it! She had no idea how concrete should feel, but she faked it and made a much-needed new water tower for an orphanage. Thank you, Mom, for showing me that life is a series of twist and turns where we often have no idea how to proceed. When those times come we need to raise our shoulders, stand tall and stride in with confidence. Thank you for your courage and determination, but most of all your grit.

~Alisa Edwards Smith

Selfie

Taking joy in living is a woman's best cosmetic.
~Rosalind Russell

I plucked it. In spite of the old wives' tales or the superstition that three would sprout in its place, I took the tweezers and pulled.

I had to. The strand of curly grey hair that poked skyward was too obvious nestled among my straight, chestnut-brown tresses.

Curly grey hair? Was that what was going to become of my locks? It was two inches long when I stretched it out. I wondered how long it had been there, silently marking time.

Underneath the discovery of my first grey hair was a sense of calm, of acceptance, the next step. For this, credit goes to my mother.

While other moms were running to the drugstore, or consulting with their hairstylists over how to "naturally" cover the grey, I watched my mom's hair evolve from black, to pepper with a side of salt, salt with a dash of pepper, and finally to what it is now: an all-over silvery grey.

Of course in my early years I was irked. Everyone else's mom had "normal" hair, so why didn't she? "Too fake," was her response.

True, but the other moms didn't look like clowns. The browns, auburns, blonds and reds complemented their skin tones and gave them a bounce in their step... at least that's what the commercials promised.

"Okay, but can't you get contacts?"

"Then I'd have to do something with my eyebrows."

"You should pierce your ears."

"Too painful," she replied.

It was a beauty argument I couldn't win. She was set on being as natural as possible. Even on the occasions when she went out with my dad, the pallet of eyeshadow sat undisturbed beside the lipstick and perfume on her dresser. I didn't even know why she bought them.

Never watching my mom fuss over her appearance has been the biggest blessing of my life. While other moms were taking their daughters for make-up lessons, perms and obsessing over morsels of food, my mom was cheering me on from the sideline during soccer, having coffee breaks the minute we got to the mall, silently teaching me balance before it was trendy.

In spite of her own feelings about beauty, my mom allowed me to explore the subject on my own: taking me to get my ears pierced when I was ten; never saying a word when I left the house wearing way too much mint green eyeliner; and laughing with my friend Meredith about whether I actually had eyebrows anymore. Thankfully the latter has sorted itself out.

But the truth remains, whatever I experimented with beauty-wise was just that: an experiment. I never did anything to make myself feel better, or cover up an inch of skin; completely the opposite: I tried things on as one would snakes — for shock value.

And my shock value wasn't like other people's shock value. Sure, while I was in my early twenties I got a tattoo, pierced my navel and dyed my hair fire-engine red. I never tried on an actual snake, never felt the need to spend millions on make-up, never wished I were someone different.

Because of my mom, and like my mom, I believe in natural beauty, the kind of beauty that comes from fresh air on cheeks, and eyes that are sparkly from mischief and adventure.

Now that she's a granny and I have three daughters of my own, her nonchalant approach to aging makes me feel safe. There's never a question or a worry that she'll say the wrong thing or push my girlies down a bumpy path of self-criticism. I love her for that.

Today I stared in the mirror examining the roots of my thirty-seven-year-old hair, wondering how much longer the brown will reflect back at me. If I'm completely honest, there is a part of me that wonders if I'll be able to carry a head of grey (possibly curly) hair. But when the wondering gets too much, all I have to do is look at my beautiful mother and know I'll be just fine.

~Alison Gunn

The Dangdest Thing

Doing the right thing has power.
~Laura Linney

"You're wasting your time. It's going to die." My father crossed his arms and glared at Mom.

She poured milk into the baby bottle, screwed on the lid and said, "Yes, I know."

Earlier that day Mom had taken me shopping at Phillips Department Store, the 1960's equivalent of a mall. On the walk home we'd taken a shortcut through the Omaha stockyards and noticed a newborn calf alone, bawling pitifully in one of the pens. Now as we prepared to go back, my father scowled.

He worked innumerable overtime hours on the Post Office docks. On this rare day off he needed to tackle his enormous honey-do list. The prospect of caring for their three toddler sons while his wife fed a doomed calf galled him.

Mom touched Dad's arm. "Honey, even if it's meant for slaughter, it isn't right to let it suffer now."

Dad rolled his eyes and stomped out of the kitchen. Mom tucked the bottle in her back pocket, took my hand, and we headed out the door.

I skipped at her side, elated by our rescue adventure. "I'm so glad we're going to save the calf."

Her grip on my hand tightened, but she walked on without answering. I slowed down and tugged at her.

"Mom, it'll be okay, right? We'll save it, won't we?"

My mother stopped and sighed. She reached down to brush the hair from my forehead. "No honey, we can't save it."

I pulled away, tears welling. "But we're going to feed it. It has to be okay."

Mom cupped my cheek with a gentle hand. "We can't save it. But we can help it now." She captured my gaze. "It's important to always do the right thing, even if you can't change the outcome."

She clasped my hand again and we headed to our task, somber now.

When we arrived the 250-acre stockyard teemed with activity and a smell that carried for miles. Even my familiarity with that odor didn't prepare me for the stench inside the holding pens. Our calf huddled in the corner of one.

A stock handler rode over as we climbed the manure-splattered rails. "Ma'am, what are you doin'?" he called.

We perched on the top rail and Mom held up the bottle. "We've come to feed the calf."

The cowboy shook his head. "Its mama birthed him then went into the slaughterhouse. That little feller ain't gonna make it."

Mom allowed his horse to nuzzle her hand. "I realize that."

The cowboy pushed his Stetson back and asked, "Then why bother?"

She reached out, stroked his horse's sweaty neck and said, "Because it's hungry, and feeding it is the right thing to do."

The man leaned back in the saddle. "That's the dangdest thing I ever heard."

She petted the horse without replying. Whether it was her determination, her evident appreciation of his horse, or her good looks, he finally shrugged and said, "Suit yourself."

He trotted away and Mom and I slipped into the enclosure. We avoided the fly-laden piles of manure and crossed to the calf. Despite its feeble struggles, Mom upended the bottle and slid the nipple into its mouth. She guided my hand to the bottle and steadied the shaky calf.

It caught on quickly, and stared at me as it guzzled the milk. Elated, I stroked its damp coat with my free hand.

The calf drained the bottle and plopped down, content. Mom smiled. "Let's get home before Dad pulls his hair out. We'll come back tomorrow."

The next day we hurried back, but found the pen empty. Mom's shoulders drooped. I buried my head against her side and wept. "It's gone. It's dead."

While she comforted me our cowboy cantered over. "Ya'll looking for that calf?"

I lifted my tear-streaked face. Mom nodded.

"It's the dangdest thing. A farmer stopped by yesterday after you left." A huge grin crossed the cowboy's face. "He took the little feller home to raise. Guess feedin' it was the right thing to do after all."

That day Mom did more than save a calf's life. Her actions impacted mine forever by imprinting the importance of doing the right thing. Her model has produced a legacy that's been passed down to three generations.

And it all started with feeding a hungry calf.

It's the dangdest thing.

~Jeanie Jacobson

Mom's Recipe for Life

Life is like a mirror, we get the best results when we smile at it.
~Author Unknown

I have a lot of Mom's recipes in a blue tin box—the pumpkin pie she made during my growing-up years, the light and yeasty dinner rolls that were family favorites, and the tender date muffins that her own mother made. Every time I see one of the cards with Mom's handwriting on it, I am carried back to the aromas in our small kitchen where she reigned. Even so, the recipe I treasure most is not on any index card. Nor did she send it to me in a letter. On the contrary, she lived this recipe all of her life but I was too blind to see and appreciate it until her final years.

My mother grew up in a small coal-mining town in southwest Iowa. My grandfather once told me that she knew no stranger; she considered everyone in that community her friend. That attitude continued wherever she lived for the rest of her life.

As a tween and teen, I cringed every time my mother addressed strangers in the grocery store or on the city bus. She talked to everyone and offered a smile. I was embarrassed.

Mom had a cheerful greeting for everyone she encountered and a question of some sort that triggered an answer and more conversation. She spoke to the mailman, the grocery store clerks, and the girls who worked in the neighborhood bakery.

"Hi Lorraine," she'd say to the woman who owned the bakery. "What did you think of Jackie Gleason's show last night?" Lorraine chatted about the show as she sliced the usual loaf of bread for Mom, then asked what else she wanted. "Half a dozen of those wonderful crullers," Mom might say. Then she'd lean closer to the counter and say something like, "Isn't life wonderful?" I'd roll my eyes and accept the free cookie Lorraine gave me even into my teen years, then hurry out hoping no one would see me with the woman who talked to everyone.

Decades later, after my father passed on, I drove the hour and a half to my mother's house every couple of weeks to spend a day with her and help with errands. She grieved for Dad for a long time inwardly but her smile never wavered. "No sense being a Grumpy Gertie," she'd tell me.

I watched as she spoke to the Walmart greeter before he even had a chance to open his mouth. "Hi. How are you doing today? Isn't it great to see the sun?" She flashed him a million-dollar smile as he helped her get a shopping cart while he chuckled.

I noticed that she smiled at everyone she passed in the store's many aisles. Almost all of them responded with a bright grin of their own. Some spoke, others nodded their heads at this elderly woman who brought a little light into their day.

What really sold me on Mom's approach to life was her experience on the senior bus, a story I've repeated to others many times. The weeks I could not be there, she used this low-cost transportation to the grocery store. After her first trip, I asked her how it went.

"Ha!' she said, "I got on that bus and what did I see? Thirteen little old ladies and one old man and not one word was spoken."

I wondered how long it would be until the somberness on that bus would change. On my next visit, Mom mentioned the girls on the bus and something one of them had told her.

"Oh, are you talking with them now?" I asked.

"Of course," she said. "One day I climbed up the steps of the bus and before I looked for a seat, I gave them a big smile and I said, 'Isn't it a wonderful day?' I noticed a few shy smiles."

Mom didn't give up. She greeted them all each time she got on the bus and before long, the whole group was laughing and talking to one another. The bus became more than just transportation.

When we went to the various stores, I observed as she smiled and chatted with perfect strangers. Some of them looked like the sourest person you'd ever met but once Mom beamed at them and started a conversation, most responded favorably. She had a man with deep frown lines laughing over a little joke she told him as she leaned on her cane. My mother didn't embarrass me any longer. I found myself admiring her.

She's been gone for ten years but I've carried on her recipe for life. I smile at people as I walk by and often begin a conversation in the checkout line. Silent, solemn people respond with smiles of their own and a bit of chatter. All it takes is for one person to initiate the smile or a greeting.

Recently, I noticed a woman ahead of me in the checkout line. Her red raincoat looked cheerful on a wet day, and I told her so. She had looked quite serious only a moment before, but she smiled and thanked me. "You know what?" she said. "I really like the color of your raincoat, too."

It's such second nature with me now that only the other day I noticed that everyone I passed in the grocery store smiled at me. Must be a lot of happy people here, I thought. Then, I stopped walking and bowed my head in a grateful prayer of thanks for the mother I had been given. It was me who had done the smiling first and all those people had responded. My mother didn't lecture but taught me by example. She'd given me a recipe for life.

~Nancy Julien Kopp

The Letter

You learn you can do your best even when it's hard,
even when you're tired and maybe hurting a little bit.
It feels good to show some courage.

~Joe Namath

My mother died many years ago when I was only thirteen. Sometimes life before then seems like a dream. However, every now and then I remember something that Mom did, and she is right back with me as if she'd never left.

Twenty years after Mom died, I became ill. My health gradually deteriorated and after many tests, I was diagnosed with Crohn's disease, an inflammation of the small intestine. I continually suffered from severe stomach pains and was unable to eat properly. My weight plummeted and I became weak and tired. I was lucky that I was given support throughout this ordeal by my husband, Peter. He helped me cope with the pain and the endless hospital appointments, but it was quite easy to feel sorry for myself.

One day, when I was sorting through some old paperwork, I found a letter from my mother. She had been seriously ill and had written to me from the hospital. I had only been eight years old at the time. It had been ages since I had read the letter, and just seeing her handwriting whisked me back to my childhood. Thinking of Mom, I could feel the tears welling up. But when I read through the letter a few times, all I could feel was guilt. Mom had been ill for most of her life, in fact since she had been a little girl. She had remained strong throughout, yet here I was giving in to my illness and I wasn't half as sick as she had been. What on earth was wrong with me?

"I was so happy to speak to you on the phone," she wrote. "Everybody is saying how good you've been, and I'm so proud of you. I know that this is all a little strange, but you're a clever girl and you know it can't be helped."

Despite being ill, Mom was more concerned about how I was coping and never once mentioned how sick she was or if she was frightened of the operation she was about to face.

Mom had developed tuberculosis when she was five years old and had spent much of her childhood and teenage years in sanitariums. Due to her health problems, she was advised not to have children, but she ignored the doctors and had me.

When I was eight, Mom was diagnosed with breast cancer and given no more than six months to live. But she was a strong-willed woman and she survived for another five years. I have always believed that it was her determination not to leave me at such a young age that kept her going against all the odds.

"You're such a brave and grown-up girl," Mom said to me in hospital one day.

Mom was lying in bed waiting to have a mastectomy. It was the first of her many stays in hospital over the coming five years and I was terrified. I certainly didn't feel grown up or brave. I knew I should be for Mom's sake, but it was hard. I felt young and useless. It should have been me comforting her, but instead she was trying to cheer me up. She seemed more concerned about me than herself.

Mom stayed in hospital for three weeks that time and I was relieved when she came home, especially as everything went back to normal on her return. However, I wasn't aware at that time how ill Mom really was. She never complained and even returned to work. I know now that she wanted to make my life as normal as possible.

The letter Mom wrote to me while she was in hospital all those years ago gave me the strength to cope with my illness many years after she was gone. Sometimes I was in so much pain that I could barely lift myself out of bed, but more times than not I forced myself to get up and go to work. Mom's illnesses had been far more serious than mine, yet she never gave up and always got on with her life cheerfully. I'm sure she knew she wasn't going to live to be an old lady, but she was determined to make the most of the time she had and to make my childhood as happy as possible. How could I just give up and not fight? Yes, some days were too bad for me to go out and try to lead a normal life, but I made sure these times were few and far between. I'm certain Mom's letter was the reason I refused to give in to my illness. She never gave up hope, and in the end nor did I.

"I love you sweetheart; be good and pray for me please, all my love, from your mommy."

And so the letter ended. Thankfully I haven't had a recurrence of Crohn's disease since an operation twenty years ago, and I'm reasonably healthy. But if I ever feel sick or sorry for myself now, I read Mom's letter. Her words of strength and love give me the power to cope with my problems and persuade me not to give up on life.

~Irena Nieslony

10

Breaking Bed

*The purpose of human life is to serve,
and to show compassion and the will to help others.*
~Albert Schweitzer

I remember how my mind swirled when my mother told me a new girl would be arriving to live in our home. Five of us already shared two overcrowded bedrooms. This new girl would be an intrusion in my life and my already limited space.

My younger sister and I already shared a double bed. Our dresser and desk took up much of the rest of the room. We had enough room to put a small end table by each side of the bed for a lamp and radio. Now the new girl was going to get a bed of her own and it would occupy the only remaining space in our room.

The next afternoon, a curly headed teenager carrying a suitcase arrived with a caseworker. The woman introduced us and Rose curtsied. My parents laughed.

The adults talked while scanning official looking papers; Rose and I stared at each other. My mother had already explained to me that most of the kids in her position had been through some kind of traumatic situation at home. I didn't want to ask questions and appear nosey, but I did see sadness in Rose's dark brown eyes.

That night, my mother said good night and the room became silent, except for my sister's heavy breathing. She suddenly let out a loud snort.

A snicker came from Rose's direction. "What was that?"

"My sister snores." Another snort and another snicker. I began giggling; Rose's snicker grew into laughter.

"Quiet down, girls," came from my parents' room.

Through all the laughter, my sister didn't wake up. Snort. Snort. We giggled again. We finally gained our composure and Rose became serious, "You know something, Margaret, this afternoon I thought you were pretty stuck up."

"Well, you came off kind of weird. A curtsy. Seriously?"

Rose doubled over in laughter.

"Shh, my mom is getting mad. We better go to sleep. We can talk tomorrow." I thought maybe everything would work out. I rolled over to get some sleep and it became silent again. BOOM! We bolted upright in the darkness.

"What was that?" My mother stomped down the hall. She opened our door and peeked in.

"Is everything alright in here?"

"Yep." I squinted toward Rose. My mother closed the door and continued to the boy's room. Rose and I jumped out of bed and peeked into the hall.

"What happened in here? Who broke the beds? You guys better settle down." My father's footsteps plodded down the hall. I shut the door until he passed by.

"What's wrong?"

"The boys were messing around and broke the beds." My parents started reassembling the beds. Not wanting to get involved, I closed the door and climbed back in bed. On her way past, my mother opened our door and peeked in.

"They're asleep."

"Well, that's where I want to be. Let's go," my dad closed the door. I listened until the footsteps stopped and began drifting off.

"Psst. Margaret, are you asleep?"

"Almost. What do you want?" Rose was moving around in her bed. "I got to tell you something."

I opened my eyes in time to realize she was stepping across the opening between our beds.

"Don't…" BOOM! Both beds collapsed. We sat on my bed staring at each other, waiting for the explosion that was sure to come from my parents. They stomped down the hall again and went straight to the boys' room to question them.

Rose giggled. "Your sister didn't even wake up." I giggled. The more we tried not to, the harder we laughed. Our door slowly opened.

"What's going on in here?" We doubled over, grabbing our stomachs.

"What did you girls do?" We couldn't answer through the tears. When we didn't stop, my mother shook her head and smiled. "I don't have time for this, I'm tired. You girls fix your own beds." She closed the door and went back to her room. I could hear my parents laughing, too. We got up, rolled my sister out of bed, and fixed both beds. She stayed asleep on the floor. We woke her up long enough to get her back into bed.

"Rose, what did you want?"

"I can't remember, now." She started giggling again.

"Oh, brother. Don't start again. We gotta get some sleep." We climbed back into bed; however, every few minutes a muffled giggle erupted. As I drifted to sleep, I decided sharing my room with this strange girl wasn't so bad.

I realized what my mother meant by finding common ground to make a connection. The laughter we shared bonded us and was worth the loss of a little space. I don't think this kind of situation was what my mother had in mind, but broken beds and laughter created a sister bond and a lifelong friendship.

Rose now lives in Washington State and I live in New York. We are both in our sixties, but each time we call each other this episode comes up and the laughter begins again.

I wish my mother could be here and understand how much I appreciate the lessons she taught me about compassion and acceptance. Without my new brothers and sisters, I might not have developed the understanding and the skills that prepared me to be a teacher's aide for children with special needs. My mother's legacies of giving and love are still being shared with those who need them most.

~Marge Gower

11

Sailing Through the Storm

A mother is she who can take the place of all others
but whose place no one else can take.
~Cardinal Mermillod

hen the dermatologist's office left a message for me to call them, I figured there must be yet another insurance snafu to straighten out. I wasn't at all prepared for what they told me.

"The samples we took from the spots on your face are both basal cell carcinomas. We'll need to set you up with a specialist to have them removed because we don't want to take any more tissue than necessary. We'll also need you to see a plastic surgeon for skin repairs."

Skin repairs? I'd barely processed the fact that I'd just been diagnosed with skin cancer and now they were hitting me with the need for a plastic surgeon. I'd had biopsies before but they always turned out to be nothing. Facing the "Big C" wasn't something I'd planned on, and the thought of having my face cut made my stomach flutter.

I scheduled the appointments and wondered what this could mean. What if the cancer had spread? Just how much facial cutting would be necessary? What would I look like afterward? It didn't take long for me to jump to the worst-case scenarios I could imagine. I could hear the doctor telling me cancer cells had spread to my lymph nodes, not to mention my future with a permanently disfigured face.

I chewed my lip and reached for the phone to call Mom. I'd always turned to her before when in trouble and wanted nothing more than to hear her reassuring voice. Yet I decided the grown-up thing to do was wait until I had a more definite prognosis.

My husband Phil walked me into the medical center. I held his hand so tightly my knuckles were white. In the examining room the doctor numbed my face before meticulously cutting away bits of skin. Then he sent me to the waiting room while the samples were analyzed. The nurse called me back in twice to have more tissue removed. It felt like hours before the doctor finally announced I could go home. The anesthetic that numbed my face kept me from smiling.

I had a small hole on the side of my nose and such a gaping hole in my cheek I could barely stand to look at my reflection in the mirror. I couldn't imagine how the plastic surgeon would be able to put me back together. I almost picked up the phone to call Mom, but again told myself to wait. No need to worry her yet. It made much more sense to call her after the reconstructive surgery had been completed.

The surgery was scheduled for the next morning. Since the procedure required general anesthesia, the hospital gave me forms to sign that boldly outlined all the things that could possibly go wrong. I wished I hadn't waited to call Mom and took deep breaths until the anesthesia mercifully knocked me out.

I woke up loopy and numb. The hospital discharged me with pain medication and lengthy instructions that I hoped Phil would remember. But as soon as I got home the numbness deserted me. I couldn't even stand to put my head on the pillow. So I swallowed pain pills and tried to sleep in a chair with my feet propped up. Fitful dozing brought nightmares of being chased by faceless demons.

The next morning, I woke to the aroma of fried eggs and bacon. I shuffled stiffly to the kitchen, my eyes squinting against the bright light. Mom stood at the stove as I had seen her do so often during my growing-up years. "Phil needed to go to work today so I came over to keep you company."

She smiled at me without a single word of reproach that I had neglected to call her. When her arms went around me in a hug that held me firmly together, my eyes misted and a hard knot dissolved inside me. Perhaps I wasn't as much of an adult as I thought.

"Everything is going to be fine," she said.

Nothing could turn out badly with Mom on duty. She fed me comfort food and freshly squeezed orange juice, her cure-all for most of my childhood ailments, and put me to bed. Fortified with good cooking and the relief that always comes from letting someone else take charge, I closed my eyes. Sleep came swiftly and dreamlessly.

Three days later, a phone call brought good news. The cancer hadn't spread. No further treatment was required. My face healed with a slim diagonal scar on the cheek and one side of my nose isn't quite like the other. But no one cringed in horror when they saw me. Mom nodded her head and said, "I told you there was no need to worry."

A few months after my surgery, Mom faced a crisis of her own. After years of problems with renal function, her kidneys shut down. She would have to go on dialysis. As was her custom, she joked with the nurses and remained calm in the face of a frightening diagnosis. Though she looked small and vulnerable lying in a recliner and hooked to a machine, her lips turned up in a rueful lopsided grin when she saw me.

"Well, this is a revolting development, isn't it?"

I smiled back at her when I replied. "It sure is. But I know everything is going to be fine."

Senseless worry about things we can't change only muddies hope. Mom didn't waste time on self-pity or energy on "what-ifs." Instead she focused on navigating the storm that entered her life like a seasoned captain awaiting the inevitable rainbow. No one could have given me a better lesson. I know I can sail through any problem that comes along by following Mom's example. All it takes is courage, a little determination, and a smile.

~Pat Wahler

12

The Cake Lady

Cakes are special. Every birthday, every celebration ends with
something sweet, a cake, and people remember.
It's all about the memories.
~Buddy Valastro

Long before the popular television show *Cake Boss* made decorating cakes a fascinating hobby to watch, my mom was whipping up her own creations in the privacy of her own kitchen. She is known around our town as The Cake Lady—Donna McCoy, the "Real McCoy" of baking.

When I was nine I helped her cater a wedding. I was so excited to finally be able to attend one of the magical ceremonies, seeing the fragrant flowers, flickering candles, beautiful dresses, and of course the centerpiece, my mom's towering creation. I was only allowed to carry a few dishes and the napkins to the table to restock. I watched my mom carefully slice into the grand cake, cautious not to tip it over. She proudly served the delicious slices to eager guests. They congratulated her on how scrumptious it tasted. She smiled and graciously thanked them.

Those hours spent at the wedding were unforgettable, but I also remember the mess we faced when we got home. Piles of dirty dishes, bowls full of icing, catering supplies stacked and ready to be washed. My older sister and I pitched in and helped my mom with the less than glamorous side of her catering business. I say "business" lightly.

She rarely made a profit because she didn't charge enough. Baking was more of her hobby.

My sister Mellanie and I always had the most amazing birthday cakes. From castles to creatures to fabulous fairies… my mom could bake and create whatever we asked. Mom would come home from working all day, throw a cake in the oven and sit up most of the night decorating it. One year, she was asked to do a Wonder Woman cake for a lady down the street. She bought the pan and painstakingly squeezed the icing tube forming each and every detail of the cake. She carefully placed the cake in a box and carried it to her car. She came back in to get more supplies. When she returned, she discovered our Boxer/Bulldog, Ginger, standing in the back seat of the car devouring the cake; she had forgotten to shut the car door! My mom screamed at the dog and I am certain shed a tear or two before she came back in and started all over.

We were proud to be known as "The Cake Lady's kids." We just weren't thrilled with the mess the cakes left behind. As teenagers, we were required to clean the kitchen before we were allowed to go out on a date. We fussed and fussed as we dumped icing in the trash, slammed pans in the dishwasher, or hand scrubbed and sanitized Mom's icing bags.

"I am sick of cleaning this mess!" I yelled at my sister.

"Agreed," she replied.

Mom would quickly remind us we were a team and she needed our help. The little money she made from cakes helped pay for my cheerleading uniform and helped my sister with college expenses, so we stopped complaining… briefly… until the next time cleanup duty rolled around.

As the years flew by, Mom still baked and decorated cakes. I had one of the most beautiful wedding cakes in the state of Georgia. It was five stories tall, sitting on top of a fountain with staircases connecting to smaller satellite cakes. Ribbons, roses, and tiny sparkles gleamed all over it. It was spectacular. My husband, a Georgia Tech graduate, had a customized cheesecake for his groom's cake and a traditional, chocolate cake with Buzz the mascot sitting on top. They were mouth-watering as well as stunning.

Our first daughter, Alison, arrived and "Grammy" made her a special first birthday cake. It was a tradition in our family: a stand up teddy bear. She stood the solid cake bear on top of a large sheet cake alongside a ball made out of cake. Alison's cake was a huge, edible toy box. She squealed with delight.

As our other four children and my sister's three children arrived, each was ushered in with a one-of-a-kind baby shower cake followed by a special Grammy-designed birthday cake every year. The kids got whatever they asked for. She still baked cakes for others, but the cakes for her own family were amazing. She always swore she would never do another one like it, then someone would order it and she could never tell anyone no.

My mom has been decorating cakes now for over forty years. Her reputation as "The Cake Lady" is cemented in our rural Georgia town. She has baked those memorable first birthday "smash" cakes for clients and later been asked to do that same child's wedding cake. Now, she is honored to be doing their grandchildren's birthday cakes.

An artist in her own right; she has never been a wealthy business-woman, but she never intended to make a profit. She was given a talent to share with others and she does so willingly. My sister and I tell her all the time to charge more money, but she does it for pure pleasure and occasionally will make a dollar or two.

She is slowly passing her legacy on to us, teaching us how to bake and decorate. My own daughters eagerly sit around the kitchen table to watch and learn her trade. We still leave the "heavy, complicated stuff" to her, but my sister has introduced the use of fondant and other modern styles to the "family" business.

I attended a wedding reception recently for some of my mother's dedicated clients. I am now an elected official in my hometown, but I stood right beside my sister, slicing cake and serving it to the guests. Old habits die hard, but I loved every minute of it.

"Did your mom do the cake?" folks asked.

"Of course," I proudly replied.

"I no longer have to clean up the mess. I get to do the fun stuff!" I whispered to my sister.

Mom taught my sister and me about life through her years of cake baking. We learned to clean up our own messes. And Mom showed us about loyalty through the way she treated her customers who supported her. Baking taught us responsibility, showed us the joy of working together, and brought our extended family together for many sweet events and milestones.

~Amy McCoy Dees

Chapter 2

Thanks to My Mom

Rising to the Challenge

13

A Strike at the Ballpark

The human spirit is stronger than anything that can happen to it.
~C.C. Scott

I entered the kitchen to find my mother looking quizzically at our Nespresso machine. "What is that, an onion?"

"No Mom, it's a coffeemaker."

"And what are those — little onions?" she said, pointing to the little pods that went in the machine.

My mother doesn't like technology or coffee, so it wasn't surprising that she didn't "get" our coffee apparatus. I thought she was just fooling around when she started calling other things in our kitchen "onions."

It was the Fourth of July and we were going to the Mets game for my mother's eighty-first birthday. My mother and sister had met at our house so that we could all drive together to the game.

As we drove down the highway my mother continued to act a little weird. When my husband executed a rather smooth move to exit the highway and avoid a traffic jam, she was overly effusive about his driving skills. We got to the stadium twenty minutes later, and my mother was still chatting away, saying strange things.

I didn't know much about strokes but it occurred to me that she might be having one. I asked for directions to the medical station and started to walk my mother there without telling her where we were going.

As we took the elevator, Mom was exclaiming that we needed to see the "emperor"—which I came to realize was her word for the new Citi Field stadium. Apparently she was making the jump from baseball "stadium" to "Coliseum" to Roman "emperor," all words with common Latin and historical roots. She kept trying to veer off course to show us the emperor while I steered her toward the paramedics.

The paramedics did their normal stroke assessment, my mother duly identified the pen they held up as a "key," and we were rushed off in an ambulance to the stroke unit at a hospital in Queens. My mother's language skills were rapidly deteriorating by then.

We were fortunate that we caught my mother's stroke within the window of time allowed to administer the drug TPA. This drug, in layman's terms, stops the stroke in its tracks, like turning off a hard drive that is starting to erase itself. But TPA is a strong anti-clotting drug and it can kill the patient too. There were some tense moments when I had to make the decision, but I knew that my mother would rather risk death than let the stroke continue doing its damage. My mother received TPA at the first hospital, survived it, and we got back in an ambulance to go to a more sophisticated stroke unit at a hospital in Manhattan.

After a stroke the brain swells from the injury and the symptoms get worse and worse. My mother went from calling things "onions" to not even knowing her own name. But despite the fact that she didn't know her name, she said that she didn't want to cancel the sixtieth anniversary party that she and my father had scheduled for the following week. When I pointed out that she was missing a lot of words and she wouldn't know anyone's name, she said, "They'll just think I'm a little peculiar... but then they've always thought I was a little peculiar."

Even at the depths of her loss, Mom retained her self-deprecating sense of humor!

When she figured out her first name and her maiden name a couple of days later, but she couldn't recall her married name, she waved it off, saying, "That doesn't really matter," which seemed a bit like a commentary on her well-worn marriage. Stroke damage is a paradox. When I matter-of-factly gave my mother a form to sign in the hospital, she did it perfectly, inscribing her first, middle, and last name. I showed it to her and suggested she sign her name and then read it back to herself when she couldn't remember it.

After a few days my mother was sent home with a diagnosis of receptive and expressive aphasia. That meant she had trouble understanding spoken and written language and also finding the right words to express herself. I made a big poster with photos of family members and their names inscribed underneath. It hadn't been helping my relationship with my brother and sister that Mom was calling them both by my name. Everyone in the family was "Amy" for the first few days.

We got my mother into a language therapy rehab program that she would attend several days a week. When they were testing her capabilities, and discovered that she couldn't pronounce R's, I intervened and explained that she was from Boston, where they "pahked cahs" instead of parking cars. God forbid they wasted precious insurance-paid visits on trying to reinstate an "R" sound that my mother never had!

My sister signed on to drive my mother to therapy and help her with her nightly homework. For the next few months, my mother diligently went to speech therapy and spent hours on her homework each night, relearning words, especially those tricky pronouns and units of time. She still has trouble with masculine and feminine pronouns, units of time, and understanding spoken letters and numbers but she regained almost all her other words or found substitute words.

Aphasia lasts forever, and even now, three years later, my mother cycles through a few pronouns before she lights on the right one, especially when she is tired. She still attends an aphasia support group. This is her new life, but she feels fortunate. She knows how lucky she was to have the stroke in front of us, so that we could get her medical help right away. If she had been home alone or asleep while having the stroke, there's no telling how bad the damage would have been.

Right from the start, my mother bravely informed store clerks and other people she met that she had a "strike" and thus had trouble finding her words. She called it a strike instead of a stroke, which seemed appropriate, since it was like her brain was on strike when it came to language.

I've been so impressed with the way my mother has handled this dramatic change in her senior years. Her fortitude, her lack of embarrassment, and her can-do attitude have been inspiring. In fact, just two weeks after the stroke, my mother and sister were back at Citi Field for another Mets game. Mom was a little anxious about going to the same place where she had the stroke but she decided to face her fear head-on.

That first day back at the stadium, or "emperor," my mother discovered the cure for her anxiety—the gigantic margaritas they sell at Citi Field. She bought one and sipped it for the entire game. And she has had a margarita at every Mets game since. Mom has found workarounds for the words that she has permanently lost and she has found a workaround for watching the Mets without having a stroke, or strike as it were, despite their dismal record!

~Amy Newmark

This Too Shall Pass

If you're going through hell, keep going.
~Winston Churchill

"Mom, how am I ever going to survive this?" I asked with tears in my eyes. My mom, who always knew the right thing to say, grabbed my hand and softly said, "This too shall pass."

Tears trickled down my cheeks as I gulped back sobs. "Oh Connie, I know what you're going through and if I could, I would take away your pain," Mom reassured. "But I promise you that it will get better and life will be good again."

I leaned hard against my mom's shoulder and let the tears flow freely. She let me cry for about five minutes and then pulled me up with her strong arms and said, "Come on... let's keep walking!" It was our morning ritual before the hot August sun of California scorched us and sent us back into the air-conditioned house.

"One day you'll wake up and cancer won't be the first thing on your mind," my mom promised. As she wrapped her arms around me, she whispered, "Life will be good again, you'll see."

"Really?"

As I blinked back more tears, my mom pushed the hair out of my eyes, like she had done so many times when I was a little girl. It gave me comfort to know that some things remained the same.

A week earlier, I had flown out to visit my parents in Brentwood, California after I finished my radiation treatments for breast cancer. I left my husband and boys—who were nine and fourteen—in Lancaster, Pennsylvania in hopes of regaining my strength and recovering from three months of non-stop medical therapy to eradicate any lingering cancer cells.

Working full-time through treatment and having radiation on my lunch break had taken a physical and emotional toll on me. As most cancer survivors will admit—and I was no exception—the end of treatment is often the most difficult. I had reached an emotional black hole and I didn't know how to climb out of it. I was a skeleton—having lost twenty pounds—and sleeping and eating were pure torture. When I was able to fall asleep, it was only for brief periods of time and then I would wake up in a cold sweat, screaming from night terrors.

Every night my mom would come into the bedroom, flip on the switch to the lamp I had as a child—with its layers of faded pink ruffles—and rub my back while she whispered the soothing words, "This too shall pass." She smoothed the matted hair from my forehead and stayed with me until I fell back to sleep.

Night after night the scenario replayed itself until we were all exhausted, including my dad, who found another place in the house to sleep. But my mom kept vigil each night, making sure that I could peacefully fall asleep.

When I was growing up my mom often used the phrase "this too shall pass" when I fell and scraped my knees, was crushed from a broken heart or didn't feel beautiful with braces and headgear. But this was different; I was forty years old and I had breast cancer! I had everything to live for—a husband who loved me and two boys who needed me—but I just didn't have the strength to keep going. And what were my boys going to do without a mother? The mere thought terrified me.

Every morning my mom had to coach me out of bed and force me to lace up my running shoes. "Come on," she gently coaxed, "you can't stay in bed all day." And then the haunting words, "You can't waste what little time you have left on this earth worrying about the future. You only have today!"

Who better to share that with me than my mom! She had battled breast cancer five years before me and she flew out to Pennsylvania when I had surgery and took care of my family when I couldn't even take care of myself. In her humble way she lived out her words every day of her life. She was a survivor and I desperately wanted to be one too!

The next day—after spending more than a week with my mom and dad—I boarded a plane back to Lancaster, Pennsylvania. My parents accompanied me to the San Francisco Airport and were there to see me get on the airplane. It was Dad who gave me a thumbs-up sign with tears filling his eyes, but it's my mom's face that I will always remember—smiling through a veil of tears and mouthing the words, "This too shall pass."

That was eighteen years ago and I can't thank my mom enough for giving me the will to live and look to the future with hope. I'm not sure of the exact day, but I was getting ready for work and had already seen the boys off to school. I glanced at the clock and realized I didn't have time for breakfast, so I grabbed my coffee mug and headed for the car. It was October—Breast Cancer Awareness Month—and while I was driving, I passed a road sign flocked with pink ribbons reminding women to get their yearly mammograms. I smiled and realized that when I woke up that day, cancer wasn't the first thing on my mind. It happened just like my mom had promised.

Many more family tragedies have come and gone, but with each one the echo of my mom's words has sustained me… "This too shall pass."

~Connie K. Pombo

15

They're My Children

An ounce of mother is worth a pound of clergy.
~Spanish Proverb

I wouldn't be writing this if I hadn't begged my mother to let me wear my hair down that day. It was a Sunday. I was seven. My sister was five. We were sitting alone in a pew in the middle of a big white church in a small Vermont town.

Our mother was up front directing the choir, my father home with the two youngest. My mother must have decided we were old enough to behave ourselves. My sister had her large doll with her, but she was more distracted by my waist-long hair that was usually tightly braided.

I like to imagine we were good for a while, at least until partway through the sermon. But the minister's delivery was pretty dry. Very soon my sister lost interest in the doll and began toying with my hair. Soon she was draping it over and around her and whispering loudly. I was pushing her away from me and too loudly shushing her. As we became more rambunctious, our patent leather Mary Janes were knocking against the pew in front of us.

We forgot all about the minister until he stopped the sermon and said in a very loud voice, "You two girls come down here and sit in front of me."

Scared, heads down, we clambered out to the side aisle and made our long way toward the minister. The church was silent. We passed in front of the choir loft and my mother motioned for us to sit in the pew nearest her. We sat down and the minister boomed: "I told you girls to come sit here in front of me." We were frozen.

My mother replied in an amazingly strong voice: "They're my children and I'll tell them where to sit."

I don't remember the rest of the service, but I know the drive home was silent. My sister and I knew we were going to "get it" when my father learned of our behavior.

She never told my father.

Consequently, he never learned of her bravery until I told him many years later. Although she was a devout churchgoer, and certainly appalled by our misbehavior in a church full of friends and neighbors, she was not cowed by the minister.

It was then I knew that of all she valued, we were the most valuable.

My sister and I still repeat to each other: "They're my children and I'll tell them where to sit."

~Susan DeWitt Wilder

16

Under Control

*Unselfish and noble actions are the most radiant pages
in the biography of souls.*
~David Thomas

om calls to let me know she is in the parking lot at the electric cooperative where I work. I walk outside to visit for a while and to see how things are going today. Each day is an adventure when it comes to my husband Jim, and Mom is his willing cohort.

Mom is parked in the shade of the Bradford pear tree with the driver's side window rolled down. Jim is in the passenger seat. Although it is a pleasant fall day, his Levi's jacket is buttoned to the top button. His ball cap is planted firmly on his head. As always, dark sunglasses hide his bright blue eyes. He happily munches on a spicy chicken sandwich and takes a sip of his Coke.

"He really likes those spicy chicken sandwiches." My mom smiles as she pats Jim on the arm. "Don't you, Jim?" He gives her a tiny smile and a nod.

"Indeed he does." I shake my head. Jim, who used to detest fast food, has developed a taste for the sandwiches.

As usual, Jim remains silent.

Mom has driven fifty miles to spend a few days with us and keep Jim company while I work. I use a home health service, but they can't furnish anyone full-time. Jim's dementia has progressed to the point he can't be left alone, so Mom has come to the rescue. Again.

My seventy-five-year-old mother is healthy and active. She's neatly dressed in jeans, a lightweight turtleneck top, and a light denim jacket. As usual, she is in a good mood. She has other things to do, but willingly volunteers to spend two to three days a week to fill in for the hired caregivers.

Our house is in the country on a gravel road. My mom likes the solitude that some of the hired workers loathe. One caregiver refused to come back after one day on the job because she was afraid to be alone in the country. Of course, it creates a bad situation when a caregiver doesn't show up, or shows up late. Because they are unreliable, I feel that I'm becoming an unreliable worker as well. I take it one day at a time, and today is a worry-free day because Mom is taking care of him.

When I get home from work, we have dinner and Mom brings out her guitar. She sits on a kitchen chair strumming and humming.

Jim plucks his guitar off its stand and settles in a chair facing her. He strums a cowboy song about having a bad day and sings a few lines. It seems to be about the only song he remembers.

"Hey, Jim, can you play 'Buckaroo?'" Mom coaxes.

He strums the cowboy tune again.

"I'd sure like to hear 'Buckaroo,'" Mom said.

Jim gives her a blank look.

Mom nods and smiles encouragement. "Buckaroo?"

Jim's eyes light up, and he lowers his head as his fingers find the melody. The strains of "Buckaroo," played flawlessly fills the kitchen. As soon as he finishes, Mom and I applaud. It is so good to hear his "signature" tune.

He puts his guitar back on the stand and saunters into the living room to watch television.

"How did things go today?" I ask Mom.

"Well, I'd say it's been a good day," she replies. "We watched several episodes of *Walker, Texas Ranger*. He only took off down the road three times today." The patience Mom learned from raising eight kids makes her the perfect caregiver. Chasing Jim down when he wanders out the door and down the road perplexes most of the hired caregivers.

Mom spends the night and is up and helping me get Jim bathed before I go to work. Her bag is packed and sitting by the door. The caregiver is due at 9 a.m., and Mom will stay until she arrives. I hug Mom, thanking her profusely as I leave for work at 6:30 a.m.

"See you next week," she says.

I wonder what I would do without her as I drive down the road, my tires kicking up dust. I try to clear my mind for work.

About ten o'clock, my work phone rings. It's my mom.

"Sharon called a little while ago and said she couldn't come today. She's having some kind of issue with her daughter."

"Again?" This is getting to be a regular problem with this sitter. Of course, the service never has a backup. "Okay. I'll take off the rest of the day and come home." My employer has been flexible with me, and I don't have anything under deadline today. They are aware of the trouble stemming from undependable sitters.

"Don't do that!" Mom says. "I'll just stay another day. At least he's watching *To Hell and Back* today instead of *Walker, Texas Ranger*." Jim has already worn out two VCR tapes of the Audie Murphy movie. "Then, I'll take him for a drive. Maybe we'll pick up some lunch in town. We'll have a good day."

When Mom stays with Jim, he usually does have good days. She has a way of coaxing his best behavior out of him. She uses patience, love, and an occasional bribe of a spicy chicken sandwich.

I swallow hard. "Thanks, Mom. I love you."

"Love you too, honey. Gotta go! Jim's heading out the door."

I hang up the phone. I'm sorry that Mom is putting her own life on hold for another day, but relieved that Jim is spending the day with a woman who loves him like a son.

"Is everything okay?" a coworker asks.

"Yep." I give her a smile as I turn to face my monitor. "My mom's got the situation under control."

~Linda Fisher

Roomies

Living together is an art.
~William Pickens

After my father passed away, I stayed with my mother to help her tackle the decisions for the memorial service and all the other things she needed to do after fifty-three years of marriage. During that time, after many long talks and many tears, we decided to try living together.

We'd always been close but we wondered if living in one house would end up being too close for comfort. Could we set parameters without wounding one another's feelings? She worried about cramping my lifestyle. I worried that she would wait at the door when I came home late. She worried I would feel the need to tiptoe around in the morning while she slept, and I fretted I'd wake her when I headed to work.

During our discussions, we both realized we had only begun to scratch the surface. Would our idiosyncrasies bug each other? I put dirty dishes in the dishwasher immediately, but she doesn't like using the dishwasher. I like white space on the walls. She likes the art gallery look. She watches television every night. I like to read or go out with friends.

We agreed on one thing without hesitation. Cleaning wasn't a priority for either of us. We'd rather create memories. That helped us finalize our decision. We felt as long as we continued to be open and honest, and not let the small things bug us, our relationship would continue to flourish.

We took the plunge and agreed to reevaluate after six months.

Because I'm a gypsy at heart and not attached to "things," I sold most of my belongings so she could keep hers. Still, she weeded through household items, sold a few pieces of furniture, and narrowed down her kitchen goods. We sorted out our duplicates and passed them on to others.

Within a month, we were roommates.

Living beneath one roof brought an inordinate amount of laughter into our lives. We giggled when we used a measuring tape and still couldn't hang a picture straight. After the third try, we stuck a nail in the wall and hung the picture. We decided our intuition was better than planning ahead.

Now, we laugh at each other's "senior moments." There are many. When was the last time you laughed so hard your cheekbones hurt? It's almost a daily occurrence with us.

We've discovered even the simplest things are better with two people. Cleaning house is less of a chore when divided by two. Yes, we do clean occasionally—when company is coming.

We agreed from the beginning not to let our different personalities become a sore point in our friendship. I know I can be bossy. She's an advice-giver. But underneath, it is just because we care. So now we listen with a smile, then use what we want and ignore the rest.

We suspected dividing expenses would have financial benefits, but it took several months before we realized how positive an impact it made on our travel budgets. We booked our first cruise together. Then I took her to Southeast Arizona to show her the birds of the Sky Islands. In Ecuador we each received our first passport stamp.

We do Bible study together and gain new insight into one another and His Word, sometimes discovering something new about each another.

Whether we're tackling a holiday decorating project or just asking, "Does this make me look fat?" we've discovered two heads are better than one. Hearing opinions from someone who loves unconditionally is an extra bonus. Of course, we've also found two minds do not guarantee things will always go smoothly. There have been times when one of us walked out the front door with different socks on and neither of us noticed until much later in the day. Like I said, senior moments occur.

The blessing I treasure the most is having my mother so close every day. I've witnessed a woman gracefully cope with the loss of a beloved spouse. I admire the life she's created since my father died. She volunteers for several charities, plays bridge during the week, quilts and donates children's blankets, and takes senior classes at the local college. She's developed a group of strong friends.

I thought she would be standing at the door when I came home late, but in fact, there are times I get home and she's still out visiting friends. At times I have to fight the temptation to call and ask, "Where are you?"

Although I'm certain it's not always easy, she greets the challenges of her new life with a smile and sense of adventure. Now, instead of praying her idiosyncrasies will not rub me the wrong way, I pray her tenacity and spirit will rub off on me.

And that six-month reevaluation we agreed to? It's been more than five years. We haven't slowed down enough to have that conversation. Perhaps we never will.

~Gail Molsbee Morris

18

Looking Back

*There is in every true woman's heart a spark... which lies
dormant in the broad daylight of prosperity; but which kindles up,
and beams and blazes in the dark hour of adversity.*
~Washington Irving

We found out that my dad had another family back in 2000. My older sister had just started working, my older brother was still in college, and I was in high school. Discovering that my dad had another family while he worked overseas devastated us. Emotionally, we felt betrayed and left behind. Financially, we were at a loss since most of the family income came from his earnings. Physically, we had lost our father. He never came home after that, nor did he make any attempt to contact us.

I was young enough to be naïve and believe that things would work out. Nothing much changed in my everyday life, except that my father stopped coming home from overseas and stopped his weekly phone calls. Since I was mad at my dad for hurting my mom, I was okay with that. But everything else stayed the same—school continued and life went on. Every now and then, Mom would remind me to not be a spendthrift or wasteful. But I was a kid. I didn't understand what was really happening.

We never went hungry, changed schools or had to face how different things really were. Only recently did I learn about the harrowing days that my mother endured. I knew she had gotten sick at some point, but never attributed it to the stress she felt over the pain, loss, and coping for her kids. I knew we had less money but I didn't know that she took out a huge loan to keep us in our schools. Now that I am an adult and paying my own bills, I can't figure out how she did it. I also recently learned my mother had to sell off properties to pay our bills. I never knew any of that was happening.

Mom never let me see how hard it was for her. She let me continue as a carefree teen, focused on my studies and my future. We remained a regular, happy family, spending weekends together at the mall. I have nothing but fond memories of those years. My siblings and I grew up to become well-adjusted happy adults, able to face things head-on, knowing that every problem is conquerable, thanks to our amazing mom.

~Clarissa Villaverde

19

The Perfect Prom Dress

I look back on my childhood and thank the stars above.
For everything you gave me, but mostly for your love.
~Wayne F. Winters

It would be maroon. My favorite color. Maroon with spaghetti straps and a cowl neckline that made it look like I had cleavage. Maybe a bow… No, not a bow. A ruffle. Crap, I messed up. I scribbled over the drawing with my blue pen and sketched a new dress. This one had a ruffle.

"Your paper on *The Awakening* is due on Friday," Mr. Minor announced. Everyone began to put their books in their bags. "Hey! The bell hasn't rung yet. You still have five full minutes. Don't pack up."

I added strappy platform sandals and a necklace to go with my dress. Writing that paper was going to suck. I'd only read half the book, even though AP English was my favorite subject and I loved flamboyant Mr. Minor. But lately, with all the stuff with my mom, it had been hard to focus on some feminist novel from a million years ago.

Then again, it was hard to focus on anything that day. I was going prom dress shopping after school.

Mom had suggested it over the weekend. I was running out the door to my best friend Laura's house when she said it: "Daddy and I want to take you prom dress shopping."

I looked down at my car keys, swinging from their red lanyard. It was February. No one goes prom dress shopping in February. But when everyone went in March and April, she'd be dead.

"Okay," I said slowly. Then, for her sake, "Sounds good."

"Oh good!" she chirped. "I'm so excited. I think we should try Ask Alice first, since that's where we found such pretty dresses last—"

"Okay, Mom," I said, suddenly unable to fake it anymore. "I gotta go."

"Oh, all right sweetheart," I heard her say, a bit bewildered, as I slammed the door behind me and drove off.

The bell rang, and I stirred from the memory. Everyone grabbed their bags and rushed from the classroom, but I packed up slowly. *My mom has pancreatic cancer.* Could I say that to Mr. Minor? None of my teachers knew.

"Have you heard from any schools yet?" he asked.

"Just Binghamton and Penn State so far."

"You won't have any problem," he reassured me, so proud that I wanted to study writing. "Keep me updated."

On the drive home I blasted my new favorite band, At the Drive-In, and sang so loud that it sounded like a sob: *March 23rd hushed the wind, the music died. If you can't get the best of us now, it's 'cause this is forever.* "This is forever"—those words stabbed straight through my heart. Denial can only distract you to a certain degree. Underneath it all, you know exactly what's going on, and that it's not going away.

When I was a block away from my house I lowered the music. It somehow seemed disrespectful to my mom, who'd been home all day instead of teaching. Guilt twisted my guts that I'd been able to escape to school while she'd been forced to retire from hers.

A Baby Story was on TV and the kitchen smelled like toast and jelly when I walked in. Instead of her usual pajamas, Mom was dressed in Gap overalls and a striped thermal shirt. Lilac eye shadow made her green eyes dance. She looked pretty. When she came over, I didn't flinch, like I'd been doing lately. Still wearing my coat and my messenger bag, I just hugged her and let my eyes well up with tears. I blinked quickly before she noticed.

"How was your day, honey?" She sat at the kitchen table, waiting for me to join her. I could tell she hoped that we'd chitchat until Dad got home and we left to go dress shopping. That's what we would have done before all this.

"Good," I said, hanging back near the fridge. "What did you do all day?"

"Oh, I read my book and watched some TV. *A Wedding Story* was on before this. It was a good one. The guy was a pilot and the girl was a flight attendant and he proposed while they were almost in a plane crash."

"Wow," I said half-heartedly, worried she'd change the topic and talk about being sick. I inched backwards toward the staircase that led to my bedroom. "I'm gonna do some homework before we go."

When Dad came home from work, I tied my sneakers quickly, concerned that if I was late that would give him yet another reason to be disappointed in me—the way he had been ever since Mom got sick. He wanted me to be there for her, and I just… couldn't. But when I rushed downstairs, he greeted me playfully: "Monkey!" I was relieved. Especially on prom dress shopping day, I just wanted the three of us to get along, like old times. Even if we were pretending.

In the car, Mom complained that the seat hurt her back while Dad tried to steer with one hand and massage her neck with the other. I gazed out the window, telling myself it wasn't really February. The fact that we were going prom dress shopping so early didn't mean anything, right?

We parked and went inside. Racks of dresses filled the tiny store.

"Ooh, Missy! Look at this one." Mom pointed at a steel gray gown with iridescent sequins. It wasn't maroon.

"I'll try it on," I started to say as she shoved the dress into my arms. She scoped out the sales rack while I browsed by myself, choosing a Betsey Johnson ruffled party dress, a glamorous red satin sheath, and a maroon and black lace gown. The hangers began to bruise my knuckles, and I headed for the fitting room.

I tried on the gray dress first. She'd be hurt if I didn't. Stepping into it, I watched the bottom swirl out like a Cinderella gown. When I emerged, Mom and Dad's faces lit up. "Oh, Missy, you look beautiful," Mom gushed. "Very pretty," Dad agreed. I looked in the mirror. Fluorescent light bounced off the sequins, making the dress sparkle as I turned. It was pretty, in a fairytale kind of way.

I slipped on the other dresses, but even the maroon and black lace dress didn't quite match the dress I'd drawn in my notebook.

"So?" Mom asked, bright-eyed. "What do you think?"

I put on the gray gown again. The saleswoman brought over matching earrings and necklaces, and a pair of heels. I pictured myself stepping out of the limo, reaching for my boyfriend's hand. Mom wasn't there, but I was wearing the dress she picked out, and that mattered.

"Okay," I said. "I'm gonna get it."

Mom and Dad took the dress to the register while I pulled on my jeans and hoodie. I knew if we had longer, we would have searched every store until I found the perfect dress like the one I'd envisioned. We'd shop at Jessica McClintock, Macy's, Bloomingdale's…

I shook myself from the daydream. It couldn't be that way, and it was stupid to wish. Stupid, stupid, stupid.

At home, I headed straight to my room and called Laura.

"Ohmygod, how was it? Did you get a dress? Is it maroon?"

• • •

More than a decade later, Laura will accompany me to dozens of bridal stores as we shop for my wedding dress. And it will only be on those trips, as my heart breaks with longing for my mother, that I will truly understand my mom's sacrifice. That despite her illness, she made something as minuscule and monumental as a prom dress into a revered mother-daughter rite of passage. And with that, she taught me how to march on, even when the situation isn't what you had planned. How to make it beautiful anyway.

~Marisa Bardach Ramel

As Long as I'm Living...

*I love my mother as the trees love water and sunshine—
she helps me grow, prosper, and reach great heights.*
~Terri Guillemets

I remember picking up the phone and calling my mom, telling her I wanted to quit my job and move to a new city to be closer to my fiancée Laura and pursue my dream of one day being a firefighter. My mom's overwhelming support was second nature. When others thought I was crazy and asked why I was leaving a "great gig," she never once questioned my decision. My mom didn't ask why I was leaving a high-paying job, taking a pay cut and pursuing my dream. Her response was, "You're going to make a great firefighter someday and I am glad you are following your heart."

It was the summer of 2013, and Laura and I had finished unpacking the U-Haul at my new apartment. After bringing in the final load of boxes, we slowly began digging through them all to figure out where to start. This was the first time aside from when I went away to college that I would not be in the same city as my parents. As a result, I took all of my belongings from my parents' house, including all of the knickknacks from the basement.

As I unpacked some of my rubber totes and boxes in the spare bedroom, I began filling my shelves with marketing books from college,

EMT books from a night class I took, and my many Chicken Soup for the Soul books. As I reached into the bottom of one tote, I pulled out a book that brought me to tears. It made me flash back to my childhood and think about my mom and everything we had faced, the struggles we shared and how we had persevered. The book was a hardcover copy of *Love You Forever* by Robert Munsch. I opened the book and read the four lines that were so familiar:

> *I'll love you forever,*
> *I'll like you for always,*
> *As long as I'm living*
> *my baby you'll be.*

The book was very meaningful for my mom and me. I remember many nights having that story read to me while we shared a spot on the couch or armchair. I almost always ended up falling asleep. Growing up, my dad's job took us to quite a few new cities, and often times he would move there before us. My mom and I would stay back until the house sold and then pack up to move where my dad was. My brother and sister were quite a bit older than me and were on their own, so they didn't make some of the later moves. I sometimes joke that I grew up as an only child because of the age difference. Because of these special circumstances, my mom and I were able to forge a special bond. That bond has been tested a lot over the past eight years. But because of everything that has happened, our connection is stronger and tighter than ever.

The past eight years I've withstood a number of life-changing events and gone through a lot of rough patches. As I met each obstacle, one thing was constant: my mom was by my side. Through an arrest, two ACL surgeries, completely switching careers and five facial reconstructive surgeries stemming from an assault, my mom never gave up on me and she never stopped praying.

Through all of the trials I have endured, my mom silently fought a battle of her own, never complaining, and never letting it intrude or affect how she cared for others. When I was a senior in high school, my mom went in for some tests, which I thought were routine. I came home from school one day, and to my surprise my mom wasn't home. There was a message on the answering machine — it was my dad saying that my mom needed to have open-heart surgery.

My mom never once let her surgery sideline her from watching a single one of my soccer games, or from asking me how my day was. My mom has been an inspiration and I attribute a lot of my own success to her strength.

So this story is to my mom, a woman with a heart the size of the earth. Thank you. Thank you for believing in me and praying for me when no one else would. Thank you for supporting me and telling me to pursue my dreams. Every time I pull into the fire station after a call, I think about how I got where I am today and what I had to go through. Without her, none of this would have been possible. To a selfless and humble woman, and my best friend:

I'll love you forever,
I'll like you for always,
As long as I'm living
my Mommy you'll be.

~Thomas Schonhardt

Mom Said No

Mothers hold their children's hands for a short while,
but their hearts forever.
~Author Unknown

As I look back on my life and the countless ways she showed her love for me, I realize there are many reasons to thank my mother. Yet, the thing I am most grateful for is that soon after I was born, she said "no."

I was a very sick child, born with cerebral palsy. My pediatrician advised my mom to put me in a home for handicapped children. He said that I would be unable to do anything on my own.

When my sweet mom said "no," that word made all the difference for me, and the direction my life would go.

As a younger woman, my mom sacrificed the carefree life that she could have had to make sure my siblings and I were fed, clothed and educated and that we were happy. My stepfather was a wonderful dad and loved me as his own. But he was a Marine and was stationed overseas a lot. My mom was often all alone taking care of my two older brothers and me. Later our family grew, and I got two younger brothers as well.

Somehow my mom managed to provide a loving and happy home while taking care of me with my health problems. Since I couldn't walk or speak, I needed twenty-four-hour care. I know this must have made life harder for my mom, but she never seemed to mind.

Mom and I learned sign language together when I was only two years old. I attended school for handicapped children for nineteen years. I then decided to further my education by attending a community college and getting my GED. I went on to graduate with an Associate Degree in Computer Science. Looking back, Mom did the right thing by enrolling me in the school for handicapped children because I learned a lot at an early age. At school, the teachers taught me how to crawl, sit up by myself, type on a typewriter, write, and use more advanced sign language so I could communicate with people better. At that school, I made lifelong friends.

When I was seven years old, our home state chose me to be the Poster Child for handicapped children. Mom took me everywhere they needed me to go for publicity tours. We had many new experiences, all thanks to my mom. She felt it was important that I have this unique opportunity.

Every time I was in the hospital, which was often, my mom stayed with me. Some of those times, it meant that she had to leave my dad and brothers for weeks.

I know I have proved that the pediatrician at my birth was completely wrong about me. He assumed that I would be unable to do anything for myself. Even though I can't walk or speak, I graduated from college. I love to write and I have my own mind. I even got married to a loving man. Recently, we celebrated our twentieth wedding anniversary.

I give the credit for all of this to my sweet and devoted mom. Because of her love for me, she did not listen to my doctor all those years ago. If she had, I'm sure I would not be who I am today. I am so grateful and blessed that my mom kept me out of a group home. If she had not sacrificed for me, I would have not known my four great brothers and had an awesome childhood with them. We had fun together, playing outdoors and swimming in our backyard pool.

Now that I am a married adult, I know how hard it must have been for our mom to stay home and have her life revolve around us. Mom always encouraged me to be my best and make my own decisions. Once I made a decision, she was always supportive and helped in any way she could. Even though I know and feel it, Mom tells me that she "loves me bunches" every chance she gets.

If Mom had listened to that pediatrician long ago, I would not have a blessed life with my devoted and loving husband, family and good friends. I would have missed out on a lot of wonderful things. I am so blessed and thrilled that my mom loved me enough to say, "No." Thank you, Mom! I love you bunches too!

~Terrie Lynn Birney

Underwear Model

There's power in looking silly and not caring that you do.
~Amy Poehler

I was singing in the choir in our little country church when I saw her. She came in through the double doors at the opposite end of the church. She had been to the restroom and now she was returning and was at the back row, welcoming guests and inviting them to stay for dinner on the grounds. The place was packed like it always was on homecoming Sunday. This was the day when families brought large boxes and baskets full of food to share after the service. We would sit outside at long rows of picnic tables covered with Southern delicacies like chicken and dumplings, banana pudding and the best fried chicken ever! (After all it, was Kentucky.)

As I sang from the stage, I watched her making her way through the crowd, smiling, hugging, and beaming with hospitality. And then about halfway up the aisle she turned her back to me and I stopped singing. In her haste to rejoin the crowd, the hem of my mother's dress had gotten caught in the elastic waistband of her pantyhose and there was the back of her white underwear for all to see. I knew I had to reach her before she got to the front of the church! But I was a kid, and by the time I got to her, I was laughing so hard I couldn't breathe, let alone speak. Through my pointing and gesturing, she finally realized what I was trying to say, and we headed for the ladies room. I was still guffawing when I saw her face. Tears filled her eyes as she smoothed down the dress in the back. I stopped laughing instantly.

"I am so embarrassed," she said. "Go back inside and get my purse. I'm going home."

"What? Home?" Selfishly, my mind raced to the chicken and dumplings and banana pudding to be served at the picnic. I had to talk her out of it.

"You don't want to do that," I began. "What about all the food you've made? And the guests you've invited! Think of them! Besides, they've already seen you now, so unless you plan on never coming back..." My voice trailed off and a slight smile crossed her face. She stared into the mirror, wiped her tears and said with resolve, "You're right. Let's go!"

I was never more surprised and impressed. At the dinner, a few women came over to laugh at her, and I cringed. But she just waved them away and acted like she couldn't care less. She finished out that day doing the same things she had done every other year, greeting, serving and welcoming others. It was about them, not her. On that day, I'm sure she never thought about the young daughter that was watching her. That single event would influence my response to teasing, bullying and embarrassing moments for the rest of my life. She probably would never have imagined that her most embarrassing moment would have turned out to be the day I was never more proud.

~Edie Schmidt

Speak Up

Don't be afraid to stand up for yourself,
you should speak up even if you don't get the answer you were
looking for; it's the fact that you said something that matters.
~Author Unknown

"No, I don't want to go to school anymore. Anyway, I can't find my backpack," I protested.

My mom looked at me, puzzled. "What's going on? Why don't you want to go to school?"

"I can't find my backpack. Besides, I don't like school anymore! Can you teach me here at home, please?"

My mom remained adamant. "What is the real reason you don't want to go to school? Is someone bothering you?"

"No! I just don't like school anymore, and I can't go to school without my backpack. That's where I have my homework."

Earlier that morning I had sneaked into the back yard and, attempting to hide my backpack, I'd thrown it on the roof. My mom walked straight into the back yard and pointed up to the roof.

"Maria, isn't that your backpack?"

My heart sank. How did she know it was up there? My brilliant plan had backfired.

At the beginning of the school year I had been so happy to start second grade. I had a few friends and we were always playing and talking about school and planning new adventures for our weekends. I had my routine. Every day after school I would take off my uniform and get it ready for the next day. I had a jump rope that I took to school and only my friends and I could use it. School was fun. After school I would tell my mom all about my day and everything that had happened.

But now I didn't want to go back. And Mom was trying to get to the root of the problem. I finally gave in and told her, "I don't want to go to school anymore because the teacher pinches me on my arm and sometimes on my back."

Very calmly Mom said, "Okay, let's go; I'm going to have a talk with her." At that moment I regretted telling my mom about the pinching. I pleaded with her to forget what I'd said.

I had the whole scenario down in my mind. I could see it. After the meeting my teacher was going to slap me and continue to pinch me and separate me from my friends. I was terrified, but my mom grabbed me by the hand and took me to school.

We arrived late. My teacher came to the door and said, "Good morning. What is going on?" I did not respond; I was paralyzed with fear.

Mom took charge by saying, "Good morning. I am Maria's mother, and I'm here because my daughter does not want to come to school anymore. She says you pinch her arm and her back."

My teacher glared at me with a piercing gaze that sent chills down my spine. She proceeded by saying, "What a little liar you are, Maria. When have I ever done those things to you?"

I wished the floor under me would open and swallow me. I wanted to disappear, but my mother courageously said, "I don't think Maria has a reason to lie, but let me tell you something. My daughter does not come to school to be punished; she comes to school to learn. And if there is a problem with her behavior, you can send me a note. I need to make sure you understand that if this punishment continues I'm going to have a meeting with the principal, and if that does not give me good results, I will go to the district. Do you understand my concern?"

The teacher changed her tone and said, "I'm sorry for this misunderstanding. It will never happen again."

My mother gave me a hug and a kiss and left. As I walked inside the classroom I heard a tender sweet voice directing me to my seat. It was my teacher saying, "Maria, take your seat. We are reading page 22."

After that magical day my life at school changed. My teacher treated me decently, and I was not afraid to go to school anymore. She never pinched me or anyone else in my class that year.

That day I learned you don't have to be a victim, and that when you speak up people listen. Even though this incident happened many years ago, that day my mom became my hero. This experience gave me the courage to speak up throughout my adult life whenever I encounter an injustice, which is something I've passed on to my children.

~Maria Calderon Sandoval

Until One Day

Force is all-conquering,
but its victories are short-lived.
~Abraham Lincoln

ot again, I thought, but all the bumping and cursing from the hallway beyond my closed door told me differently. I may have been but four years old but the muffled sounds of sorrow had become all too familiar. As I sat on my white canopy bed, I would often turn up the volume on my little thirteen-inch television set and pretend that my life was as sweet as the cotton candy pink throw pillows that surrounded me. Just like my father had instructed me to do so many times in the past, I sat and waited and minded my own business until he came for me. Until one day... I didn't.

Maybe I was being disobedient. Maybe I was just curious. Maybe I was just a small girl whose desire to match sounds to sights overcame her desire to be safe in a land where laugh tracks had perfect timing. As I cracked my bedroom door I was startled by a gruesome sight that took a while to decipher. Eventually, I realized that the arms and legs I was seeing belonged to two people—my father and my mother—and my father was suffocating my mother with a pillow while she fought back.

Had my eyes deceived me? How could my father—my provider and hero—hurt my mother, who was my other provider and hero? Suddenly my mother reached out and yanked the phone cord, sending the telephone crashing to the wood floor. In that instant, I came eye to eye with two people I had never met before: a violent, angry man I called Daddy, and a vulnerable, listless woman I called Mama.

Mama stretched for the phone but couldn't reach it. She begged me repeatedly to hand her the phone or call 911. With every plea from Mama came a threat from Daddy not to touch the phone or else. If I had had the courage to take just one step towards Mama I would have been her saving grace that day. But I was more afraid of the malice in Daddy's voice than I was the urgency in Mama's. Retreating back to my room, I shut the door, turned the volume up on my television, sat on my white canopy bed and pretended that my life was just as sweet as the cotton candy throw pillows that surrounded me.

Until one day.

One day, my mother, brothers and I stopped running away from home.

One day, we stopped returning to the battered women's shelter.

One day, we stopped hiding at my grandmother's house.

One day, we stopped pretending we didn't see the bruises, busted lips, and blackened eyes.

One day, our father was gone for good.

One day, I no longer had to pretend.

And for that, I say, thank you.

Thank you for deciding that our mental health was more important than the stigma that came along with being a divorced single woman with three young children.

Thank you for deciding that struggling to provide for us was worth more than the security of an extra paycheck.

Thank you for not letting us grow up with domestic violence.

Most importantly, thank you for leaving my father, whom I loved dearly.

It was the best choice you could have ever made for you, for me, for us.

For that, Mama, I thank you.

~M.G. Lane

Safety Arms

A mother's arms are made of tenderness
and children sleep soundly in them.
~Victor Hugo

I don't remember the day my mother saved my life. But for her, the memory of that day is vivid. When she recalls those events, she's thirty-five years old again and I am a tiny bundle in her arms.

It's early March, but the icy wind bites like it's the depths of December. My mother tucks the blanket even tighter around me as she hurries to the clinic door. I am two months old, and this is our third visit to the doctor this week. Each time a different face says the same words: "It's nothing. Just a simple cold, ma'am." Today is no different. My mother leaves feeling frustrated, convinced that my constant congestion is something more. At home, she keeps me closer than normal, constantly monitoring my breathing and worriedly stroking my baby fuzz hair.

When I wake up that blustery Thursday morning, gasping for air, her arms are around me with quick sureness, running me out to the car. We fly past stop signs and red lights, my mother periodically wrenching one white-knuckled hand from the steering wheel to jiggle my car seat as I rasp. "Breathe, Alana! Breathe!" she cries out. Small tears that fall onto my bluish face are mirrored in my mother's sapphire eyes, desperation finally taking over.

We reach the hospital, and her safety arms are around me again.

"This baby can't breathe!" my mother shouts, her voice ringing out above all the beeping. Even as tubes and doctors surround me, her arms never let me go, and I breathe in sweet air.

Now I'm twelve years old, and those same arms enclose me as I crumple onto the cold, blue-green slate of the kitchen floor. She whispers soothing words. My sister's head rests on her shoulder. A few feet away, my older brother slumps against the wall, holding our dog Dotch's head in his lap.

The doorbell rings. My mother pauses, looking up at my brother and silently asking him to be strong. She attentively unfolds my sister and me from her arms, then looks at each of us. Her blue eyes soften, and if I were older I might glimpse how hard the situation is for her too. "It's going to be okay," she promises quietly. The veterinarian is waiting. Standing up, my mother kisses each of us on the forehead before approaching the door. She is completely composed as she smiles and politely welcomes the veterinarian.

We knew this day was coming, and our parents had prepared us for it. Yet putting our beloved fifteen-year-old dog to sleep is harder than all of us had imagined. When the moment finally comes, my mother prepares a spoon overflowing with peanut butter—Dotch's favorite treat—to distract Dotch from the hovering needle. My mother's warm fingers enclose mine. The vet murmurs a string of words, but I don't hear. As Dotch's eyes close for the last time, I fight back tears inside those safety arms.

Today I'm seventeen, and for most people that means the times for dependence are over. It's early September, and I am applying to colleges. My fingers type out essays, addresses, achievements, awards. I stare for hours at the computer screen until it's all I can see, and I am overwhelmed. Suddenly, I feel young and unsure. When did I go from child to adult? Behind me, the door creaks open, interrupting my trance. My mother enters carrying a bowl of steaming soup. "How's it going, honey?" She sets the bowl in front of me as I groan in response.

Standing up to stretch, I suddenly ache with stiffness all over my body. She holds out her arms, and I sink into them. For the first time that day, I feel comfort and safety and strength; it's all going to be okay.

And I realize that dependence is not a weakness; rather, it is the appreciation that with someone by my side, I am much stronger than I will ever be alone. My mother's support is and will always be unfaltering. Each embrace brings strength; each small word encourages me to pursue my dreams. No, I may not remember the moment my mother saved my life so long ago. However, looking back, I see that this was not a one-time occurrence. My mother saves my life every day.

~Alana Patrick

No Matter What

Every plan in life is different. Each leads to its own perfection.
When we allow hope and love to exceed fear, we will experience
harmony in everything we do.
~Johnny Tan

My mother tried to have a baby for fifteen years. When I was finally born after a C-section when the umbilical cord wrapped around my neck, I was her miracle baby.

Later, my mother had to come to grips with my autism diagnosis. This was especially hard after my father died when I was three.

Lucky for me, my mom recognized my potential and didn't listen to all the negativity that she heard from doctors. She also married my stepfather Bruce, who has become my real father and who I call "Dad."

Recently, while visiting with my parents one Saturday night, I asked my mom to talk about my childhood challenges.

"Well, your dad and I took you to Johns Hopkins to see a specialist when you were about twelve." She turned and looked at my fiancée for a moment before continuing. "Amber, that was the longest car ride ever. For twelve hours, he would not shut up about an Elmo doll. Bruce and I wanted to throw Elmo out the car window."

"Sorry about that. I'm surprised you didn't send me to live with Elmo," I retorted, laughing.

The doctors at Johns Hopkins, like those back home, told my

mom I would have problems. It was at Johns Hopkins that doctors discovered that in addition to the autism, there was frontal lobe damage to my brain and that my development was three to four years delayed. I stayed in an observation room for about a week. Eventually, doctors sat down with my parents and explained what was going on.

"Ms. Stocks, Tyler is a smart child and a friendly child. He can develop normally. He just needs to be around other kids and participate in sports," a doctor said.

My mother made sure that I was always around other people. I played baseball with the neighborhood kids, and I participated in basketball and football in high school.

Mom held me when I had meltdowns and accepted me when I failed to talk and made grunting noises instead. She made sure that I remembered to take my lunch to school every day, that my shirt wasn't inside out again, and that I wasn't trying to wear the same smelly outfit I wore to school the previous day. Most importantly, Mom spent hours meeting with my teachers and gathering all my paperwork and medical documentation to ensure that from elementary school through high school, I received my academic accommodations.

My mother's tenacity and compassion illuminated the darkness for me and helped alleviate the fear and anxiety I had about school. She even worked multiple jobs so that I could receive private tutoring sessions. She made sure I got the best education possible.

I graduated high school and received the same diploma that the rest of my class members did. I didn't have to settle for a GED or a vocational high school completion certificate. I had struggled for four long years and my mother had struggled with me. In many respects she had to become a high school student all over again. The algebra just about killed us.

I had made it and the graduation ceremony was glorious. After it ended, I embraced my mother while trying to hold back the tears that were flowing down my face. "I did it Mom, I did it."

"Doctors told me you would never graduate from high school. I knew you could. Look at you now. Your dad and I are so proud of you."

Now I am a published writer and student at East Carolina University. All because of Mom. She gave life to my dreams and goals. She believed in me when others did not. In the end, I wasn't just a problematic autistic kid who couldn't do anything, who had to live with his mom and dad the rest of his life.

My mother taught me how to survive in the world. She advocated on my behalf. She was my best friend when times were tough. She has been with me through thick and thin. When I couldn't walk, she carried me. When I couldn't talk, she graced me with her smile. Her determination and courage have truly been uplifting. She made up her mind from the moment I came into the world that God had a plan for me. My mom gave me the eyes to see that plan. My mom is the reason I am what I am today.

~Tyler Stocks

Chapter 3

Thanks to My Mom

Maternal Mischief

Catastrophe

Life is either a great adventure or nothing.
~Helen Keller

If I were a betting woman, I would have said the odds were overwhelmingly against my mother going to a tattoo parlor, but there she was. Growing up, my mother taught me many things, mostly by example, and today was proving no different.

Today's lesson was about ingenuity, a trait she cherished. When she first told me her plan, calling it her last option, I decided I'd better go with her. That's how we both came to be standing on the threshold of Wicked Ink.

A cheery bell signaled our arrival. The clerk behind the counter greeted us with a wave and asked for a moment while he finished rolling what looked like a poster for a customer. I'm not sure who I expected to be working in this shop, but his welcoming eyes and nice smile were not only a pleasant surprise but also a comfort. I mean, this was my mother we were talking about.

While we waited, Mom pretended to admire the samples that covered the walls in dizzying rows, everything from fierce dragons to colorful butterflies. And skulls. I saw her eyes go wide.

"You still think this is a good idea, right?" I asked her. "Because we can leave."

"We're here, let's see it through." She fumbled in her purse for a Tums. "I'm at my wit's end."

The shopper left and we couldn't delay any longer. I put a firm hand on her back and propelled her forward. She tightened the scarf that covered the lower half of her face, mortified that anyone might see her, and made her way over to the clerk on shaky legs.

"Hello, how can I help you?"

"I'd like to speak to someone about—" she hesitated, "a problem," she finished in almost a whisper.

"You'd like to get a tattoo?"

"No. Definitely no," Mom said quickly. "I'm a kindergarten aide," she added, as though that explained everything.

"I see," he said, but of course he really didn't. "And?"

I could tell that she was fighting the urge to bolt. "I figured you guys were ink experts, so you'd be able to help me."

He leaned his elbows on the counter. "That's true. About the ink. So, do you want to tell me about it?" When she didn't respond, he pointed to a curtained-off section and added, "We could go in the back if you'd like."

Mom let out a grateful breath. "Yes, please."

We followed him to the area and she settled herself in an artist's chair. She didn't seem to know whether she should put her legs up on the recliner part or not. She tried it both ways, and settled for sitting sideways and ramrod straight. He seemed to sense her fish-out-of-water moment and waited patiently. She slowly lowered her scarf, a simple act that I knew took all her strength.

I had to give him credit. His eyes widened but he didn't gasp or say anything. I was sure he'd seen worse. He snapped on a light and stepped closer. "That is impressive," he finally said.

Mom could tell from the look on his face that he was holding in his laughter. "Don't you dare laugh at me," she said in her best teacher voice.

His eyes twinkled. "I'm more of a dog man myself, but those are great cat whiskers. May I?" he asked, as he lifted a hand. At Mom's nod, he gently examined her face. "Let me guess, indelible ink?"

"Yes." She flashed him an embarrassed smile.

"Your cheeks are quite red. What have you been doing?"

"My daughter went online and looked up ways to remove ink. We've tried everything: hand sanitizer, rubbing alcohol, even hair spray. They're not as dark as they were, but even make-up won't cover them."

"How did this happen, if you don't mind my asking?"

"Today my class was doing face painting, and we were having a great time. The kids wanted to do my face, so I let them. I shut my eyes so I wouldn't get anything in them, and when I opened them… well, as you can see, I'm now a cat. I didn't even know there was a marker in the box of paints." Mom tucked a loose strand of gray-streaked hair behind her ear. "I've washed it and creamed it. It won't come off."

"Don't worry; it will wear off in a week or so," he said.

"Oh, no," she wailed. "I can't be a cat for a week. Open house is tomorrow night."

He snapped his fingers and his face lit up. "You're Mrs. Somers. My nephew is in your class. Jacob Murphy?"

"Yes, we've got Jacob this year. He's a great kid."

The thought of her class made my mom's face light up despite her situation. When my daughter started kindergarten, my mom wanted to be a part of it so she signed up to help. She read books, helped with the arts and crafts programs, and generally assisted the teacher. She loved it and had been in that classroom for three years.

He leaned back against the supply counter and crossed his arms. "I don't think I can help you."

At the look on her face he quickly added, "No, I mean I can't help you because I don't work here."

I suddenly realized he didn't have a single tattoo himself.

"Len, my uncle, owns this shop." He held out his hand. "I'm Ethan. I come in and do his books. He'll be right back. He ran to the bank. I'm sure he'll know what to do."

"You think so?" Relief flooded her face and for the first time since it happened she began to relax. "It is a little funny," she admitted.

Just then the doorbell dinged. It was Len, who proved to be as charming as his nephew. I noticed when they were introduced and shook hands that he held mom's a few beats longer than necessary. Sure enough he had a remedy. As he applied the remover with gentle dabs of soaked cotton, he flirted shamelessly. It made me smile to see Mom laugh and even get a bit flustered at his attention. Fifteen minutes later, Mom was appreciative and whisker-free. Len insisted on walking us out to the car, opening the doors for both of us. Mom settled herself in the passenger seat and turned to thank him once again.

"If you're free this Saturday night, I'm playing guitar at the art café around the corner," he said. "Any interest in coming with me?"

She was very interested.

"Make sure they don't ink stamp your hand to get in," I teased.

"Don't you worry about it," she said as we pulled away. "If they do, I know a man."

~Jody Lebel

28

Eating the Evidence

There can never be enough said of the virtues, dangers, the power of a shared laugh.
~Françoise Sagan

The jig was up, I thought, as the U.S. Federal Inspection Service Agent tore open my knapsack and flung my neatly packed contents helter-skelter. All too soon she would discover my secret stash of goji berries. I suspected there might be a problem. My brother said they could be confiscated. I didn't anticipate that my mother's banana would be the culprit or that I'd be held for questioning and nearly arrested for its possession.

We had spent two weeks visiting my brother and sister-in-law in Hong Kong. I had sampled so many delectable examples of Chinese cuisine. The goji berries particularly enchanted me. These diamond-shaped beads stud Cantonese puddings, stews, and soups like bright red jewels. I love their sweet fruity taste. When I saw them on the grocery shelf, just hours before our flight left for San Francisco, I bought them as a reminder of our delightful adventure.

Our trip had been the first time my mother and I had traveled together for longer than three days. I had some trepidation. A conversation with her is not complete without her saying, "What would people think if you do such and such?" She also worries about the outcome of things, assuming they'll end badly. Usually I groan and roll my eyes, but I've also become adept at planning for worst-case scenarios. I worry too much about what people think of me. I even worried what she would say if I did something outrageous. I wanted to just be myself and not have her comments interrupting my flow on our vacation.

The trip had actually gone without a hitch. Because I was enjoying her company, I wasn't concerned with what she or anyone else thought of me.

When I purchased the goji berries, my mother and I also bought bananas to eat on the plane. My brother, who has flown the Asia-U.S. route many times, warned me about the berries, so I took precautions, hiding the sealed packet deep within a black bag. He didn't comment on the bananas.

My mother and I both stored the bananas in our carry-on items—mine in my handbag under the seat in front of me, and hers in her roll-along knapsack in an overhead bin several rows behind us.

As we settled into our comfy padded seats, the soft airline blankets covering our legs, she said, "We must remember to eat our bananas."

"No problem," I said. "I'll eat mine for breakfast."

The engine roared, the lights dimmed, and our plane took off into the clouds, on time after midnight for the twelve-hour flight back to San Francisco. At 2:30 a.m., the flight attendant brought our dinners and customs forms. My mother pointed to one item on the moss-green rectangle. It read: I am bringing fruit/vegetables back to U.S. soil. "I checked 'no,'" she said.

I was surprised, but then I rationalized: by the time we arrived we would've eaten our bananas. I trusted my mother's decision. "I will, too." I knew I wouldn't have a problem.

A few hours later, my mother said, "I would like to get my banana."

"How will you do that?" I didn't know if she had the upper body strength to reach into the far left corner of the bin, drag out the knapsack, and maneuver it to the floor, especially since she had complained about its weight as we trekked through Hong Kong. Had it been stored over our row, I would have offered to retrieve it. Since I had the aisle seat, I knew I wouldn't hit anyone on the head with it, if it fell.

But it rested above someone else's row. The thought of getting it down made me worry about dropping it on the man in the seat below the bin. "I know what you could do—wait for the plane to land, get someone to help you with your bag, then eat your banana."

"Oh no, Eva, that wouldn't be legal."

She changed her mind as I ate my bananas. "Could you eat my banana, too? I'll give it to you after we land."

Maybe her lack of sleep kept her from thinking clearly. It was unlike her to suggest such a thing.

"Of course," I said, planning to eat it right after we deplaned.

Just then, we hit turbulence. I gripped my armrest and gritted my teeth as the plane jumped and bounced and bumped, jerking and shaking through the air.

By the time we taxied to our gate, I was clutching the seatbelt, eager to be the first to unclasp it and race off to find the bathroom. Neither of us mentioned the banana.

When I caught up to my mother, we made a beeline for baggage claim and then to Federal Inspection. Right after we went through the doorway, we dropped our bags to the floor and rested. She said, "I still have my banana. You'll have to eat it now."

Since I was used to her extreme moral self, it didn't occur to me that she could be anything but. Still, I glanced around, remembering my flight back from Ecuador the year before when a dog had sniffed my carry-on for drugs. I wondered whether German shepherds had been trained to sniff out bananas. I didn't see any dogs drooling, waiting to pounce. We were safe.

"Here," my mother said, "turn around so no one will see you."

I did as I was told. Even though I am forty-seven and she is seventy-five, I have moments where I am as obedient as when I was growing up. Unpeeling the banana, I stuffed giant-sized bites between my lips. I didn't feel good about what I was doing. What if I got a stomachache?

Halfway through eating it, an officer strode over, looking official in his black shirt, black pants, and gold U.S. Customs insignia. "May I please see your passports?"

"Is this about the banana?" I asked.

He nodded.

"I can explain. It was in my mother's knapsack. She planned to eat it on the plane, but didn't have a chance, so she gave it to me. We both knew it was wrong, but…"

He held up his hand to stop me. Oops. My mouth went dry. At any moment he might whisk us off to federal prison. A newspaper headline flashed through my mind: "Woman Held for Possession of a Banana."

He said, "You can hand in your banana to the agent and you won't be in trouble or you can keep eating it. Your choice."

For a mini-second, I was tempted to keep eating it. I needed the potassium to give me strength. But I also valued our freedom, so I discussed the matter with my partner in crime. My mother decided she'd hand it in. It was, after all, her banana. I felt sad giving it up. What a waste of a good banana.

We filed behind the other passengers in line for inspection. Recalling my brother's cautionary words, I leaned over, whispering to my mother, "I wonder if I should mention my goji berries."

"The less said, the better," my mother muttered.

Hard to believe, I missed her usual lecture about what people would think and the doom that would follow my misstep. I wondered what had happened to the mother I knew, who obeyed every rule, every time, the one who raised me to be honest and ethical.

My stomach tightened. I had narrowly escaped being arrested over a banana, but what if someone found out about my berries? Why wasn't she concerned with what the federal inspection agents would think if they discovered her daughter's stash of goji berries?

Seizing my knapsack, an agent said, "Did you bring any fruits or vegetables?"

I scrunched up my face, feeling awkward. "Goji berries," I sighed.

"Show me." The zipper squealed open as she pawed at assorted packages.

I dug and dug, overturning containers and rustling plastic bags. The berries were invisible, even to me. Later in my apartment, I found them, squished beneath parcels, but at the time neither of us could detect them.

"What had you seen?" she consulted the man inspecting ghostly images on a digital screen.

"A carrot," he said.

"Oh, a carrot." That explained everything. I felt the sharp corners of a box and opened it, revealing a wooden acupressure horn, curved like the letter J. "Did you mean this?"

He nodded, and the agent said I could gather my things.

As the doors swung open for our grand entrance, my mother and I doubled over laughing. She had shown a different side of herself, and even though we nearly got arrested, love swelled inside me, linking us. I wouldn't trade that for anything, not even a banana.

~Eva Schlesinger

The Mailman

A mother is the truest friend we have when trials, heavy and sudden, fall upon us; when adversity takes the place of prosperity.
~Washington Irving

In the summer of 2013, at the ripe age of nineteen, I left home to spend nine "wonderful" weeks in Army Basic Training at Fort Sill, Oklahoma. Prior to leaving, I solicited advice on how to survive basic training from active duty soldiers in our church who were stationed at a nearby Army base. I also received a lot of unsolicited advice from several retired soldiers who had "been there and done that" many years ago. As the advice piled up, I noticed that no matter where it came from, young soldier or retired veteran, there was always one common admonition: avoid the attention of your drill sergeant! I was repeatedly told to keep a low profile, avoid the limelight, and try to make it through basic training without my drill sergeant ever knowing my name. So that's what I set out to do.

During the first week of basic training, I was so good at keeping a low profile that I was virtually invisible. But then, Mom intervened. After I had left her crying and waving goodbye on the doorstep when I departed, she anxiously awaited the first letter from me to give her my address. All "new soldiers" were required to write home on our first day at Fort Sill to provide anxious parents our address and to hopefully avoid having our anxious parents call our drill sergeants. As luck would have it, my first letter got lost. So back home in Alabama, Mom was convinced that something terrible had happened to me. After a week of not hearing a single word, Mom wore down my stepfather (a retired Army officer) until he finally called Fort Sill and spoke to my drill sergeant. I was then called out of my platoon, by name, by my drill sergeant, and escorted to an office where he instructed me to call home — now! He listened intently as I assured Mom, "All is well. Don't worry." So much for keeping a low profile!

After that, I crept back into "stealth mode" and succeeded at melting into basic training anonymity, at least for one more week! Because that's when Mom learned that my long-time girlfriend had sent me a "Dear John" letter, breaking up with me. That's all it took for my anxious mom to turn into a "mama bear" determined to make sure that her little wounded cub was okay.

So once again, Mom went to work on my stepfather, pressuring him to use his knowledge of the Army system and any connections he had to contact Fort Sill to check on me. I don't blame my stepfather; a man can only take so much nipping at his heels from an angry, anxious "mama bear." Finally, knowing if he didn't do something, Mom might hop in her van and drive 1,200 miles to see me, my stepfather caved and called an officer he knew at Fort Sill. Within thirty minutes of his call, I was again called out of my platoon by the loud, booming voice of my drill sergeant. "Private Waterman, come here right now!"

With a pounding heart and wobbly knees, I ran to stand in front of my drill sergeant. He gestured to an officer standing nearby and told me to go with him. The officer was a chaplain. Oh no, I thought, something bad has happened at home and the chaplain has come to give me terrible news. Instead, the chaplain said, "Your mother is worried about you because of the Dear John letter and somehow she contacted my superior officer and he ordered me to check on you."

After assuring him I was fine, the chaplain prayed with me and said he would contact my mom to reassure her. Then he sent me back to my drill sergeant. So far it was proving very difficult for me to follow the sage advice to stay off my drill sergeant's radar. Now, not only did he know my name, he knew my mom's name as well!

After that, Mom didn't initiate any more calls to Fort Sill. Instead, she shifted her focus to keeping my spirits high. I appreciate her for doing that, but how she went about it for my remaining weeks in basic training didn't help to lower my profile. She gave my address to everyone she knew, told them about the "Dear John" letter, and asked them to write to me. As the wife of a pastor of a church with over 2,000 members, Mom knew a lot of people! And if that wasn't enough, she also posted the same request on Facebook, Twitter, and Instagram! The result was that instead of overcoming the phone calls and being an invisible soldier, I started to receive a lot of mail. It was ridiculous—and embarrassing! I got letters from people I didn't know, from places I didn't recognize, from somebody and anybody who read a random post about a broken-hearted young soldier and wanted to encourage me.

Every day in basic training, usually at the end of the day, there was a "mail call," the only time when all 200 of the soldiers in my company were assembled. A sergeant would read the names from the letters and then pass them through the group to the lucky soldier. Again, so much for keeping a low profile! After Mom started her letter writing campaign, I got so much mail that I was ordered to sit next to the drill sergeant, the one I was doing my best to avoid, in order to save time passing so many letters to me through the group.

Instead of going through basic training quietly and unknown, I became one of the best-known soldiers to my drill sergeant. He told me, "You're the new record holder at Fort Sill for the number of letters received during basic training, over 400 letters in just nine weeks, an average of over ten letters every day! Congratulations!"

Even though it disrupted my plan to be an "unknown soldier," I must admit that Mom's concern and love lifted my spirits and enabled me to successfully complete basic training. Once again she proved that she is always there to help me, and I will never forget how she did it.

Oh, by the way, I may have been a bit invisible after all. I don't think my drill sergeant ever remembered my name because he just always called me "The Mailman."

~Zachary Waterman

Neither Snow, Nor Rain, Nor Gloom of Night

I know how to do anything—I'm a mom.
~Roseanne Barr

The rain came on fast, with those big fat drops that appear out of nowhere, and before I knew it my doll and I were drenched! My friend Susan and I had been playing with our dolls in the alley, watching our big brothers play kickball and carefully guarding our dolls from the big red balls flying in our direction.

But now the skies were dark, with thunder and lightning raging. Dozens of kids fled to their homes. I raced down the alley with my carriage and my doll blanket. It wasn't until I was safely inside that I realized, to my utter dismay, that my doll Susie (whom I had named after my playmate) was missing.

Is there any childhood panic or despair like that of a five-year-old girl whose only doll has been lost in the rain? So my sweet, beautiful mother went out into the dark and the rain to look for her. I was hysterical, crying for Susie and frantic that she would be washed down the alley and lost forever.

Later, the door opened and my mom walked in, shivering and soaking wet. She did not have Susie. I started howling again, but she hugged me and told me that as soon as the sun came up the next day we would go out and find her.

And so we did. She enlisted my dad, my brothers and sister, and all our friends on the block to search up and down the alleys and streets for Susie. It was the first time in my short life that I realized my mother was not completely magical, for after an hour or two even she, with all her wondrous powers of healing and fixing and making things wonderful again, couldn't find my beloved doll.

I don't remember what happened next. I suppose I cried and cried. But I think my mom must have promised that everything was going to be fine, because I was overjoyed but not surprised when, two days later, she came into the house carrying Susie.

"Kathleen, look what happened! The doll hospital called to say that someone found Susie and brought her into the hospital. They cleaned her up and fixed her hair (my brother had cut her hair the year before) and got her a new dress because her other one was so muddy. They heard that we were looking for her and they called us to say she was all better and ready to come home."

I looked at my magic mother and my beautiful doll. Susie must have been very sick, because her skin wasn't nearly as cuddly, and her eyes weren't exactly the same color, and her red hair was kind of orange now. I missed her red plaid dress, but the new blue dress they gave her in the hospital was pretty too. I hugged her and told her how much I had missed her and how happy I was that she was home.

Fast forward to a Wednesday morning twenty-five years later. I was singing with my music class, an exuberant group of kindergartners. One of the little girls had her doll with her, and she was singing and dancing with her around the piano. Suddenly, a cloud lifted from my memory. The blazing sun of realization finally dawned. I started giggling to myself, then laughing like a crazy lady. At the five-minute break, I marched straight into the faculty lounge and dialed the familiar phone number of my childhood.

"Hello," said my magic mother.

"That wasn't really Susie you brought home that day, was it," I accused.

"I've got the dumbest kids in America," she said.

She'd been waiting twenty-five years for that phone call, and she didn't miss a beat when it finally came.

She remains my magic mother, the one who was so chilly in the air-conditioned restaurant in Hawaii that she took the tablecloth off and wrapped it around her shoulders. The one who, a year before her death, was so tired of looking at the brown and dying flowers in the front yard that she got a spray can and painted them bright purple.

Her magic wasn't strong enough for the cancer that claimed her, but the memory of her love and tenderness with her children can still, after all these years, heal our broken hearts and bring our lost loves back to us.

Neither snow, nor rain, nor gloom of night was going to keep my magic mother from consoling her little girl. She was going to find Susie, whether she had to swim to her, or dig her out of the mud, or enlist the "doll hospital" to do it. And you know what? She's still rescuing me, still consoling me, still loving me, twenty-nine years after her death.

That's the strongest magic of all.

~Kathy McGovern

Mom's Cuss Jar

Pull yourself together and use what you have.
~Betsy Cañas Garmon

With a house full of kids from toddlers to teens, Mom was a full-time homemaker while Dad worked at a local factory. To keep food on the table and a roof over our heads—and most likely to enjoy some peace and quiet—he volunteered for overtime whenever he could.

Dad was a strict disciplinarian and head of our household, but Mom was the heart of our home who lovingly maintained order. She made sure we got to school on time, finished our homework, and stuck to our promises to give up something—usually candy—during Lent.

Then one spring, her orderly world turned upside down. Dad was hospitalized with pneumonia and was unable to work for more than a month. Mom assumed Dad's role as the breadwinner, but she needed a job that allowed her to stay home during the day. With just an eighth-grade education, the only work she could find was as a late-shift waitress at a diner that catered to a rowdy, but generous, crowd.

After a long day of cooking, cleaning, and taking care of her family, she donned her uniform and rode a bus to work. She'd come home just before bedtime, bone-tired, but relieved she'd earned a decent living and proud of the fact that she'd learned how to make dishes we'd never eaten before, like hot German potato salad, mostaccioli and meatballs, and, my favorite—mayonnaise cake. And most nights she brought home leftovers.

As I helped count her tips, I asked, "Why do you have to work so late, and why do we have to eat leftovers from the diner? Are we poor?"

She sighed as she brushed my hair. "There's no shame in being poor, honey, and no shame in hard work. Besides, my boss and the people I wait on are good to us."

After working a few weeks, another thing she brought home was a salty vocabulary. Whenever she got stressed, which usually happened when we misbehaved or after bill collectors called, she'd spout a string of swear words. And she wasn't alone. One of my brothers accidently broke a toy and swore, using a word from Mom's new vocabulary.

When she punished him, he whined, "It's not fair! You say it all the time."

That night before leaving for work, Mom plunked down an empty pickle jar on the kitchen table. She stuck a piece of masking tape on front of the jar and, in big black letters, printed "CUSS JAR" on it.

"What's that for?" I asked.

"I'm giving up cussing for Lent," she said. "Every time I say a bad word I'll put money in the jar. Not-so-bad words cost a nickel. Stronger ones cost a dime. And the real bad ones, like your brother said today, cost a quarter."

"Where will you get the money?" I asked.

"From my tips," she answered. "I'm keeping my job after your daddy goes back to work so we can catch up on bills. But I plan on using the change in my cuss jar to buy you kids something special for Easter."

It didn't take long to figure out the more we acted up, the more she'd cuss, and the more she cussed, the more money there'd be for us. We started bickering to get her to lose her temper and swear.

Mom caught on right away and announced, "New rules for my cuss jar."

Grinning, I hoped she'd increase her bad-word fee.

Instead, she said, "From now on, every time you kids do something to make me cuss, I'll take money out of the jar. The more you misbehave, the less money there'll be for Easter."

After her talk, we acted like angels—at least we tried. And Mom stopped cussing most of the time. When she did slip up, it was usually only with nickel words, and by the end of Lent, even those were scarce.

On Easter Sunday Dad carved our Easter ham, and Mom presented us with large solid chocolate rabbits, buying them with the money in her cuss jar.

Thanks to Mom, I learned lessons that have lasted a lifetime: Moms aren't perfect, but being a mother is the hardest, and most important, job on earth. No matter how dismal things look, never give up hope. And no matter how many times I make a mistake, keep trying to improve—just like Mom did with her cuss jar.

~Donna Duly Volkenannt

32

The Bahamas Mammas

The art of mothering is to teach the art of living to children.
~Elaine Heffner

As a teenager, I became interested in learning about my mother's life before she became a mother. I spoke to my aunts and uncle and witnessed my mother's interactions with them.

My mother was the oldest child in a family of four children. Her parents were immigrants from Italy and she grew up during the Depression. At the age of ten, my mother was charged with all the household responsibilities while her mother went to work. At a time when most children focused on themselves and their needs, my mother supervised the other children, cooked, and cleaned. My aunts and uncle recall that while they were growing up my mother was consistent and firm with them, with a smile on her face and a song in her heart.

My mother graduated from high school, got a job, married my father, and started her own family. Her four children came every two years and she had a house filled to capacity before the age of thirty. In addition to working full-time, she managed to attend each child's school and sporting events, and keep us all on the straight and narrow.

Having learned about her abbreviated childhood and knowing that my father was really her "fifth and worst" child, I decided that when I completed graduate school I would take my mother on the first of what would become our annual mother-daughter trip. Since I landed a very lucrative job, I told her to pick any place she wanted to go and I would make it happen. She had never been more than fifty miles from our home and so she was thrilled and overwhelmed at the prospect.

For the first three years, we went to Bermuda, Arizona, and Charleston—the three locations she picked. However, during my fourth year after graduate school, I opened my own business, and my finances were very limited. I didn't want my mother to know, so I didn't let on when she said she wanted to go to the Bahamas.

I searched for the least expensive way to make this trip happen and ended up with a "package" that included airfare, transfers, and accommodations. Even now, when I think about the terms of the package, I cringe. The airplane was ancient and tiny, the transfer to the "resort" was via a barely running school bus, and the accommodations… well, let's just say that we had to share the hotel room with the native bugs and insects and tolerate the smell of moldy sheets.

After a perilous flight and a death-defying bus ride to our hotel, we and 200 other passengers were tired, cranky, hot, and disappointed. To make matters worse, there was only one person working the registration desk, and we had to stand in a long line under the blasting Bahamas sun to get our room key.

Since there was no place to store our luggage, we carried and dragged our suitcases along with us in the line snaking toward the front desk. Just when I thought things could not get worse, the late afternoon rains common to the Bahamas blew in. While both my mother and I had tried to keep a positive attitude up to this point, this was the last straw for me.

However, my mother had another idea. She turned and looked at me with a twinkle in her eye, and I knew we were in trouble. My mother has this habit of doing the most outlandish things at the most unanticipated times. When I see that twinkle in her eye, I know she is going to do something that will be outrageous, unexpected, and will probably embarrass me.

With a quick kiss on my cheek, my mother strolled over to the swimming pool, took off her glasses, and jumped in fully clothed, shoes and all, screaming "Yahoo!" The line of disgruntled passengers all paused and turned to look at me with facial expressions that ranged from amazement to disgust.

What's a child to do with a mother like that? At least I was smart enough to take off my shoes before I ran over to the pool and jumped in next to her. Several other people joined us in the pool. Of those who did, we spent considerable time with two young women who were lifelong friends and a husband-wife team; we soon dubbed the group of us the Bahamas Mammas (much to the husband's chagrin).

Not surprisingly, we ended up thoroughly enjoying that vacation, and I have stayed in touch with our Bahamas Mammas for the past twenty-five years. They were a great comfort to me when my mother passed away. We all left the funeral, went to the beach, and ran into the ocean fully clothed, yelling "Yahoo!" I am confident that my mother looked upon us with a twinkle in her eye.

~Judith Fitzsimmons

33

My Mother's Wig

Red is the ultimate cure for sadness.
~Bill Blass

My mother has taken to wearing a wig. Not just any wig. Not even a wig that suits her. Oh no, my mother's wig is shocking in every respect. It's bright red, with burnt orange streaks. It couldn't be mistaken for anything other than a wig. No one looking at such a frail old lady could ever believe she was meant to have hair that color, not even if she were fifty years younger.

The first time I saw it on her, I cringed with embarrassment. How could she? How could she wear something so false and not realize she looked stupid? She might be getting old, but she is far from senile. She's still as sharp as a tack, my mother. So why wear something so dreadful?

My dad bought her a different wig. One closer to the soft brown color her hair used to be when she still had hair. She wears that one to please my dad if they go out somewhere together. At home, she doesn't bother wearing either of them, but for hospital appointments, on goes the red monstrosity.

I sat with her once while she was having chemotherapy. Her skin, almost white and wrinkled like parchment, made the red stand out even more. The nurses took no notice of her red mop; neither did the regulars who called out their greetings across the chemo ward. But newcomers, fear etched on their faces, looked around, saw the wig (how could they miss it?) and whispered comments to their companions. Smirks replaced stricken expressions — for a moment or two, at least.

Eventually I had to ask. "Why did you choose that color, Mum?"

"I've always wanted to be a redhead," she answered, but I knew that wasn't the real reason. I could hear in her voice that there was more to it, so I waited.

We don't often talk. Not proper talking like many mothers and daughters. We're so different and yet so much alike. Sometimes we meet on the same planet, but it's rare. I love her, I know she loves me, but most of the time we can't communicate.

However, every so often we come together at the right time and she'll tell me something, or I'll open up to her. Maybe once every ten blue moons we have a moment of truth. On that day in the chemotherapy ward, out of the corner of my eye, a bright blue moon sailed into view.

Mum turned to me. "Standing in the corner over there is death. He's following me around and in this place he reminds me he's waiting." She smiled, but it was an effort. "I am not going to give in to him. If he wants me, then he has to fight for me and I'm not going anywhere. Not yet."

She broke off as another regular came in. "All right, Myra?" Mum called over. "How's your grandson?"

Mum carried on a conversation until the woman called Myra was hooked up to her drip and then she turned back to me.

"Sometimes I get scared. I know the doctors say I haven't got long to go, but I'm not ready to die yet. I'm fighting this the only way I know how. I'm not clever with words like you, but I feel better if I wear the red wig on chemo days. I don't know how to explain it, but it helps me fight death. It's my way of telling him to get lost."

As we were leaving, she made the rounds of every patient. She knew their names, their condition, family details. She knew who lived alone, who was scared, who was doing well. I could see on their faces that she'd made them feel better. This sick old woman with her ridiculously bright red hair made each and every one of them smile.

She's dying, my mum. When she's gone, and it won't be long now, the only thing I want to remember her by is that red wig. Red for courage, red for defiance, and red for vitality—the vitality she showed right up till the end.

~Lorraine Mace

Top-Priority Delivery

A mother's love for her child is like nothing else in the world.
It knows no law, no pity, it dares all things and crushes down
remorselessly all that stands in its path.
~Agatha Christie

As an aircrewman in the Navy, I made numerous trips from Norfolk, Virginia to the Caribbean. Homestead Air Force Base in Florida was a good place to stop for gas. It was even better since my mom lived nearby and would meet us at the terminal for a short visit, bringing a tin of chocolate chip cookies. The crew got to know my mom as adventurous and full of surprises.

On one occasion there was a security situation and we couldn't leave the airplane. There would be no visit and no cookies. I heard the pilot yell as he laughed. "Hey Schaf, what'd your mom do now?" I looked out and saw a K-9 security car pull up. In the back seat, behind the dog's cage, was my mom. She got out of the car with the security guard, who was carrying a tin of cookies. I met them at the back of the airplane as the crew watched. She hugged me and the guard handed me the tin. They got back in the car, and laughing, they left.

Somehow with her charm and determination, she convinced the guard the tin was a high-priority delivery. Maybe she slipped him a few cookies. Much to the delight of the entire crew, the cookies didn't make it to where we were going. They never did. I would always get off the plane with an empty tin, a smile and another fond memory of mom.

To my brother Bob: if you ever read this, "Nanner, nanner, I got cookies, and you didn't."

~Rick Schafer

Chapter 4

Thanks to My Mom

Love and Acceptance

I Was So Wrong

There is no love without forgiveness,
and there is no forgiveness without love.
~Bryant H. McGill

My mother was young when she had me, practically a child herself. By seventeen years old, she had become a mother, lived through the torment of broken homes, and survived a car accident that broke her back and nearly paralyzed her.

For as long as I could remember, my relationship with my mother was strained. After high school and college, when I had moved on to a professional career, I continued to avoid her. I made excuses not to visit, even on holidays.

When my girlfriend and I decided to elope, the first thing I felt was relief that I wouldn't have to deal with a wedding and my family being present. I sent my mother a text message early that evening giving her the news. At 2:00 a.m. when she saw it on her phone, she called me. She thought it was a joke. When I told her it was true, I could hear the tension in her voice. It wasn't hurt or disappointment... it was worry. Her voice trembled as she went through her list of questions: "Are you serious?" "Are you sure?" "Is this really what you want?" "Is she pregnant?" After that, I expected her to ask me when I was coming home or for her to complain that it was a big event and she wanted to be there. She didn't, and I began to realize how much I had disappointed her with this and many other decisions.

I called her back the next day to ask if my wife and I could visit after the wedding. She sounded very excited at the prospect. I set the date and a couple weeks after the wedding, my wife and I made the trip from upstate New York to Maine.

My mother invited some family to the house. It was early October, so the weather was still nice enough to have a cookout. Most of the family was quiet, seemingly shocked that I had actually gotten married.

The family tried their best not to bombard my wife with questions. A large percentage of them had never met her, including my mother. She tended to the guests, remained in the background until everyone had left and it was just her, my wife and me in the kitchen at the table. My mother put a cup in the Keurig coffeemaker and then disappeared into the back room. I heard her shuffling around in her closet. She returned a few moments later with a cardboard box labeled "Joseph."

She didn't ask my wife if she wanted to see what was inside. She didn't make a joke about pulling out embarrassing photos of me naked in a tub at age two. She quietly opened the box and looked at me. She got up to get her coffee, mixed her French vanilla creamer into it, and sat back down at the table. It was hard to know if she was doing this for my wife or for a few moments of nostalgia for herself, or even me, but I know I was the most affected by what happened next.

There were no embarrassing photos in the box. There were no photos at all. My mother had saved nearly every one of my art projects, stories, and report cards. She pulled the things out one at a time, took a second to glance at each one and set it on the table. My wife laughed at some of the crayon masterpieces where angry strokes had made it difficult to see the lines I was supposed to color inside. My mother smiled at each item she took out, and occasionally a tear ran down her cheek.

Then my mother began to pull out letters and poems she had written to me. I had no idea these existed. She handed each poem and letter to me with a solemn expression on her face. I tried to imagine her at nineteen, twenty-one, and twenty-five years old drafting notes to her small child. I took the notes and letters she had written and read them. I thought about all the years she had collected those things. I looked through the dates on them and kept reading until my mother had finished going through the box. I didn't have memories of the letters she wrote, but I remembered the time periods—times I wouldn't talk to her or I'd shut her out for reasons I can only find shame in now.

I resented my mother for things she had no control over, for the poverty we suffered through, for my biological father never being around. My mother kept writing those words, kept spilling her love for me onto those pages because I was too stubborn to accept her words. There were times, most of my life actually, that I shunned every hug she tried to give me. I'd roll over in bed at night, away from her, when she tried to tuck me in.

All of those years, my mother kept my things, some of which I know she had to pick out of the trash. She kept telling me she loved me even when I wouldn't listen. Then, she sat at a table, at the quintessential moment of my manhood, and went through all of those moments again—decades of time lost. I can't imagine how difficult that must have been.

I stayed awake that night, reading and re-reading my mother's writing. My wife and my mother had gone to bed, and I sat alone at the kitchen table, my hands shaking cigarette smoke into chaotic dances, trying to find a way to apologize and knowing that even with another lifetime, I could never match the love she gave me in just one of those poems or letters.

~Joe Ricker

A Bowl of Soup

Only the pure in heart can make a good soup.
~Ludwig van Beethoven

"Lunch is almost ready." My mother's accented speech rose up the stairs like a heat-seeking missile. The target, my defenseless stomach, never stood a chance. That woman knew how to cook.

I could see her in my mind's eye, all five feet of roundness standing at the base of the steps, peering up at the empty landing, a wooden spoon clasped in her arthritic hand. Which housecoat and apron had she donned for this day? It didn't matter, really. All of the worn and faded garments looked alike—comfortable, practical and frugal—just like her.

If you searched for Old World grandmothers in a German travel book you'd find my mother's face smiling up from the page, a set of oversized dentures marring otherwise delicate features. Even after decades in the States, her softened "th" sounds and sharp letter V gave away her heritage. Never much of a talker, she still labored at finding the proper English translation for words and ideas she wished to share. And when frustrated or upset, she wouldn't even try. Thoughts shot from her lips in a wild blend of German and English, with a sprinkling of her own hybrid thrown in for good measure. Confusing? Yes. Amusing? Undeniably. But we didn't dare laugh.

"Okay, I'll be right down." I rolled over on the bed, hating my room, my body and my life. What had I done to my future? Here

I was, twenty-two and very pregnant, curled up on a chenille '60s bedspread in a baby blue room I'd occupied at age six. I was as stuck as a beached whale.

Back home with Mom and Dad—that had never been part of the grand plan, but a series of devastating circumstances had returned me to this space. In the course of one week, I'd discovered I was pregnant, lost my job as a dental assistant, and ended the relationship with my boyfriend, the baby's father. One consequence of the split? Homelessness. I shuddered as the door to my carefree existence slammed shut.

I battled depression daily, convinced of my worthlessness. I, myself, had been an unplanned—and to my mind unwanted—surprise late in my parents' marriage. I fought to belong, to fit in with them and my much older siblings. My neediness hung in the air, heavy as a shroud.

But Mom didn't care for hugging, and gushing shows of affection embarrassed her. Physical touch wasn't part of her upbringing. Her early life had revolved around the struggle to survive. To hear her say 'I love you' to me or anyone else would have required a birth, a wedding or a death. As my childhood passed, I hungered for those words.

Rebelliousness defined my teen years, and the current situation hadn't won my parents' favor more than any other catastrophe I'd dragged them through.

Yet, these two good people had reopened their home to me. Survivors of the Depression and World War II, both knew how to build, mend and grow almost anything. They'd learned the ins and outs of scraping to get by, a tough lesson I knew awaited me as a single mother. I'd study under the best, and this time, I'd keep my eyes open.

Just as the past three months had challenged me, autumn offered a welcome change of season, and perhaps an improvement to my health, both emotional and physical. I'd experienced morning, afternoon, and evening sickness and everything in between. Particular smells triggered nausea with uncanny reliability. Whether I dined in a restaurant, shopped the mall or endured a job interview, the enemy struck hard and fast. Eating induced vomiting, which inevitably brought on humiliation. My appetite went AWOL.

Trudging downstairs, the tantalizing fragrance of Mom's cooking pulled me to the table like a baby to a bottle. And I was hungry — famished. My mother had discovered the cure for my queasy stomach.

Soup. Every day. In every way imaginable, but always from scratch. Egg drop, chicken with homemade noodles, twelve bean or lentil soup filled my bowl at the mid-day meal, as predictable as the noonday sun. It was often accompanied by a warm slice of Mom's homemade bread spread thick with sweet butter. From the moment she rose until lunch was served, Mom's attention focused on me, the baby and our health.

"So, what did you make today?" The ancient pot, its base no longer flat, wobbled on the trivet. Steam rose, silent witness to the flavors awaiting my palate.

Ladle in hand, Mom smiled. "It's stew. One of your favorites."

"Thank you." I lifted the chipped bowl from my setting and handed it to my mother. Her deft fingers gripped the rim as she poured the rich broth and chunks of meat and veggies in — first one scoop, then another. If I hadn't stopped her, she would have served the entire pot to me and scrounged up something else for herself and my father. She would give all she had, just as she'd done all my life. Even if it wasn't much, it was enough.

So what if my mother never actually said out loud that she loved me? She didn't need to. She lived those words with a richness that overcame our poverty, in a language anyone could understand. One I yearned to master.

Luther, in a letter to Zwingli, once wrote, "… God is hidden in the soup… " I believe it.

I know love was. I tasted it gratefully. And I was filled.

~Heidi Gaul

Nothing Wrong

*A man travels the world over in search of what he needs
and returns home to find it.*

~George Moore

I sat in the back seat of my family's overcrowded Nissan Altima slumped against the door. My stepdad drove while my mom filed her nails in the passenger seat next to him, staring out at the occasional graffiti mural along the freeway, typical of the city, but less so of where we were coming from, the suburbs.

My two younger brothers joined me in the back. The baby was about one, the middle one six, and I was eleven.

I don't recall where the family was headed that day. And that isn't because this particular event happened such a long time ago. It's because a lot of the peripheral details from that day were overshadowed by a conversation that took place during that particular car ride on that particular day.

As the car rolled on, my mom stared in the rearview mirror at my baby brother in the back seat. He was chewing on his foot, oblivious to her adoring gaze.

My mother blew him a kiss. And then she turned to my stepfather and said, "What would you do if your son turned out to be gay?"

The implication in the question was that being gay was something undesirable. My mouth immediately became dry. My intestines felt twisted. I froze, hoping my stillness would make me invisible. If being gay was something undesirable, then, at eleven years old, I knew I was undesirable in my mother's eyes. Tainted.

Miles later, when the conversation had long moved on, I stared at my baby brother—his wide, bright eyes, his shining, blond hair, his rolls of baby fat. How could any of that be anything other than beautiful?

I secretly hoped that for his own sake he wasn't tainted. Like I was.

•••

Eleven years after that car ride, I was drinking coffee with my mother. It was just the two of us that night. I was back home for the summer, and since our favorite television show, *Survivor*, was on hiatus, we were watching a movie on Lifetime, *Prayers for Bobby*, based on a true story. It was a real tearjerker. I think we decided to watch it because the title character shared a name with me. It dramatized the real-life story of a Northern California, small-town, Christian mother who in the 1980s could not accept her son's homosexuality.

Shortly after turning twenty, her son Bobby ends up killing himself. He jumps off a bridge straight onto a traffic-heavy highway one night.

Towards the end of the film there's a scene where the mother, portrayed quite well by Sigourney Weaver, is speaking to a pastor at a church in complete and utter desperation. She's trying to come to terms with the possibility of her son not having made it into heaven because he had sinned. She still cannot allow herself to properly grieve, even though it has been many months since her son's passing.

That's when I heard my own mother grumble something underneath her breath. I looked over and saw she was speaking directly to Sigourney Weaver portraying this character inside the television. My mom was clearly overwhelmed by the woman's hardheadedness. Soon enough my mother was not speaking softly. She was downright yelling at the television, saying, "C'mon, lady. Don't be stupid. Get over it. There was never anything wrong with your son to begin with!"

~Bobby Bermúdas

My Mother's Hands

Gratitude is an art of painting an adversity into a lovely picture.
~Kak Sri

Many years ago, while my son David and I were taking a bus to visit my parents, we sat across from two passengers who were undoubtedly mother and daughter. They each carried a guitar case and chattered excitedly. As they rose for their approaching stop, the younger woman grasped the older one to steady her against the lurch of the bus. When their fingers intertwined I noticed they had the same hands, identical in shape, length, and even similar, subtle calluses from decades of plucking guitar strings.

I envied the obvious closeness they shared, wishing that I had that kind of relationship with my own mother. Apart from our eye color and build, she and I had very little in common and had never bonded over mutual interests.

My parents immigrated to Canada after World War II, arriving with little more than the clothes on their backs, three small sons, and the few possessions they could carry on board the ship that brought them here. I was born shortly after.

Mama and Papa were extremely strict, impatient, and distant. My mother also had some severe mental issues that prevented her from being the loving, demonstrative parent I yearned for. Our home was usually filled with turmoil, and laughter was rare.

My parents struggled to provide bare necessities, squirreling away every extra penny to eventually buy their own home. Aside from dealing with language barriers, Mama was terribly antisocial. She preferred an environment that demanded little human contact, so, from the time I was eight, she spent almost every weekday scrubbing floors, washing windows, dusting, ironing and cleaning for others.

Evenings after work, she did more of the same at home, adding cooking and laundry to the list. What little free time she had was spent sewing, knitting, or crocheting—something that, to her disappointment, I could never master when she tried to teach me. I preferred to slip into the imaginary world of books to escape the dreary atmosphere I grew up in.

That afternoon, when we finally got to my parents' house, my father took David out to splash around in the wading pool they kept for him. I stayed inside with my mother. I offered to make tea and was relieved when she accepted. It gave me time to gauge her mood from the kitchen. I could never be sure if she was going to be pleasantly warm or cold and tight-lipped.

As the tea steeped, I observed her. She seemed calm, happily working on her latest knitting project. When I handed her the mug, she glanced up with a rare smile and I relaxed.

I watched her quietly for a few moments while she concentrated on a complicated series of stitches. Trying not to stare, I studied her hands. They looked nothing like my smooth, carefully manicured ones. Her nails were cut short, the fingers twisted, rough-skinned and knotted from years of hard work.

"Are you hungry?" she asked in her heavy German accent as she put her needles aside and sipped her tea. "You want I make you sumptink?"

"No thanks, Mama," I declined politely. Now that my parents were retired, their freezer and pantry bulged with food for the times their children visited.

I reached over to admire the sweater she was making. The intricate pattern was emerging, each stitch tight, precise and perfect. "This is beautiful," I told her softly.

"Tanks," she murmured, then proceeded to tell me how she'd seen the design on a vest a woman was wearing at the supermarket that morning, and couldn't wait to get home to duplicate it.

Her face became animated as she spoke, the way it always did when she was excited about her latest creation, even if it was a simple doily. Normally I would lose interest, but that day I listened intently.

Eventually, like all conversations do, the topic changed. Before I knew it, my mother began to reminisce about her childhood in Germany, her love of school, and how disappointed she was to abandon her studies in the sixth grade when her father decreed she had enough "book learning." He needed her to help out full-time in the family butcher shop and bakery, shattering her dream of becoming a nurse. I heard the bitterness in her voice before she went on to discuss the war's impact on her life.

It was then that she nervously resumed her knitting, avoiding further eye contact. Her voice became agitated when she related how her father forced all his daughters to smuggle items to the enemy that could have resulted in immediate execution if they were caught.

Mama recounted the many times she narrowly escaped death herself, naming friends and family she lost, including her own mother who died in her arms from a shrapnel wound infection. The hair on my arms rose as she narrated how she and Papa escaped from Germany, and how close they came to being caught and shot.

It was the longest my mother ever talked to me. As the memories flooded her mind and slipped from her lips, I recognized the familiar anxiety that usually set off one of her emotional outbursts. I immediately changed the subject.

"Why didn't you go back to school here in Canada and study to be a nurse? You would have been a good one," I added.

"Four babies, no money," she said in her fractured English. "I worked so you all could finish school—get nice, easy jobs."

My father and son came into the house then, and the conversation ended. My mother's experiences, however, remained in my thoughts as I reassessed my many childhood resentments.

The birthdays and Christmases without gifts became insignificant. The embarrassingly shabby rented house of my youth suddenly became a haven now that I was aware of my mother's sacrifices to help provide a better permanent home, food and education. Hated handmade clothes that were always fashioned to "grow into" seemed prettier in retrospect. And most importantly, the "crazy woman" everyone teased me about when she succumbed to one of her spirals of erratic behavior became a heroine and survivor in my eyes.

As I looked at her knotted, wrinkled hands, I realized that, though I'd had a difficult childhood, this woman who had always been both a stranger and parent to me had suffered an entire lifetime of loss and grim bleakness.

When I left that day, Mama actually leaned into my goodbye hug instead of simply tolerating it with her stiff unyielding body. For a brief moment, I experienced the mother-daughter bond I'd always craved. When we pulled apart, I raised her work worn hands to my lips, kissed them and whispered "thank you" into her ear. Her eyes softened, and then grew expressionless again as she returned to that impenetrable safety bubble she'd grown like a skin around herself.

We would continue to have our ups and downs for years to come, eventually becoming completely estranged as her illness progressed and her defensive hostility escalated. That day, however, I felt nothing but gratitude for the woman who spent her entire adult life ensuring that none of her children would ever have her gnarled and roughened hands.

~Marya Morin

39

An Ordinary Life

*I've seen and met angels wearing the disguise of
ordinary people living ordinary lives.*
~Tracy Chapman

Mom turned seventy at home in Tennessee this year and celebrated with a trip to visit family in the Midwest. We sat on my red brick patio in the Chicago suburbs sipping iced tea. I was in a funk and though we talked often on the phone, it was easier to share my troubles face to face. I was second-guessing the years I spent focused only on family and felt my individual achievements didn't measure up. My nest was empty and my plans for an accomplished life seemed like silly daydreams.

Mom listened and then I waited for her wise words to spur me to action or transform my attitude. Instead, she wiped the condensation off her glass, squinted her blue eyes against the bright sun, and said, "I always thought there was something special in store for me, too. Turns out, I was ordinary."

She said it matter-of-factly, with a twinge of longing. The implication was that looking back on her eventful life, she was average, nothing special. Her revelation shocked me. I looked out over the many shades of green in the back yard and shared the first memory that came to mind. I asked if she remembered a certain Friday night after I'd dropped out of college.

It was around 8 p.m. and I was home with no plans. Again. The past months had been rough. I'd had a disastrous freshman year and had recently split up with my boyfriend of five years. I was new at work, and my high school friends were scattered at college or busy with boyfriends. I was nineteen and adrift. I felt abandoned and ashamed.

I paced our living room while my mom and stepdad watched a movie in the family room downstairs. They'd invited me but the only thing worse than spending Friday night alone would be watching movies on the couch with my parents. Even my younger siblings all had plans.

Looking back now from the comfort of my home and family, it's easy to recognize the signs of depression. But I'd grown up in a family without much self-reflection. I was one of five kids raised in a string of rented houses by a single mother. She often worked double shifts as a waitress, machine operator, or bartender. She rarely made it home for dinner or even before bedtime. We were self-sufficient, thrifty and practical. We were also close-knit and optimistic. Mom was busy and had no time to dwell on sad things. If we had a bad day, a hug and a quick "you'll survive" were usually enough.

Tonight was different. For the first time, I thought, maybe, I didn't want to survive.

That was new and scary. I'd never felt hopeless before. I had turned on the radio and changed into a burgundy leotard and black tights, thinking exercise might improve my mood. My stomach ached and I folded my arms over it trying to contain the sad, empty feelings. Nothing helped.

My mind was racing. Why did he break up with me? Why couldn't I hack it at school? Were normal kids my age at parties? Did my siblings think I was pathetic? What was wrong with me? My throat tightened and it was hard to breathe.

In a trembling voice, I yelled for her. "Mom? Mom!"

"Yeah, Suz?" she called over the television noise.

"Can you come here? Please?" I felt guilty about interrupting her. Tonight was her night off and she was relaxing with my stepdad.

Mom came upstairs, took one look at my red, tear-stained face, and wrapped me in her arms. She was little, 5'2" and 125 pounds, but tough. She had grown up poor, the second of five — just like me. She was a daddy's girl, but also fierce and independent. She had little respect for men unwilling to work as hard as her and didn't remarry until my senior year in high school.

Growing up, we missed having her home nights, but she never missed an assembly at school. We collected bottles for milk money but I got new cleats when I made the softball team. We shopped at yard sales and thrift stores but she bought my brother a new suit for his first homecoming dance. She was our Wonder Woman.

At nineteen, I was two inches taller than her, but I let her rub my back as I sobbed. I felt comforted by her touch and the faint whiff of her vanilla and coffee scent that penetrated my stuffy nose. I hiccupped, unable to take a deep breath.

"What's wrong?"

"I… I've got no friends, no boyfriend. What's wrong with me?" I dragged my arm across my face trying to compose myself but more tears fell.

Mom took me by the arm, sat me at the dining room table, and brought me a kitchen towel for my face. Then, my practical-by-necessity mom grabbed a yellow legal pad, a pencil and a ruler from the kitchen drawer and saved my life.

She didn't know it at the time, but I'd had a fleeting picture in my head of how to end it. I'd never thought that before and I never have since. But I did that night.

Drawing a line down the middle of the pad, she wrote "PRO" on one side, "CON" on the other, and started listing all my positive qualities and accomplishments.

"Pro, you're smart." I rolled my eyes. High school was over and my honor roll triumphs were old news. College courses required effort, unlike many of my high school classes, and I'd spent more time social-izing than studying. "You're a wonderful big sister, writer, dancer…" She nudged me with her elbow. Even my brothers inherited our mom's rhythm and we loved music and dancing. "You make delicious fruit cocktail, love to read, give great presents…" On and on she wrote. "You're funny, you type fast, love to sing…"

She added a few CONs to make it fair. "You miss spots cleaning the toilet, you shed hair everywhere." She moved back to the PRO side, listing the things she loved about me, listing the things my family valued.

I don't remember how long this went on but she missed the whole movie. As she sat writing, my tears dried up and my breathing became easier. It wasn't the items on her list that rescued me. Most parents believe their kids are great. It was her calm strength and the presence of mind she showed when making the list. She believed in me when I didn't believe in myself.

I finished telling her the story about that long ago night, reached for my iced tea and watched Mom's eyes widen in surprise. "Of course I remember that but I just thought you were upset." She hadn't realized what her presence meant to me that night.

Despite all she went through, Mom created magical Christmases with no money and turned popcorn dinners into celebrations. She taught us to laugh at ourselves, told ghost stories and encouraged us to stick up for others. She still makes quilts for each grandkid, bakes legendary bread pudding and occasionally jitterbugs in the kitchen.

I put my glass down, reached for her hand and told her the truth, "There is nothing ordinary about you."

~Suzanne M. Brazil

40

The Cleaning Gene

There's something wrong with a mother
who washes out a measuring cup with soap and water
after she's only measured water in it.
~Erma Bombeck

In our family, the cleaning gene definitely skipped a generation. The fact that my DNA was missing that particular gene wasn't as evident when I was a child. My mother taught me very early in life that my room was my responsibility. I had to make my bed every morning and put away my clothes every night.

When my mother, in her guise as drill sergeant, checked my room on a daily basis, I always passed inspection. Some days, that meant racing two steps ahead of her to put away a couple of things at the last minute, but I still managed.

Then I grew up and moved out. My first apartment was a studio. With so little room, I had to keep it neat and clean. That and the fact that I never knew when my mother might drop in unannounced. Fear, as they say, can be a great motivator.

So, I continued to make my bed and put away my clothes every day. If I left an occasional dish overnight in the sink, hoping the dish fairy would wash it, I was soon disabused of that notion. It was always there the next morning, still as dirty as before. Guess my mom was right. The dishes, like the rest of the apartment, were indeed my responsibility—a good lesson to learn.

Vacuuming and dusting, on the other hand, were a lower priority for me. As I pointed out when my mother wrote her name on the dust on my coffee table, "They're putting up a building right next door. Of course it's going to be dusty."

The drill sergeant was not amused. She gave me "the look" and stood guard as I dusted the table and everything else in the apartment.

When I moved to another city, my inner slob moved in with me. While my mother worried about me living on my own almost 400 miles away, I reveled in the freedom. One dirty dish morphed into a sink filled with dishes. My bed retained a just slept-in look for weeks on end. My vacuum cleaner, a gift from my mother, stood forlornly in the closet. I'd pat it every so often and promise I'd use it—eventually.

Every time my parents visited, I would go on a whirlwind cleaning marathon. By the time they walked into the apartment, it was neat and clean. I'd even make the bed, mostly because my parents would be sleeping in it while I got the couch. As my mother did her inspection tour, a hint of a smile on her face, I'd trail behind. "Not bad," she'd say. "But I wonder what it would have looked like if we'd come in a day earlier than planned."

I'd grin.

Over the next thirty years, I moved four times. When my father got sick, my parents stopped visiting and my inner slob took over my house. She smiled at me when I rooted in the sink for a somewhat clean glass. She cheered when I mounded the blanket on my bed for one of my cats to sleep on. She played hopscotch down my hallway, using a rather large fur ball as her stone. My mother would have been appalled, but my inner slob and I were quite content.

After my father died, my mother started visiting again. I would send my inner slob out for the day as I raced around doing dishes, chasing down fur balls, and throwing out piles of newspapers that were threatening to take over my living room. While the house still had a lived-in look, at least I wouldn't have to worry about a visit from the health inspector.

My mother disagreed. She'd walk in, take one look around the house and say, "Why don't you clean up? I'll even pay for a cleaning woman."

I'd stifle a groan and imagine a huge pile of newspapers tumbling over her. Just for an instant. "Thanks for the offer, but I'd have to spend days clearing all my books and papers before she could even start to clean. And I'd never be able to find anything." Then to make my mother happy, I'd grab files, books, half-written articles and lesson plans from their perch on my coffee table and dump them in my already overcrowded office.

For the rest of the visit, my mother would walk around the house, mentally consigning me to the guardhouse for failing inspection. For my part, I'd wash the dishes, throw out the newspapers every day, and try to keep ahead of the cat hair that decorated the furniture. But I'd refuse to make my bed. "Can't," I'd say, "it would disturb the cats."

All that changed on her last visit. When she walked into house there were dishes in the sink, newspapers in the living room, and enough cat hair to knit another cat tucked into every corner of the house. Apart from the guestroom, which I never use, every other room had a decidedly messy look.

"Didn't I teach you anything about cleaning when you were growing up?" she asked. She glanced at the sink. "Maybe just do a couple of dishes?"

"Nope," I said. "They're quite happy where they are." I gave her my best imitation of a drill sergeant. "And I expect them to be there tomorrow morning when I wake up. Don't even think about doing them yourself."

Before she could object, I continued. "You taught me a lot about cleaning when I was growing up. More importantly, you also taught me to make my own decisions. For that I thank you and for so many other things you taught me and did for me. It's not your fault I've decided I'd rather read a good book than do the dishes, or play with the cats instead of making the bed, or…"

"… I get it," she said.

And she did. When I woke up the next morning, the dishes were still there. She had even added her own breakfast bowl and plate to the pile. I grinned to think that I might actually be having a bad influence on my own mother, that she might allow her own inner slob to peek out. She can thank me for it later.

~Harriet Cooper

41

Learning to Forgive

*Each day of our lives we make deposits in the memory banks
of our children.*
~Charles R. Swindoll

he flashing lights of the patrol car came out of nowhere. With my heart racing, I pulled over to the side of the road. I had just gotten my driver's license earlier that year. And now, a ticket!

I decided not to tell Mom what I had done. I would save my lunch money for the next few weeks and pay the fine myself. That way I could keep driving and not be grounded.

The next week I came in from school and, propped on my dresser, was a letter addressed To the Parents of Darlene Carpenter. The envelope was already opened, so I slid the letter out. It explained to my parents that I had received a ticket at 8:15, Sunday night, for not stopping at a stop sign near Dallas Love Field Airport.

My hands were shaking. 8:15. Sunday night. I was at church at 8:15, Sunday night. Every Sunday night. I sat ten pews behind Mother and Dad. How was I going to explain this? I was afraid to come out of my bedroom because I knew Mom had already read the letter.

I changed out of my school clothes, did my homework, straightened up my room. I formed all kinds of lies in my mind to explain how they sent the letter to the wrong address. I kept listening for her footsteps coming down the hallway to my door. I heard my dad come in from work. I was sure she was telling him, and they both would appear at my door any second with some form of punishment.

My sister came in from work, and my little brother came in from playing outside. Still, no word from Mom. In a few minutes I heard Mom calling us for dinner. I reluctantly left the safety of my bedroom. I wasn't hungry, but I forced food down. I couldn't look at Mom. When dinner was over, I began cleaning off the table. Mom instructed me to wash and dry the dishes as she walked out of the kitchen.

Okay, I thought, she's going to wait until bedtime to give me my punishment.

To my surprise, Mom said nothing about the ticket that night or the following week. The letter disappeared off my dresser. I tiptoed around the house for the next few weeks. I did my chores plus anything else I could find to do to help Mom. My transgression was never discussed, and I finally got past my fear.

Years later I sat at Mom's kitchen table and asked if she remembered me getting a ticket when I was sixteen. She said she did, and I asked why she never punished me.

"Oh, it was enough watching you punish yourself," she replied.

I looked up and saw the laughter in her eyes.

"You know where I went that night?" I asked.

"No, but I bet you remember," came her answer.

"I went to see Elvis. They said on the radio that he was flying into Dallas Love Field at 7:30. I told my friend at church, and we decided to sneak out as soon as church started. If we went straight to the airport, watched him get off the plane, and went straight back to church, we could just make it before the last Amen. When I saw the stop sign, I looked up and down the streets. No cars in sight anywhere. I kept going. I don't know where that policeman was hiding. The sad part is that Elvis had come and gone by the time we got to the airport."

Mom laughed and asked me if it was worth it. I thought for a moment and then said,

"Well, at the time, I was so scared that I didn't think so. But, looking back, I realize that I learned a lot that week."

She stopped stirring the beans on the stove, and with spoon still in hand, asked what I learned.

"I learned what forgiveness is. I know you didn't approve of me going. But, you forgave me for going without me even asking you to. I learned to do what's right. Not because of my fear of you, but because of my love for you. I wanted you to be proud of me again."

Mom smiled. Her big brown eyes misted up. She had done her job as a mother.

Thanks, Mom, for teaching me to do what's right even when no one is watching.

~Darlene Carpenter Herring

She Already Knew

I would maintain that thanks are the highest form of thought;
and that gratitude is happiness doubled by wonder.
~G.K. Chesterton

I was fourteen. My girlfriend at the time was in southern Georgia while I was in Metro Atlanta, and we had only met online, never in person. We'd gotten into the habit of staying up late on the phone, even falling asleep sometimes, because my sisters or parents would constantly interrupt during the day. Nighttime was the only time we were sure to be unbothered.

I'd gotten comfortable in the routine: my dad would fall asleep on the couch, Mom would help him sleepwalk into their bedroom, my sisters and I would each go to bed, and my mom would turn in for the night after cleaning whatever dishes were left in the kitchen. I'd hear my mom's door shut and immediately text my girlfriend for her to call me.

This particular night, however, my mom was taking a very long time to go to bed. My girlfriend grew impatient, so I let her call but warned her that I would have to whisper until my mom went to bed.

What I didn't know was that my mom was in the living room, on the other side of my bedroom wall, reading a book with no intention of stopping any time soon. Eventually, I got too complacent and loud, and she heard me. My heart jumped out of my chest when she burst through the door, hissing at me to get off the phone and go to sleep. I quietly whispered what had happened to my girlfriend and hung up, burying under the covers so that I wouldn't have to face my mom's glare.

The next day, I was a wreck at school. I knew my mom wanted to talk to me about why I had been up so late, but we wouldn't have a chance to be properly alone until she drove me to orchestra that night. At school, I was constantly expressing my worries to my friends, all of whom already knew I was gay, asking them what I should say. I've always been a generally good kid; I wasn't used to getting in trouble, but there simply wasn't any credible excuse I could give to my mom to explain why I had been up so late without coming out to her.

Then I thought about what my mom's reaction would be if she did know it had been my girlfriend I was on the phone with instead of just a friend, like she'd thought. Her being my girlfriend was the only reason I would stay up with her on the phone, after all. I voiced the idea to my friends. Although they said that it was a brave decision to make on a whim, I had their support in whatever happened.

I wasn't particularly worried about my mom's reaction, necessarily. I'd been thinking about what would happen if I came out to her for a while; I didn't think that she would go so far as to kick me out or anything, but I had absolutely no idea what her opinions were on LGBT issues. I was sure she wouldn't hate me, but that didn't mean she would accept my sexuality.

Usually, I would sing along to the radio when riding in the car, especially when it was just my mom and I. However, that night, the ride to orchestra was spent with me in silence, constantly wondering when she would bring up the late-night phone call. When she dropped me off, she assured me that we would talk on the way back home.

Well, that didn't assure me at all. It only served to make me more nervous, so during rehearsal, I forced myself to get completely lost in the music we were playing so that I wouldn't have to think about what was to come. As soon as I started packing up my violin, though, all the nerves came back. I felt sick to my stomach, wondering what was going to happen once I told my mom that I was gay.

We were five minutes into the car ride when she asked me, "So, what made you think it was okay to be on the phone at two in the morning?"

This was it. This was my chance. I willed for my voice not to crack as I spoke, but it felt as if my heart was trying to claw its way up my throat. "Because she's my girlfriend," I replied.

There was only a half-second pause: "Okay, so why did you think it was okay to be on the phone at two in the morning?"

I was shell-shocked. Out of all of the reactions I'd imagined, I definitely hadn't thought that my mom would simply gloss over my Big Coming Out Moment.

That wasn't the case, however. After chastising me for staying up on the phone and promising me she'd take it away if she caught me again, my mom started asking me about my initial answer. She asked if I was gay, and then how I knew; I told her yes, and that I'd simply never wanted to be with a boy, but girls had always gotten my attention.

She was completely fine with it all. "If I'm being completely honest," she told me, "I kind of already knew." Apparently I'd had a fixation with girls since I was little, be it the pink Power Ranger or my fifth-grade student-teacher. She promised that she didn't love me any less or any differently.

That was nearly six years ago. Since then, my mom has been my support system within the adults of my family. When I came out to my dad and he didn't react very well, she was right there to reassure me that everything would be fine. She asks how my girlfriend is doing when I'm dating someone, and she can always tell when we've broken up. She doesn't question my clothing choices and lets me be who I am.

A lot of people don't get so lucky when they come out to their parents. A lot of teenagers are kicked out onto the street simply because of who they love. My mom has been the most accepting, loving parent I could ever wish for. I knew I was lucky to have her before I came out, and that belief was confirmed once I'd told her the truth.

I know that she'll always be by my side, supporting me in who

I am and what I do. She's the best mother I could ask for, and I will never be able to thank her enough for that.

~Ayanna Bryce

43

She Put Her Book Down

> *The most important thing in communication*
> *is to hear what isn't being said.*
> ~Peter F. Drucker

The early morning sunlight brightened and warmed the hospital waiting room as we awaited the results from my mother's latest surgery. I feared the worst, and that led me to contemplate specifically what it was that made my mother so special to me. Like most children, I believe that my mother is the best mother that anyone could have. How could you feel otherwise about the person who gave birth to you, fed you, cleaned up after you, kissed your boo-boos better, cared for you when you were sick, held you close when your first love broke your heart, and did millions of other things for you, too?

As I enjoyed the warmth of the sunlight it dawned on me that the most extraordinary thing my mother did for me — the one characteristic that illustrated everything about her as a mom — was that she always put her book down.

When I was a teenager, I was so wrapped up in myself that I felt my issues were the most important and weighty things in the world. Also, like most teenagers, I would keep my worries and concerns to myself and try to figure things out on my own, since no one else could possibly understand what I was going through.

But every so often I could not ignore the need to talk to someone and I would drift into my parents' bedroom to unburden myself to my mother while she was sitting in bed reading.

As the mother of five rambunctious children, she would often retreat to her room in the evening for some "down time." I'm sure she viewed this as her time to relax, unwind, and get away from the pressures of caring for a husband and children, even if only for a few moments. Yet even though this was to be her time for herself she would never close the door to the bedroom. This was because she and my father had stressed to us that we were always welcome to talk to them about anything, at any time.

I would sit on the edge of the bed and begin with some idle chitchat as I worked up my nerve to talk about what was bothering me. My mother would always do something remarkable — she put her book down. The impact of that simple act still resonates with me today, many decades later. How easy would it have been for her to sneak peeks at her book and act as if she was listening? But she put the book down, and in so doing demonstrated to her child that he was loved, accepted, and cared for. She never once complained that I was interfering with "her time," she never asked if I could come back later, and not once did she act as if my thoughts or concerns were stupid, irrelevant, or silly. She simply put her book down and actively listened to her child for as long as was needed.

In the decades since then I have tried to embrace the lessons that my mother silently taught during those mother-son conversations. I have noted that many times when someone comes to me and strikes up a conversation, I almost automatically put down whatever I am reading so I may give this individual the same gift that my mother gave to me. I strive to remember how it felt to know that what I had to say was important to someone else and what a wonderful and powerful message can be sent by simply putting the book down.

The warm sunlight was a good omen, the surgery was successful and this "love letter to my mother" isn't a posthumous one. Is my mother special? She most certainly is special in so many ways; not the least of which is — she put her book down.

~Dale G. Jackson

44

Love in Four Panels

You can give without loving, but you can never love without giving.
~Author Unknown

I can tell you the exact second I realized just how much my mother loved me. Of course, I knew she loved me in that same abstract sort of way that everyone knows their parents love them, but I had never given it any thought past that. Some days I believed ours was a case more of happy coexistence than any sort of deep love.

After I graduated from college, finally moving back home, I found that I was drowning in books. My years away at school had led to the accumulation of more and more books, and so by the time I came back, my shelves were overflowing and in a state of total chaos. Fiction was not alphabetized, reference books were stacked under chairs, thin volumes of poetry and plays were stashed between brick-sized novels. Things had gotten so out of hand over the years that I wasn't even all that sure what titles I had. So I decided that that summer I would do a massive inventory, cataloging and filing and properly shelving every book I owned.

This turned out to be a much bigger job than I had initially anticipated. I threw my house into an even greater state of chaos as I meticulously wrote down all the information about every book, placing each in temporary stacks and shelves, wherever I could find a flat surface. One night I set out to manage one of the more difficult tasks of my inventory madness: cataloging all the comic books.

As a young child, I read comic books almost exclusively. Not the kind about superheroes, but the kind that you could read in the newspaper. *Calvin and Hobbes*, *For Better or For Worse*, *Garfield*, every Bloom County book ever made. I sat on my bedroom floor, feeling nostalgic as I flipped through them. I had read every one of them multiple times, over and over till I practically had them all memorized.

One of my mother's favorite rules of parenting was, "Let a child read whatever they want, because at least they're reading something." It had proven to be a good way of looking at things, since I had grown up to become an avid, if not obsessive, reader of books of all shapes, sizes, and genres. In fact, books were probably what I loved more than anything else on earth. And all my love for books could be traced back to hours spent reading comics. They taught me to love reading, but also taught me how to have a sense of humor about my life and myself, which was another thing that my mother strongly believed everyone should have if they wanted to navigate the world with as little self-loathing as possible.

I smiled at yet another pocket book, *Wizard of Id*, as I set it aside and glanced at my papers. I was up to nearly 400 comic books, 175 of which were pocket books, fragile little things with yellowed pages from the 1960s that somehow had managed to survive my childhood. And that was when it occurred to me that I hadn't bought a single one of them. My mother had.

This fact was so obvious to me that I wondered how I never thought about it until then.

Why had I never noticed? All the Christmas gifts made up of rectangular packages? We had never been a very wealthy family, and as I sat in my room adding things up in my head, I was staggered by the amount of money my mother must have spent in her crusade to make me love reading. Out of the 1,164 books I owned, nearly all of them were bought by my mother. She could never turn me down when I asked for a book, always willing to buy whatever title had caught my eye that week. We spent hours in the bookstore in the mall, me excitedly awaiting the new Lemony Snicket book or the next *Garfield* treasury.

So much time, so much money, so many stacks of paper and ink, many of which had changed me, made me the woman I am now.

Never in my life had I ever been so aware of just how much my mother loved me.

While I sat on the floor surrounded by the printed evidence of my mother's love, I heard her footsteps in the hall.

"Hey, what do you want for dinner?" She stopped in my doorway, staring down at me looking shell-shocked, surrounded by towers of comic books. "What on earth are you doing?"

"You bought all of these for me."

"Yeah?" she said, not quite understanding what I was getting at.

"Nearly every book I own, you bought for me."

"Well of course I did," she said. "You liked to read them."

We weren't the most demonstrative people, rarely baring our hearts in any way to anyone. But even if my mother never said "I love you" to me a single time out loud for the rest of my life, I knew she loved me. I had 1,164 I-love-you's, all sorted by genre and alphabetized, thousands of pages of evidence to remind me of her love.

So a few months later, when I opened a birthday present and found yet another book, I smiled, and thought to myself: "I love you, too."

~Karen Wilson

A Miracle Mile Miracle

One good mother is worth a hundred schoolmasters.
~George Herbert

"I'm ditching school tomorrow," I announced proudly to my friends at the lunch table. Their eyes grew wide, and who could blame them? This was big news. My friends and I were not exactly the kids who skipped school.

"You are?" one friend asked. "That's so cool!"

Another friend was clearly impressed. "Aren't you worried about getting in trouble?"

Before I could answer, my best friend Bridgette piped up. "She can't get in trouble. Her mom is going to call in and tell the school she's sick, even though she's not." She rolled her eyes and added, "They're going shopping."

"Oh, well, that's a different story," my friends said. "Skipping school with your parents' permission hardly counts as ditching."

The truth was out and my cool factor had taken a serious nosedive, but I didn't care.

I shrugged and grinned. "That might well be true," I said, "but the fact remains that while you all are taking an algebra test tomorrow, I will be maxing out my mom's credit card on the Miracle Mile."

My friends groaned, but I knew that deep down they were envious of my Mom-approved day off from school.

Shopping with one's mother on a school day might not be as cool as ditching class for more nefarious purposes, but in my book, it was just as much fun. And better still, our shopping day was an annual event.

My mom worked at the library in our small town, and every November, the library rented a charter bus and drove it to the Miracle Mile in downtown Chicago. The trip's timing was especially fortunate for me, a teenage clotheshorse with a mid-November birthday. This meant that I could have almost anything I wanted on the trip and Mom would give it to me as a birthday present. If I found too much stuff, Mom would just hold some back for Christmas.

It was the one day of the year when the answer was always "yes."

On the two-hour bus ride to the Miracle Mile, Mom and I chatted and made our plan of action for the day. Mom always asked if there was anything special I wanted, and she made finding that item a priority. This was back when "Guess" jeans were a must-have item for anyone who was trying to look exactly like everyone else in middle school.

This was also back before the "cool" brands came in children's sizes. Nowadays, my daughters and I just pop into Justice for all of their must-have items. But back then, "Guess" jeans started in a 24-inch waist.

And for me, a 13-year-old who looked about nine-and-a-half, finding cool clothes that fit was challenging to say the least. But Mom was not to be deterred. On those shopping trips, Mom and I found many of my most desired items. I wore them to school proudly—and always with a belt. Luckily for me, wearing jeans rolled up was all the rage in those days.

Although I was tiny, I had the same clothes as my classmates. At the time, it felt like a miracle.

The shopping was great, and the food was fun too. We always went to this deli that named their sandwiches after important people in Chicago. Mom and I always ordered the Hammy Sosa with waffle fries. We split the sandwich so we had room for two of their giant hot fudge sundaes, whose clever name escapes me now, nearly twenty years later.

These shopping trips were an annual thing for Mom and me throughout my middle school and high school years. One year, when it was time to book the trip, Mom and I were barely speaking. Long story short, Mom didn't like my boyfriend at the time. (It was all her fault. She acted as though one motorcycle ride through the church auditorium made him a bad guy or something. I tried to tell her he was just misunderstood, but she was so unreasonable about the whole thing....)

Anyway, I liked the guy and Mom didn't. We tried to develop an "agree to disagree" relationship, but it didn't seem to work. I was determined to point out my beau's positive attributes, but Mom just couldn't see past his black leather jacket and motorcycle. (Although the black tire marks in the church sanctuary were really the crux of the problem.)

Despite our strained relationship, I knew that missing the shopping trip was not an option. It was too special and too much fun.

And the truth was that I missed Mom. Not that I would have admitted it.

During the bus ride that year, Mom and I talked about our shopping plans, but little else. We both seemed to be avoiding the motorcycle-riding elephant in the room. But that day, Mom bought a Harley Davidson T-shirt for my boyfriend.

"It's a Christmas present," she said with a shrug and a small smile.

But to me, it seemed like a miracle. Mom was accepting my guy. Despite her feelings about him, she was acknowledging that I was growing up and was entitled to make my own choice. (Never mind that "my choice" dumped me sometime around January 3.)

Mom and I haven't shopped on Miracle Mile in many years. She still has opinions about my choices, but as I've grown up, I've learned to listen to her advice. She's smarter now... or maybe I am.

Mom and I bargain shop these days, hitting the outlet malls for kids' clothes and kitchen gadgets. The days still include lots of girl talk—and giant hot fudge sundaes.

Those Miracle Mile shopping days are some of my best childhood memories. Somewhere along the way, Mom became more than just my mom. She became my friend.

And that, I think, was the best miracle of all.

~Diane Stark

Cooking Up Love

Food is symbolic of love when words are inadequate.
~Alan D. Wolfelt

I was three or four years old when Mom placed a miniature rolling pin in my hands. It was a smooth wooden cylinder with tiny red handles, much smaller than the one Mom used to make cookies or roll out piecrust. My younger brother and I sat at the kitchen table, its surface lightly dusted with flour. She taught us how to flatten balls of dough and push cookie cutters in the dough to make shapes. Eventually we'd form the dough into a ball and flatten it again and again. Sometimes we would roll out the dough with our hands and create dough-shaped snakes. We felt important helping Mom in the kitchen. She involved us because she wanted us to take an interest in making food, but more than that, she knew food is about love. Food brings people together.

Some of my fondest memories growing up were coming home after school to the smell of freshly baked banana bread in Mom's kitchen. A homemade treat was always waiting for my brother and me after a long day — a chocolate chip cookie, a cherry pie, or homemade potato rolls. The food seemed to say, "I love you, and I hope you had a good day at school."

When we were sick, she made homemade chicken and noodles and cared for us while we lay on the couch all day, cozied up with a blanket and a bubbly cup of 7 Up.

After I gave birth to my twin boys and life became chaotic, Mom came to our home with a comforting smile and a roasting pan full of Salisbury steak, homemade mashed potatoes, and gravy. She brought along a bowl of fresh fruit, a few dozen cookies, and an apple pie. After spending three days in the hospital and coming home feeling exhausted and overwhelmed, I'd never tasted anything so good. Mom knew we wouldn't have much time to cook, so she brought another dish we stored in the freezer for an emergency. It didn't last long.

Whether it's a baptism or a birthday party, Mom brings a hot pan of macaroni and cheese, baked beans, and sweet corn. I don't have to ask. Occasionally after hauling a load of food into our house, she will disappear outside, open up her car trunk, and pull out a veggie tray and dip from a cooler, along with a thermos of coffee to serve our guests. "Oh, if I bring all this stuff, you don't have to do as much work," she says.

My boys love going to Grandma's house because her kitchen is stocked with treats. This summer when we visited her acreage, her candy dish overflowed. A pumpkin pie rested on the counter. With all the goodies around, I was mortified when my boys asked for ice cream. Mom didn't even flinch. She served three huge bowls of ice cream topped with chocolate syrup and sliced strawberries, and my boys dug in. It was 10:30 in the morning.

When my husband and I went away overnight and Mom stayed at our house to babysit, she brought a double batch of cut-out cookies. Her cookies always match the season: leaves and pumpkins for fall, Christmas trees and snowmen for winter, and flowers for summer. They are all decorated beautifully with colored frosting and sprinkles. When we returned home a day and a half later, my sons reported they had eaten all the cookies. Not even a crumb remained.

"Grandma said next time she will need to bring a triple batch," my son said with a grin. Mom laughed and said she was glad they didn't go to waste.

Mom filled my pantry with treats while I was gone: cake mixes, peanut butter, and potato chips. She even bought ham for sandwiches. My freezer is full of her apples, already sliced in three-cup portions, which is convenient for pie making. She brought twelve freezer bags of sliced apples and said I can use the apples to make one pie per month for the next year. And that's what I plan to do—using her prize-winning piecrust recipe.

Mom brings food to elderly friends, invites the neighbors in for a cup of coffee and a piece of cake, and shows up with enough food to feed an army when families are grieving. It's what she does to show she cares.

When my grandma passed away, Mom invited people to her home after the service. We ate sandwiches, told stories, laughed, cried, and devoured Texas sheet cake brownies. The food and fellowship nourished our souls.

At times Mom has struggled to express her emotions or to say the words, "I love you." It's not easy for her. Even so, I have never doubted her deep love for my family and me. I find it in my pantry and in my freezer. Love is her decorated cookies and her frozen apple slices. Food sustains us and comforts us. Mom loves by doing. She loves by cooking, baking, and sharing with others. I am grateful for the ways she fills us up with her kind of love.

~Tyann Sheldon Rouw

Chapter 5

Thanks to My Mom

The Best Cheerleaders

47

Writing What You Know

*Fill your paper
with the breathings of your heart.*
~William Wordsworth

"Why are you boys making all that noise up there? What are you doing?" my mother shouted up from the kitchen. It was Saturday morning and my brother David and I were off on yet another adven.ture. I was six and he was five, and jumping from one bed to another had pushed things just a little too far.

"We're just playing 'stories' Mommy," I replied.

"Well play a little more quietly."

Playing "stories." Ever since I was a little boy, I would make up stories to play with my brother. We had fantastic adventures in which we fought space pirates, giant monsters and mad scientists. I still create fictional stories that I try to get published and that I hope will eventually allow me to quit my day job. But being a crime reporter for a major market newspaper isn't too bad; I mean at least when I tell people I'm a writer I can add that it's how I pay the bills. For that I can blame my mother, Betty Ann Miller.

My mother loved books. She was always reading her novels, histories and romance magazines. When David and I were toddlers, she read us stories before bedtime. *Grimm's Fairy Tales* — "Sleeping

Beauty" and "Cinderella"—and heroic Greek myths, though "Sleeping Beauty" was my favorite.

So I suppose that I came by my unwavering desire to be a published novelist naturally. My mother graduated from high school but always regretted that she never went to college. She was a stay-at-home mom, and our growing family squashed the notion of returning to school. Soon, along came Marilyn, Harold-Fitzgerald, William and Christopher.

When I was nineteen, I borrowed from the library a copy of the *Writer's Market* to learn how I could begin publishing my stories. Naturally, as a huge fan of the science fiction genre, I looked to submit a piece to *Amazing Stories*. So I came up with a story I called "The Space Masters." They were a trio of futuristic intelligence agents looking to take down a gang of space pirates who had been troubling peaceful worlds. I worked at a fast food restaurant at the time flipping burgers, and when I came home I jumped into the world of the Space Masters.

"What's that you've been working on?" Mom asked me one night.

"It's a short science-fiction story," I replied.

"Really?" she asked. "Well I'd like to read it when you're finished."

"Sure," I said. "I want you to read it before I send it to New York. I'm going to try and get it published." I showed her the *Writer's Market*, and she seemed impressed and left me to my work. Now, in retrospect, I can see that she had already read it and I'll explain why. Several days later I finished "The Space Masters" and proudly handed over twelve typed sheets of paper. I went back to my room and played a David Bowie album while I waited. I could hear her and my father talking about it but I didn't eavesdrop. I just knew they were going to love it.

About an hour later she called me downstairs. Daddy was smiling conspiratorially. "Did you like it?" I asked.

Instead of four stars and two thumbs up she said, "You have a gift, Lawrence. Yes, I like it but why don't you write about what you know?"

"But what do I know?" I said, a little disappointed. I was only nineteen and all I knew was school, flipping burgers for minimum wage and growing up in West Philadelphia. What the heck did I know?

"You should try writing about what you know and see where that takes you."

Writing about what you know.

Looking back, I can see that I was born and grew up at the turning point in American history—the Civil Rights Movement. My great-grandmother, Emma Hines, wrote letters to Dr. Martin Luther King, Jr. and he wrote her back, though I have no idea where those letters are. I remember his assassination and the riots that followed. I lived in the time of President John F. Kennedy and Bobby Kennedy and Malcolm X and Medgar Evers. And I remember when each of them was killed for trying to make America into a better nation in spite of itself. Today I am a crime reporter for a major city newspaper, *The Philadelphia Tribune.*

My twelve-page science fiction story didn't see publication, but my news articles have won awards for the paper and gotten me guest spots on *Nancy Grace*, various local radio shows and fifteen minutes of fame on *NBC Nightly News*. I wouldn't have done any of that if my mother hadn't given me a love of literature. I write about what I know, the shared experiences of life in urban America. True, I write about things that are tragic and heartbreaking, but sometimes I get to write about good people doing good things and trying to make life better for everyone. With the Internet, a reporter in Philadelphia has no idea who is reading his work. It could be a student working on a dissertation or a young reporter working for a college newspaper, and sometimes they call to ask if they can quote you.

My mother didn't live to see my first published magazine article or any of the ones that followed. She never got to see my first freelance story for the *Tribune* or the day they made me a fulltime reporter. She never got to read my first front-page story, which I know would have made her so proud. But I'd like to think that she's looking down from heaven, along with Daddy and both sets of grandparents and a legion of uncles and aunts, and they're saying: "You go, boy!"

See Mommy, I'm writing about what I know. Thank you.

~Larry Miller

48

Pilots and Princesses

The future is called "perhaps," which is the only possible thing to call the future. And the only important thing is not to allow that to scare you.

~Tennessee Williams

I tried to sob quietly into the pillow the nurse had brought me as I lay on the hospital cot in my daughter's room. Jennifer was asleep so I had to cry softly. I'd cried too loudly the night before and awoken her. She'd asked me not to cry because it scared her.

What she couldn't understand was that being scared was the very reason I was crying. Here it was just a week before Thanksgiving and my sweet six-year-old was lying in a hospital bed, newly diagnosed with Type 1 diabetes.

My parents had arrived our first night in the hospital to pick up Jennifer's two little sisters, allowing my husband and me the opportunity to focus on Jennifer and how to manage her diabetes. My mom had pulled me aside and offered calm words of encouragement. "You can do this, Carol. You know you can. You're strong."

I thought about her words now as I lay on the cot, not sleeping. My mother knew as well as anyone that I wasn't a needle or blood person. I had to put my head between my knees just to have my finger pricked. Now doctors were telling me that we would need to prick

Jennifer's finger several times a day and do twice-daily injections. These prospects concerned me, but in my heart I knew my mother was right. I would do whatever was needed to take care of my little girl.

But that wasn't why I was crying.

I cried for Jennifer.

Just that morning, she'd commented about how glad she'd be when she got better and could go home and not have shots anymore. She'd cried when I gently explained that the shots weren't going away; they were keeping her well. Last week her biggest concern had been what color feathers to put on her pinecone turkey. Now, her whole life was practically inside out.

Then there had been the doctor's visit. He'd stopped by as a part of his rounds, just as Jennifer finished her lunch. He looked at the mostly untouched plate of cold canned green beans, a turkey loaf blob, and some oozy, melting, green, sugar-free Jell-O with chunks of canned fruit, and pronounced what I can only assume he believed to be words of wisdom: "You know, Jennifer, eating for you isn't going to be like it was before. You're like a car. You have to eat the right things to make your engine run smoothly. Don't think about how food tastes or if you enjoy eating it. Just remember, it's fuel and you need it. It's important."

Fortunately Jennifer was more interested in the new coloring book and crayons her daddy had brought her than she was in her doctor, so she wasn't really listening. But I was. The doctor's words and the uncertainty of how life was going to change for Jennifer were the reasons for my tears. How would she handle birthday parties, trick-or-treating, or her Easter basket? Thanksgiving was a week away and she'd been planning to help make a pie for dessert.

This was my baby. I wanted the world to offer her everything. It seemed like a big part of her childhood had been taken away, and I didn't know what to do about it. The tears continued to soak into my pillow.

The next day brought more diabetes management lessons and unappetizing meals. A mid-afternoon visit from her sisters provided a happy diversion for Jennifer and a chance for me to have a few minutes to visit with my mom. We stepped out into the hallway, and I told her about the lessons, Jennifer's questions, the uneaten food, my faltering progress with the injections. She listened patiently and offered a hug along with gentle words of encouragement. It helped tremendously, but my biggest fear, Jennifer's future, was an issue that no amount of kindness or support could alleviate. I wiped at the tears on my cheeks. Jennifer needed my support, and I needed my own mother's support as well.

"What exactly are you afraid of, Carol?" my mother asked compassionately. "You know you can take care of her. You don't have to do it by yourself. She has you, and her daddy, and lots of extended family who love her. You know all that, so what is it that's making you cry?"

The calmness and soothing tone of her words reassured me enough to reflect on what was scaring me. I searched for the right words to convey my biggest fear, Jennifer's future. I remembered something I'd read in one of the many pamphlets and instruction booklets left for us to read as part of our diabetes education plan.

"It said in one of the manuals that diabetics can't be pilots. She's only six. I don't want any doors closed for her future. She can't be a pilot, Mom."

The gentle tone my mother had taken throughout the past few days disappeared. Gone was the look of gentle empathy. In its place was a loving but steely look of determination. She spoke her words kindly, but with great resolve.

"She doesn't want to be a pilot. Last time I checked she was planning to be a fairy princess. I'm pretty sure none of the diabetes education materials rule that out."

Her words provided just what I needed at that moment: a good solid dose of reality. I was reaching far into the future and looking for problems. My mother knew how to keep me grounded in the present. She gave me what I needed and because of it, I was better able to give Jennifer what she needed.

My mom was right of course. As a grown-up, Jennifer doesn't have any desire to be a pilot. She also outgrew her plan to be a fairy princess. She is, however, a wonderful mother, thanks in many ways to my mom, who knows how to mix just the right amounts of tenderness and encouragement to keep her family grounded, but not afraid to soar.

~Carol Henderson

Letters from Home

When life gives you a hundred reasons to cry,
show life that you have a thousand reasons to smile.
~Author Unknown

Just over a year ago, I went through one of the most challenging experiences of my life. After exhausting the mental-health care that we could find in Canada, we were left with one last option. I had to go into residential care in the States, thousands of miles from home.

My mom had been there with me through the past four years of struggles and darkness, and never a day went by without her supporting me. She accompanied me to the States, and three plane rides later it was time to say goodbye. With tears in our eyes, we parted, not knowing when I would be released or when I would see her again.

I felt more alone than I had ever felt in my whole life. But after a few days, the letters started to arrive. As I opened my first piece of mail, I felt the desperation fade away. Even though I was far away, my mom reached across the distance to take my hand and walk with me along the path to getting better. She wrote to me every day.

The letters were funny, cajoling, and most importantly a reminder that I was not forgotten. Although working full-time and running a household, she would get up two hours early each morning and make sure that my letter was written before she did anything else in her day. Even though she was exhausting herself, she made sure that I had the strength to face another day in treatment.

The other residents would often look at my mom's eight-page letters and shake their heads in wonder. "How does your mom make time to write all of that?" they would ask.

On Wednesdays, she would write me stories. When I was a little girl and could not sleep, she would make up stories about my pets and the adventures they had under a pink and purple sky. I had not thought about those stories since I was little, but now every week there would be a new installment. In one of the stories, a character was wandering around a marsh and... well, I will let my mom explain it:

There were the usual bull rushes, and water, grasses and land. That was "normal" but what was not normal was the fact that everything was well off kilter. No, the plants weren't wearing kilts, thank goodness for that would be really weird, no it seemed that the people, the frogs, the insects the birds they were all wearing kilts! Talk about weird. Charlotte felt that she had landed in the Scotland of the swamp world. It was weird to see tartan everywhere; and how the heck did the insects make such tiny kilt pins?

The stories went on like this, bringing tears to my eyes because I was laughing so hard. During free time I would pull out her letters and let the flame of determination grow. I knew what she was doing. She was giving me a reason to laugh, and in doing so she gave me a reason to fight my illness and get better. She was throwing me a lifeline, and it was my responsibility to take hold and pull myself out of the quicksand of the last four years. Every day another letter arrived, each one preventing me from being sucked back into the swirling vortex of my mind.

I started working harder with my therapist, and paying more attention in the groups. Before I knew it, I was making leaps and bounds away from my illness. I quickly reached each new level, and I was given more freedom at the facility. I could call home more often, and my mom and I would laugh at whatever she had written in my latest letter.

Finally, it was the day that I thought would never come. There was a knock on the door and my family stepped in, my mom in the lead. The next twenty minutes were filled with screaming and laughing, crying and hugging.

In total I was at the treatment facility for ten weeks less a day. The average stay is around six months. I was released with flying colours and have not had a relapse since. And it was all due to my mom's perseverance and her determination to never go a day without writing me. Even though she was far away, her letters from home reassured me that she was walking beside me every step of the way.

~Rachel Loewen

A Book for Mama

The road leading to a goal does not separate you from the
destination; it is essentially a part of it.
~Charles DeLint

I slid my hands across the cardboard carton, savoring the sensation of the shallow paper ripples under my fingers. Although I was anxious to view the contents, I wanted this moment of delicious anticipation to last.

My mother's face filled my mind as I considered how proud she would be if she could have been here. The box held my first solo book, a novel dedicated to the woman who always believed I would succeed as a writer one day: my mother.

Mama sowed a love of words in my heart when I was quite young. Little Golden Books and other children's stories were read aloud to me. Other little girls might have gotten toys or candy as rewards for good behavior at the doctor's office. I earned a new book.

As I became able, I started reading the books back to her. We ran through the children's section of the local library in short order. By the time I was old enough to get my own library card, I was irretrievably hooked on the fluid pattern of words and sentences that make up written matter.

Mama handed me my first library card with great ceremony.

"This card makes you rich," she said. "With this card, you can go anywhere, see anything, and learn about anything. You can be whatever you want to be."

She was so right. As I traveled the world through my library card, I began to write my own stories and poems. When the time came to write a dreaded "paper" in school I celebrated, because writing was fun to me. I wrote book reviews for the student page of the local newspaper and little bits and pieces for other publications. I served on my high school newspaper. Over the years, I wrote training materials for employers, content for the church bulletin and press releases for organizations.

Mama always encouraged my reading and writing, even when she had to fuss at me for burning a pot while I was distracted or losing track of time and not being ready for whatever I was supposed to be ready to do. There weren't many things I could do right in my mother's eyes (typical of many mother-daughter relationships, I suspect) but she always approved of my writing.

"When are you going to write a book?" she asked, and repeated the question over the years.

My work appeared in a lot of places, but not in books for a long time. In 2012, a short essay I wrote was accepted in an anthology book. I was able to show Mama my name in an honest-to-goodness book. I wasn't alone in it, and my name wasn't on the spine, but I was in a book.

A second anthology accepted a story later that year. Mama was thrilled to see my name in the Table of Contents, but wanted to see it on the outside of the book.

In 2013, her health deteriorated and I lost her. The pain of that loss inspired a poem that found a place in yet another anthology. I could still hear her asking about a book. I got to work in earnest on the novel bouncing around in my subconscious.

In early 2014, a year after I said goodbye to my mother's physical presence, my first solo book was published. The carton holding the first delivery of the volume was the one I stood caressing.

When I opened the box, I spent another moment looking at the array of books before I lifted one from its nest. There on the cover, my name appeared, as it did on the spine. I opened the book to the dedication page for the biggest unveiling of the day.

"Dedicated to the memory of my mother, Mary Catherine."

Thanks to my mother's never-ending encouragement, I have a book on the shelf with my name on the spine and her name on the dedication page. A volume of poetry and one of devotions followed. Another novel is in the works and anthology appearances multiply. While I wish I could have seen her face as she read the dedication, I take comfort in the fact of her wish being fulfilled.

Thanks for believing in me and my dream, Mama. We made it.

~Mary Beth Magee

Mom's Lawn Chair

Oh, my friend, it's not what they take away from you that counts.
It's what you do with what you have left.
~Hubert Humphrey

om loved her role as a grandma to my three kids. Besides making a point of doing something special with them each week, she was obsessive about being at all of their school programs and athletic events. Over the years, she spent countless hours at basketball and soccer games, and cross country and track meets. She was as well-known a sideline fixture as most of the parents. Through most of their childhoods, Mom, in her fifties and sixties, was very active and energetic—young at heart. Most people guessed her to be ten to fifteen years younger than her actual age. She thought nothing of driving long miles for my kids' many events.

Then the unthinkable happened. Shortly after her seventieth birthday, she started getting dizzy often and then began having ministrokes. She spent countless hours with specialists, even traveling to the Mayo Clinic to get answers. She was finally diagnosed with multiple systems atrophy (MSA), a rare and rapidly progressing neurological disorder that is fatal. We watched as her body systems failed one by one. Throughout it all, Mom managed to maintain her positive outlook and sunny disposition.

As the disease progressed, another spring soccer season came around for my youngest daughter. By that time, my older two children had graduated from high school and had gone off to college. Mom could no longer travel to away games, but perhaps realizing her time on this earth was limited, she was determined to be at each and every home game that my daughter played in that season. Even though she was using a walker and motorized scooter to get around at home, she didn't like to take them out in public.

"Mom," I said as the season began, "let me stop by your house and take you to the games. We can load your walker in the car and take it with us."

"Absolutely not," she replied. "I don't want to be a burden. I can drive myself."

Since the soccer complex was only about a mile from her home, I acquiesced. The little bit of freedom she had left meant the world to her. So she drove herself to each and every game that season.

She absolutely refused to bring her walker, stating that she would look like an invalid. Instead, she left behind the bagged soccer chair, which we all carried over our shoulders, and started bringing an old lightweight, woven lawn chair with an aluminum frame that folded flat. She would maneuver herself out of the car, place the frame of the chair on the uneven ground in front of her and make her way very slowly to whatever field my daughter was playing on that day. She gradually inched the chair in front of her as she went, leaning on the frame for balance. Along the way, she turned down any and all offers of assistance. Although much less sturdy than her walker, the chair did manage to keep her from falling to the ground the majority of the time. When she did fall, she would laugh and stand back up, brushing herself off. Fortunately she never sustained any serious injuries.

At the field she would set up her chair and cheer Ashley on with her usual enthusiasm. When the game was over, my daughter and I would walk slowly behind her to the parking lot. She still refused any help. She would hold her head high and try to appear as independent as she could. Already embarrassed by the way her pants fit over the adult diapers that were now a necessity in her life, she wanted to save as much of her dignity as she could. Sometimes, if I was lucky, she would allow me to put her chair in the trunk while she got into her seat and fastened her seat belt. I wanted to follow her home to make sure she made it safely, but she didn't want that. Fortunately, her husband would be there to help her when she arrived.

That season was to be her last. She made it to each and every game before passing away quietly in her bed later in the year. The determination, independence, and love for family she exhibited throughout her last spring in our lives has been an inspiration to my daughter and me ever since.

~Jill Haymaker

Footprints
in the Sand

The relationship between parents and children,
but especially between mothers and daughters,
is tremendously powerful,
scarcely to be comprehended in any rational way.
~Joyce Carol Oates

Together we left our mark on the world.
Not a huge one—
Just two sets of footprints
side by side in the sand.
With the ocean vast and furious before me
and the waves reaching relentlessly to pull me in,
I should have been afraid.
But with you by my side to protect me,
be my lifeguard should I need one,
I felt fearless.
Courageous even.
And I knew that even when the water
washed away our footprints,
together we would create new ones.
As we withdrew from the shoreline,
you would remain by my side,
gently guiding me

and doing your best to protect me
from what might lie ahead,
all the while being my friend.

~Jennifer Lynn Clay

Mom's Dreams

Some see a hopeless end, while others see an endless hope.
~Author Unknown

One of the things I love about my mom is that she has always been a dreamer. My mom is almost seventy-five years old and you know what she did this spring? She planted an orchard! A pecan orchard. She's imagining in a few years she will stroll along the orchard lanes with a basket harvesting pecans. In five years she'll be almost eighty! But that's my mom.

I was in junior high when she married my stepfather. They are a match made in heaven—both dreamers and very happy. It's like she and my stepfather are these old vaudeville actors and they have this tired old bit, talking about their dreams, that they trot out every show like they are fresh and new. All you can really do is watch the show and smile and nod and try to act sincerely interested.

When I first heard their dreams, I believed them, every word. But by the time I was sixteen I began to wonder when all these things were supposed to happen. By the time I was eighteen I knew they were never going to happen. My mother and stepfather didn't have the business sense to make a million dollars, so they had to rely on dreams instead. It worked for them.

I think deep down they didn't want the dreams to come true; that's not what their dreams were for. The joy was in the wanting, not the possessing, and they were rich in want. Usually, folks burn out on the wanting and give up their dreaming. Not my folks, not my mom. Her dreams never stopped feeding her.

My wife and I are more pragmatic, especially my wife. I just accept that is how my mom operates, but it drives my wife up the wall. "How can they be so silly?" As if there was an answer to why puppies and kitties are so cute. They just are.

It worked when I was lying in a coma in the hospital with a traumatic brain injury. The doctors were advising my family to start looking into long-term care facilities. Everybody was advising my fiancée that she should make a quiet exit. No one believed I would be anything more than a vegetable.

Except my mom. As I lay dying she said, "Mike is going to be alright. You watch, he'll come through this better than ever." And my then fiancée, now my wife, always the pragmatic one, chose that one time to believe my mom's dream talk. And that one single, solitary time my mom's dream was spot on. Her whole life of dreaming was worth it just so that she could give Linda a foundation of hope that one time to build her own dream and wait for me to get better. We've been married more than a quarter century now, and it's all thanks to my mom.

~Michael Strand

The Sun, the Moon, and the Stars

No language can express the power, and beauty…
of a mother's love. It shrinks not where man cowers…
and… sends the radiance of its quenchless fidelity like a star.
~Edwin Hubbell Chapin

I stared straight ahead as trees and houses rushed by, my stomach in knots. I had to tell her, but I didn't know how she'd react. Tears came to my eyes as I looked at my mother behind the wheel and said, "I don't want to feel like this anymore." I was fifteen and it was the first time I'd talked about my depression. She looked back at me with damp eyes and promised, "I'll do whatever I can to get you the help you need." We'd fight this together.

A few weeks later, as I entered therapy and started on the lifelong quest of finding myself and escaping depression, my mother handed me a card. Alone in my room, blinking through the tears, I read the two small yellow notepad pages that she'd tucked in the card. Her curved, round handwriting spelled out all the good she saw in me: creativity, talent, a future. "Don't ever forget how very special you are to me," she wrote. My mother knows how to speak to my soul in the rhythms that move it.

I don't know what she thought I'd do with the letter, but I was sentimental and pasted it into my scrapbook, even if I didn't believe what she'd said. She often repeated her positive words to me, but I'd roll my eyes and think, "Sure. Moms have to say those things, even if they're not true."

My depression deepened despite her efforts, and dragged me into addiction. For six months after my eighteenth birthday, I stared at my mother across a circle of metal folding chairs. Some of my family had given up on me during the year of my heroin and cocaine addiction. But no matter how much I sulked or screamed, my mother made the two-hour drive every week, on a work night, to bring me a smile and a hug and her ever-present arsenal of optimism.

During one of her visits for family counseling, my mother gave me another card, this one with golden suns printed on the front. Inside, she reminded me of the things she'd said in her earlier letter. In her calligraphy, she'd written the Serenity Prayer—a favorite in the circles of addiction. I always found the most uplifting part to be what comes after the most popular lines. The part that says it's not going to be easy, but if you take one step at a time, you'll get where you're going. My path was treacherous, but I had my mother by my side, dragging me along and holding me up.

Words were the only thing I had most days in rehab, and I kept my mother's card tucked into a journal, close by my side. I scribbled plenty of anger and heartbreak and guilt upon my journal pages and discovered the release that comes from writing out emotions. I started to believe my mother's words—maybe I could be something and do something worthwhile with my life. During my darkest days, she was the sun in my sky, reflecting her light upon me. And I started to see past my despair.

When I celebrated one year drug-free, my mother looked at me with pride in her eyes, and there was another card. The front was blue with gold stars and a colorful image of a sun reaching out its rays to a smiling moon. This image was the perfect representation of that year. We'd come through it, and we were still shining.

I managed to piece my life together as I entered my twenties. I earned my GED, collected a few college degrees, got married, and had a daughter. Even a good life has its moments, though, and I had taken my mother's advice when she'd said, "Read this list of encouragement from time to time." I keep the card with the sun, moon, and stars and the letter filled with my mother's words in my scrapbook on the bottom shelf of my bookcase, in easy reach. It's a good reminder of where I've been and how I got out—with determination and a constant cheerleader by my side.

I'm sure at the time my mother had no idea how important a few sheets of notepad paper filled with encouraging words would be to me. But as a writer, words have always been an integral part of my life. They are the blocks with which I build my worlds. When I started my writing career, I had my walls of hope and confidence repeatedly torn down through rejection. I needed a way to build myself up and keep going in the midst of the negativity that threatened to drag me back to depression. So, I took her list of encouraging words from so many years ago and expanded on it.

I sat at my computer one day after facing a particularly difficult round of criticism. I'd already whined and wallowed in self-pity and given up ten times in my head. Something had to change. The yellow notepad pages from so many years ago returned to me, along with my mother's constant words: "You can do this!" My fingers hit the keys and I created a new document file. This time, I pasted words of praise in black letters on a glowing white screen.

My "Pick Me Up File" can be accessed from my computer, phone, or any device that will connect to the Internet. With just a few taps or clicks, whether I'm sitting at home or in line at the grocery store, I'll find words of inspiration and positivity from friends, family, colleagues, and even a few strangers. These words are an echo of the letter my mother wrote me two decades ago. Days when I feel down or think I should give up, I pray and read the words that remind me that I am neither worthless, nor hopeless, nor talentless, and that my dreams will come true.

In everything I put her through, my mother never gave up on me. And no matter how dim the stars or how far from my reach, my mother adds rungs of encouragement to my ladder to make the climb easier. She's the one who said from the start that a degree in creative writing made complete sense, when it seemed pointless to everyone else. She never stopped believing in me and I know she never will. She has been my loudest cheerleader through every hurdle, no matter how large the crowd that booed me.

When I had my first short story published, she wasn't surprised. "You're on your way. You're just getting started," she said. I signed a copy for her and wrote, "To my mother: My first inscription, on my first publication, to my first fan." My dream had come true and rested in my hands. But then, according to my mother, the stars were never out of my reach.

~Denise Drespling

Finish It for Me

My mother made a brilliant impression upon my childhood life.
She shone for me like the evening star.
~Winston Churchill

My husband Jim and I fell in love while we were both in college. We married the same fall he started law school, and I buckled down to finish my undergraduate studies.

A year later, I was determined to find a job with my liberal arts degree, but in a college town the best paying jobs went to graduate students who taught beginning courses while pursuing advanced degrees. I enrolled as a master's degree student in French literature. My teaching stipend covered our basic living expenses.

Fast-forward two years. Jim had finished law school and was studying for the bar exam. He had a job waiting for him and soon we would move to a nearby city to start our post-college life.

I had completed all my graduate course work and was plodding through the final stages of my thesis, translating and analyzing an obscure medieval French literary work.

That's when it happened. The French use the elegant word *ennui*, which covers a multitude of ills: boredom, fatigue, depression, or just plain feeling "stuck." I could go no further with my thesis. Every day felt like moving through mud. I didn't want to share my dismal state with Jim; he was totally consumed with bar exam preparations. I knew my friends would dismiss it as a bad case of almost-ready-to-graduate-itis.

I was daydreaming about walking into my thesis advisor's office and saying "I quit" when the phone rang.

"Hello?"

"Hi, sweetie, how are things going?"

My mom? How did she know? But then she always seemed to know when I was down, even though she lived half a country away and we didn't talk that often. My anguish tumbled out.

"I don't think I can finish my thesis, Mom. I just can't find the motivation. I doubt if the degree will ever do me any good. I'm ready to settle down and start a family."

Mom paused. "If you don't want to finish your degree for yourself, finish it for me."

Her words went straight to my heart. Mom had been a child of the Great Depression. Even though she was a talented pianist, she had turned down a scholarship to Juilliard to get a full-time job and contribute to the family finances.

She never made it to college. Neither did my dad. They had both told me on numerous occasions how proud of me they were. At that moment I realized how selfish I would be if I didn't go ahead and finish.

"Okay, Mom," I sighed. "I'll do it for you."

I successfully completed my master's degree and went on to teach college French and start a family. A few years later, after both kids were in school, I decided to make a career change and found myself back in school for three years to obtain a law degree. Mom was delighted, of course. I sailed along on my own motivation until it was time to study for the bar exam.

The bar exam, I knew from Jim's experience, was a grueling two days of essay questions with complex legal scenarios. Without passing the bar exam, one cannot be licensed to practice law. It's the "golden ticket" to being a lawyer, regardless of how many law courses you take.

Studying for the bar exam took up most of the summer. A small group of us met each day and grilled each other, sometimes late into the evening, drinking cup after cup of coffee to stay awake.

As the bar exam date loomed nearer, I felt more and more panicky. "I'll never be able to remember all this stuff," I thought. "I don't know why I ever thought I could be a lawyer. I'll never find a job at my age, anyway. Why put myself through this misery?"

My anxious mind dredged up every negative message it could think of. I was on the verge of quitting when Mom's words came floating into my consciousness: "finish it for me." Those words were my lifeline. I summoned a picture of my mother as a young woman, looking straight at me with her deep brown eyes. She nodded her head as she smiled, and I felt her heart reaching out to mine.

All my anxiety drained away. Two days later, I marched into the examination room with 200 other candidates and began to write. Whenever I faltered, whenever the old negative feelings threatened to take over, I heard Mom whisper "Finish it for me." Her words magically melted all the fears.

Six weeks later the letter came, informing me that I had passed the bar exam and requesting my presence the following week at the State Supreme Court to be sworn in as a practicing lawyer. Only then did I call Mom and let her know how her words had once again sustained me.

Although Mom's no longer physically with me, her heartening words—"finish it for me"—continue to inspire me to press on, to accomplish that next goal, whether it's writing an essay, planning a workshop, or dreaming up a special dessert. Thanks to Mom, I'm up to the challenge!

~Maril Crabtree

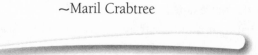

The Pie Chart of Me

*At times our own light goes out and is rekindled by a spark from
another person. Each of us has cause to think with deep gratitude
of those who have lighted the flame within us.*
~Albert Schweitzer

The infamously rigorous International Baccalaureate program
was always the most popular topic of discussion for everyone, from seasoned alumni to anxious Pre-IBers. Stories of
sleepless nights sustained by cans of iced coffee and mental
breakdowns at 1 a.m. were passed around like urban legends.

Those of us entering grade eleven didn't have time to be fazed.
But the panic first started setting in when we received our physics lab
on the third day of school.

"This is harder than anything you've done," our teacher chuckled—almost snidely—as he passed around the instruction sheets.
"No one will get above ninety." My confidence was shaken as I looked
at the page of tauntingly unfamiliar symbols.

With a heavy heart, I managed to make it through the rest of the
school day. When I finally dragged myself home, my father only added
insult to injury. Pointing out my lack of progress in the SATs, my dad
reiterated for the millionth time that I would not be able to get into a
prestigious American university without good SAT results.

The last straw was the e-mail from the Red Cross. As the vice president of my school's Red Cross chapter, getting rejected from the Regional Red Cross Youth Council was a possibility that never crossed my mind. It simply couldn't happen. Not only was the Red Cross my passion and inspiration, but it was also what I relied on to set me apart from all the other college applicants with ninety-five percent averages.

My future had seemed so bright and certain, yet in reality it was so fragile. Any small blockage could force me to veer off the narrow path to success. I felt like a rubber band—it can only take so much stretching before it snaps. After that e-mail from the Red Cross, I snapped.

I ran out of my room and the first person I saw was my mother, the woman who left behind her family, her friends, and her life in China to emigrate to a foreign country just so I could receive a better education and have a brighter future. The woman who gave up her highly esteemed job in Beijing and could only find a job as a part-time office assistant in Toronto. My mother had spent her life bringing me to the most advantageous starting point, and yet I did not have enough stamina to reach the finish line.

When my mom finally noticed me, I was already a sobbing mess. "What's wrong, baby?" she asked, her face a mixture of alarm and worry.

My answer was "everything," and so that's what I told her about. My mother let me blabber on and on.

After I was done, she stared at me with so much emotion in her eyes. Her brows were furrowed as she bit her lip. I recognized the expression on her face. It meant she had too much to say and didn't know how to get her message across, which rarely happened. The only other time I clearly remember seeing that look directed at me was when I was six and took a bouncy ball home from kindergarten. It was years later that I learned that, at that time, she thought she was a failure as a parent because I didn't understand the fundamental principles of integrity and honesty.

"This pie chart here," my mother began hesitantly after a long silence, tracing a circle into the felt table cover with her forefinger, "represents your time."

At this point, I was thoroughly confused. Rarely has my mother chosen to use mathematics to prove a point; it just wasn't her forte. It was me, rather, who had such a dominant left-brain that I saw the world around me in numbers and statistics.

"Eighty percent is school work," my mom carefully darkened the majority of her impromptu pie chart.

"Ten percent is the SAT and ten percent is extracurricular activities."

It made sense. I mentally recorded everything my mom was saying.

"But most importantly, at one hundred percent," my mother's voice was starting to shake and she was tracing the circle so furiously that it was starting to look like a shapeless blob, "is your mental health."

I stared at her, a little dumbfounded, because that just didn't make sense. She looked back at me with the same look as when six-year-old me asked why it was wrong to take home the kindergarten's bouncy ball. It was a look that said "Trust me" in the most affectionate way possible.

"Nothing is more important than your health, Aileen. Why do we want you to go to a good university? Because you are more likely to have a good, well-paying career. Why do we want you to get a good job? Because you'll be less stressed if you're financially stable. This, right here, this is not healthy. This is not happy. If you feel so burdened by every little mistake and mishap along the way, then this isn't worth it. If you're happier working flipping burgers, so be it. There's absolutely nothing more important than your physical and mental wellbeing."

Maybe, to another girl in another family, such a lecture was the norm, but not to me. My parents did not immigrate halfway across the globe so I could be healthy. Yet I couldn't help the immense relief I felt in my chest. A rubber band doesn't have to keep stretching. A rubber band that wraps around your hair during the day and is allowed to rest on your nightstand at night won't ever snap.

That night, my mother and I stayed up all night chatting about my plans for the future, yet there was no impending sense of doom. The incessant fear of failure no longer seemed so terrifying.

To an outsider, perhaps nothing changed. I was still the girl who arrived at school at 7:30 a.m. to study before tests and stayed behind until 5 p.m. to get as much extra help as I could. Yet to me, everything changed. When I received a less-than-satisfactory result, there was no calm façade that crumpled as soon as I was safely hidden in a bathroom stall; there was only me carefully analyzing my mistakes so I could improve in the future.

I'm still reaching for the moon, but I'm no longer afraid. For I know that if I miss, I will land right in my mother's arms.

~Aileen Liang

57

Chicken Soup for the Soul

"Doing Life" with Mom

A daughter is a little girl who grows up to be a friend.
~Author Unknown

"Okay, Diane, you're doing well," my obstetrician said, snapping off her rubber gloves. "You're dilated to eight centimeters, so it shouldn't be much longer."

As a first-time mom, I didn't know that "not much longer" meant another seven hours. But on that day, I was clueless about more than just the birth process.

My husband sat on one side of me, holding my hand and reminding me to breathe. My mom was on my other side, crying quietly into her hands.

"It's all right, Mom," I assured her. "It doesn't hurt that bad."

"Yes, it does," she murmured. Her eyes looked vacant, almost hopeless, and it scared me. I wondered if she knew something that I didn't.

Hours later, when my son was born, not breathing and with the cord around his neck, I forgot about Mom's tears and focused on my newborn son. His initial Apgar score was one, and I was terrified we'd lose him.

But Jordan rallied, and we were able to take him home within the week. It was exciting and scary, and incredibly busy, and Mom's odd behavior at the hospital was forgotten.

But days later, she called me, nearly hysterical. She told me that my dad was leaving her. They'd been married for almost thirty years.

"I didn't want to tell you now, when you should be so happy, but I couldn't help it. I need you, honey," she said, sobbing.

Over the next few months, the sound of Mom's tears became as familiar to me as those of my newborn son.

Because she lived far away, we spent hours each day on the phone, her talking and crying, me just listening and doing the little I could to offer comfort. I sent hang-in-there cards and pick-me-up flowers and tons of pictures of her first grandbaby.

It wasn't much, but it was all I could do. And I felt it was the least I could do for her after all she'd done for me. But still, it was sometimes scary to realize that Mom and I had completely reversed roles. After a lifetime of counting on Mom to be there for me, I had become the caretaker and she was more the child. It was frightening, but it was our reality for a season.

A few years later, Mom remarried, and my sister and I were her matrons-of-honor. Mom's new husband was a wonderful man and I was happy for her.

Things were finally back to normal.

And then my own marriage fell apart. By then, I'd had a second child and had two young kids to take care of at a time when I could barely care for myself.

But Mom stepped in. She was there in ways that only a mother could be. She provided an emotional strength neither of us knew she had. She took care of my kids when I couldn't. She just did what had to be done.

Sometimes it felt good to be taken care of, to let her do her thing. But after a while, I realized that her thing should have been my thing. It was fine to let her be my mom, but she was also being a mom to my kids—and that was my job. I pulled it together because I had to. My kids needed me.

But I still needed Mom.

One day, I was feeling particularly emotional, and I tearfully thanked Mom for carrying me for the last few months.

She smiled and shrugged. "You did it for me, honey."

I smiled back. "Yeah, I guess I did. We've always been there for one another." It was something I was infinitely grateful for, but at the same time, I didn't like feeling so dependent.

A year later, I was back on my feet. I had a job I loved, and I'd met Eric, the man I would eventually marry. My life was definitely on the upswing.

My relationship with my mom has evolved over the years. Throughout my childhood, she held my hand and wiped my tears. And for a time, I did those things for her. I then experienced a second childhood, where I needed Mom more than ever before. And she didn't let me down.

We've always been mother and daughter, but through the years, we've changed roles depending on the circumstances. One of us has stepped up when the other was hurting and in need. We were there for one another during the worst times of our lives, and now we're enjoying the good times together. Currently, what I need most from my mom is her friendship.

Life goes in cycles. Sometimes we feel strong, and we're able to lift up a friend or a loved one. At other times, we're the one who needs the support.

Those ups and downs are just part of the roller coaster we call Life.

And I'm so thankful that I get to "Do Life" with Mom in my corner.

~Diane Stark

Just One More Chapter

Children are the sum of what mothers contribute to their lives.
~Author Unknown

"Please just one chapter, just one!" I tugged at my mother's apron and begged. I gazed up at her with what I hoped was my most beguiling expression as I held the book in my hand.

She paused from washing the dishes to look down at me. At five years of age, I couldn't yet read on my own. Nevertheless, I already loved books and words with a passion. It was my mother's doing. I couldn't remember a time when she didn't read to me.

"All right." She dried her hands on a towel and turned to me, an understanding smile brightening her face. "Dishes can wait. Now where were we?" She took the dog-eared volume from my hands and headed for the rocking chair in the living room with me so close on her heels that when she paused to check the wood stove, I bumped into the back of her legs.

I curled up beside her between the cane arms of the old cushioned rocking chair and she began. An amateur actress, she read with great expression. I found it positively magical as her voice took me deep into the story. The lines between real and imaginary blurred as I listened.

She read to me often, and she also took me with her to rehearsals of the latest play in which she had a part. Sitting in the shadowy front row of our town's old opera house, I'd swing my feet and mouth the lines I'd learned along with her as she practiced.

We weren't wealthy, but my mother saw to it that there was always money for books. She delighted in my joy at each literary acquisition, and once I learned to read she accepted my long absences from family activities as I lay stretched out on my bed, with my dog beside me, to read. And when I shyly showed her my attempt at writing a mystery novel, she greeted it with joyful exuberance. She must have known the road to becoming a published author was as difficult as becoming a professional actress, yet she was determined I should give it a try. Some would call me a dreamer but she never did.

When I was fourteen, my mother was diagnosed with ovarian cancer. While other family members were deeply concerned, I ignored her disease. After all, she was my mother, my most understanding and sharing partner. Nothing bad could happen to her. Nothing could separate us. I withdrew into what is called in fiction writing "the willing suspension of disbelief."

A year later I learned that denying facts wouldn't make them go away. My mother grew steadily worse. Heavily medicated, she sometimes failed to recognize me when I came home from school. My aunt had moved in to care for her and discouraged my attempts to find the parent I'd known inside the fog of pain and drugs.

"Your mother has to rest," my aunt would say. "She can't be troubled with trying to remember you and your stories."

Having been denied my literary companion, I retreated into my own world of making up tales, fanciful stories where there were no devastating diseases and where best friends weren't torn apart by illness. I wrote late into the night in my Hilroy scribblers and hid them under my bed. Later I'd read my compositions in whispers to my dog. I had no one else with whom to share them anymore.

Finally my mother had to be hospitalized. Each day after school I visited her. Sometimes she knew me and we'd reminiscence about books and stories. She'd ask what I was working on and I'd tell her, sometimes even read her a short piece. Sometimes she'd manage to stay alert long enough to comment favorably at the end; other times she'd have drifted away by the time I finished. During the long walk home from the hospital on one of these latter days, I choked back tears of anger and frustration. "How can I ever become a writer if you're not here for me, if I can't depend on you for one more chapter?"

The afternoon before the evening that she passed I went to the hospital, a short piece I'd entitled "Twilight Encounter" stuffed into my pocket. It described the beauty of a moment I'd shared with a deer I'd met in an autumn twilight and how darkness had slowly brought down nature's curtain on the scene.

Unusually bright and lucid, she enjoyed the piece so much it brought tears to her eyes. "Beautiful, just beautiful, Gail." She smiled, her face so thin and pale she bore little resemblance to the bright, lively mother I remembered. "Never, never give up writing. You have a gift."

Her words brought joy to my heart. I bent and kissed her. "I never will, Mommy," I promised.

Fifteen minutes later, when the nurse informed me it was time to go, I took her hand as I always did before leaving.

"Remember, dear, I'll always be there for just one more chapter." She held my hand in a surprisingly strong grip.

I kissed her and left.

She passed away that evening. I returned home and began ripping up those Hilroy scribblers. Nothing made sense; life was too cruel to try to capture in words.

Suddenly, as I was about to tear yet another story in two, I recognized it as a Christmas tale, one I'd written before my mother became ill. It told how each year she'd manage to purchase my currently most longed-for books to put under the tree, how she'd hide them in her cedar chest until the big day, and how I'd discovered her hiding place and would sneak in each night prior to December 25th with a small flashlight to read them. I thought that was the end of the yarn but then I'd discovered she'd known of my crimes almost from their beginnings. And understood. My thirst for words had driven me into this life of petty larceny.

As if struck by an epiphany, I suddenly knew I had to go on with my writing. I couldn't let her down.

I stopped my self-vandalism and sat down with the pages in my hands. A half hour later I was working on it, finishing the piece. Years and many published stories later, it would appear in *Chicken Soup for the Soul: O Canada* under the title "The Secret of the Cedar Chest."

My mother left me years too soon. I wish she'd been granted the time to read my published books and articles. I wish she'd been able to share my ups and downs as a writer. And yet somehow I believe she has, that she's always been somewhere nearby, smiling and nodding, vindicated in her decision to urge her daughter to be a writer.

And in doing so, she left me with a wonderful gift, the ability to find my heart's pleasure, the icing on the cake that has been my life. She fostered my love of words and shaped it into a beautiful, lifelong positive addiction. While my family, friends, and dogs have made up the wonderful reality of my years, writing has been the ethereal magical bit that tops it off.

And sometimes, late at night, when I'm attempting to finish a book or article, when I'm weary and wondering if it's worth the struggle, I hear her voice, "There's always time for just one more chapter."

Thanks, Mom. I love you. Here's another chapter just for you.

~Gail MacMillan

The Courage to Wait

Courage is what it takes to stand up and speak;
courage is also what it takes to sit down and listen.
~Winston Churchill

I f I wrote a book called "All the Things My Mom Did Right," it would be a long one, but not too long. My mom never liked conversations that went on too long, especially emotional ones. She'd sit in her favorite chair (the recliner my brother and I splurged on for her birthday one year, and that she later reupholstered to suit) and listen for almost an hour to my latest heartfelt tale of woe. I always had so much woe.

As a teen growing up in a divorced home and then as a young adult trying to pay for university and find love, there was plenty to "bellyache" about—as my mother would call it. She had more to complain about than I did, but somehow she always put my feelings before her own. She'd listen as I talked.

Then she'd start to squirm. It was as if her emotional buttons were being pressed one by one as she listened to my stories of small betrayals. I ignored her unspoken signals. Blindly, I forged ahead, analyzing every conflict in detail. My mother hated conflict. But she "stayed in the game," as she'd say, and listened patiently—often past her own tipping point.

After the divorce, she'd turned her attention to the second chance that grandchildren offer the bereaved or disappointed. The only trouble was, the grandchildren never came. She was left with a daughter whose emotional needs were still unmet—and who wanted to talk. Looking back, I can't believe the courage and patience she showed in listening to me all those (uncomfortable) hours.

Then one Christmas the whole family met at my mom and step-father's house on the farm. My mother was stirring up her annual stuffing—breadcrumbs, white onion, pepper and celery salt—when my stepfather's mother made an innocent comment about me not being married—yet. This, of course, was my mother's long-held dream: that I would marry and have children she could dote on. She'd already bought a cupboard's worth of clothes and toys at yard sales for when "the grandbabies came." Despite all life's setbacks, she was a staunch traditionalist (and so was I).

In that awkward moment, I stood motionless, staring at the red and white tablecloth covered with poinsettias. I searched for something to say, a reason why I wasn't "married with children"—yet. My mother saw my distress. She read the signals and put down her spatula and walked over to where I stood. She put her arm around my shoulder. On my behalf, she said, "Dayna doesn't need to be married. She's perfectly fine how she is."

That was one of her rare displays of affection. But it was not rare for her to take a stand. Those simple words and that small act of love set me free from my own (and everyone else's) expectations. In one stroke, she put us both on more solid emotional and psychological ground.

Five years later I walked down the aisle, much to my mother's joy. Two healthy, active grandchildren were soon there to dote on. And dote she did! Grandchildren are great for those who want to simply love!

She got out the little green wagon that she'd found at a yard sale and she took them to the local ball game. She sat and colored for hours in the solarium and she got down on the floor to play trains. She sewed Christmas stockings for them and stuffed scrapbooks. She created pastel needlepoints for the nurseries. Her fridge and walls were covered with smiling photos. And, of course, she listened to every long tale of joy I shared with her.

I learned a lot about my patient, longsuffering mother by watching her play with her longed-for grandbabies. It was like we both had a second chance at sharing happy memories.

Sadly, my mother died of lung cancer while the children were still young. I miss her very much, but I'm thankful for who she was—a traditionalist who could still support her daughter when she deviated from the norm! I can only hope to parent as well as she did.

~Dayna E. Mazzuca

Chapter 6

Thanks to My Mom

The Wisdom of Mothers

Confessions of a Latchkey Kid

Men are what their mothers made them.
~Ralph Waldo Emerson

I was a latchkey kid, but I never knew it. I remember the first time I saw the term "latchkey kid" in a newspaper headline. The words conjured up an image of a tragic waif locked in a lonely hovel. Then I started reading the story. It was about kids who had working parents and who came home from school, let themselves in, and sometimes had to make their own dinner.

It occurred to me then that somewhere a sociologist was probably writing a book about this terrible waste of human potential—a book explaining how latchkeyism is a contributing factor in juvenile delinquency, alcoholism and the nuclear arms race and telling parents that allowing their children to return from school to an empty home is somehow immoral.

But back when my younger brother, David, and I came home from school to an empty house, while our mother was out making money to feed and clothe us, we never realized we were being abused. I think we actually enjoyed it.

When I was nine or ten years old, I remember coming home, letting myself in with my own key, plunking down on the couch and doing exactly what every other kid my age was doing—sitting like a vegetable and watching cartoons until my mom came home and screamed that it was time for dinner.

Once in a while my brother and I would cook dinner—not frequently, mind you, since that would have meant missing *Spider-Man*—but once in a while.

Yes, I confess, the absence of a parental presence in our home forced my brother and me to learn how to cook. As a result of this inhumane treatment, we're both completely at ease in the kitchen and my brother still makes one of the best lasagnas I've ever had. As scary as this sounds, we even learned how to do our homework without being nagged.

One of the reasons latchkeyism is considered such a crisis today is because there are maniacs out there. The assumption most people seem to make is that there were never any crazy people out there before. But there were and—this is the terrible part, so if you're easily frightened you may want to skip this—my mother knew it.

Do you know how I know she knew? Because she told us. "Don't open the door for strangers," she said. And we didn't. If anyone we didn't recognize came to our house, we'd leave the chain on, open the door a crack and tell the person to come back later.

She also told us that if we were ever frightened for any reason we should call someone immediately. There was a list of numbers by the phone almost as long as the Yellow Pages—the police, the fire department, the hospital, friends, relatives and, of course, our mom's office.

So do you know what we did when we were frightened? We called someone.

I remember one evening when I was about thirteen or fourteen and old enough to babysit. My brother and I heard some noises outside, so we phoned a family friend and he came over and checked it out. It turned out to be some kid from the neighbourhood throwing rocks at the windows. But it could just as easily have been one of those dangerous strangers and we were reassured that we had someone who would come right over when we called.

Yes, I was a latchkey kid and so was my brother. Both of us survived our latchkey years and—you'll have to take my word for this—I think we've both grown up to be fairly responsible adults because we learned to look after ourselves at a fairly early age. So I guess I just have one thing left to say about my tortured life as a latchkey kid.

Thanks, Mom.

~Mark Leiren-Young

61

Tell Them You Can Do It

Confidence is a habit that can be developed by
acting as if you already had the confidence you desire to have.
~Brian Tracy

I f I had to choose the one piece of motherly advice that has made the biggest difference in my life, it would be "Tell them you can do it." The funny thing is, Mother didn't actually give this advice to me. It was meant for someone else entirely. I'm just lucky she happened to repeat the story to me.

My family lived in the same town that was home to the state's oldest university, the University of Florida. Students from the College of Education frequently sought internships with teachers in the local public schools. Mother took on an intern from time to time, even though it usually meant extra work for her.

Mother's interns often sought her help with applications, references and the like because they hoped to find full-time teaching jobs when they graduated. A counseling session with one of them prior to a job interview led to the advice that has stuck with me ever since.

I don't know whether the intern actually asked for Mother's advice—probably, she just mentioned the upcoming interview. For some reason, Mother told me about it the same day, after she got home from work. "I told her, if they ask you if you can teach math, or geography, or even home economics, you tell them you can do it. Whatever they want you to do, you tell them you can do it."

Mother wasn't an overly confident person. Yes, she had two college degrees and yes, she had years of teaching experience, but she never expected any special recognition or praise. She didn't seek it, and she usually didn't get it. When I was young, I didn't fully comprehend all that my mother had accomplished.

The first in her family to graduate from college, Mother told me she had been terrified when she left her small hometown. Headed for Florida State College for Women, she was afraid of having to return home because she couldn't cut it. But she didn't fail. She graduated at age nineteen, taught for several years, and then landed a job as administrative assistant to the College of Education dean at the University of Florida.

While Mother was working at the university, she took graduate courses and continued her education, eventually earning a master's degree. It was there she met her one and only, the man she eventually married. Mother and Daddy were devoted to each other, sharing a lifelong love and mutual respect.

My mother was an accomplished lady in her own right, but she often took a back seat to my father, who, as the primary breadwinner, had a more exciting job as principal of our local high school. Although he was a quiet and humble man, Daddy was recognized for his leadership skills and frequently served in highly visible roles in church and civic organizations. Daddy was in the limelight, and Mother pretty much stayed in the background.

Unlike Mother and her intern, I never applied for a teaching job. I earned a law degree and then went to work for a law firm. For the first five years of my career, I felt woefully ill-equipped to handle just about everything that crossed my desk. I found transaction work painstaking and confusing, courtroom appearances scary and intimidating. But I kept that to myself. I told the big guys I could do it. And I did, even though I was quaking inside.

Later, when I went to work at a corporation, I became an expert in a number of fields I had previously known nothing about. The job demanded it; there was no one else to do it, so I did. Ultimately, I was asked to add management of the company's internal audit department, including the top audit job, to my responsibilities, despite the fact that I was not an auditor and did not have a financial background. I told them I could do it, and I did.

The biggest rewards in my career, and the most gratifying experiences of my life, have come as a result of stretching beyond my comfort zone. I've seen the same principle at work in the lives of younger people I have mentored. No one gets ahead by underestimating what she can do.

Years after Mother advised her intern on how to handle that critical first job interview, I told her how much her wise counsel had inspired me, even though I was not its intended recipient. I asked her why she had given that particular piece of advice to her protégé.

"I knew how much she needed that job," Mother said.

Mother wasn't into fakery or boasting or dissimulation. She just knew that deep down beyond the nattering voices that tell us we can't do the things we'd like to do, there is a boundless well of ability and grit. It will bubble up to the surface if we just let it.

I'm glad I had the opportunity to thank Mother for the advice that has been so helpful to me over the years. Even so, I am not sure she understood the extent of its impact. It is with me still, encouraging me when I'm tired, intimidated or overwhelmed.

"Tell them you can do it." Mother's words ring in my ears, firm resolve underscoring each one.

Echoing her voice, I whisper to myself, "I can do it."

And then, I do.

~Mary Wood Bridgman

62

Be Nice

Be kind whenever possible. It is always possible.
~Dalai Lama

I lived at home while I went to college, and I appreciated the extra time with my family. I respected my mom's wisdom and I actually took her advice! One day particularly stands out for me, a day when a simple piece of advice became a lifelong lesson.

I don't remember what I was upset about, but I remember vividly that I was talking on the kitchen phone to someone, a classmate or a boyfriend, and there was an issue. Mom was busy as usual with household tasks and she wasn't one to eavesdrop or interfere. But for some reason she knew as the call went on that my mood was not improving. Suddenly she stood before me with a tiny scrap of paper. On it were two words and a drawing. She handed it to me with a smile and then left the room to get back to her projects.

I looked at the tiny paper in my hand. It read: "Be Nice" and had a smiley face drawing.

I heeded her advice. From that point onward the conversation took a friendlier tone. By its conclusion the tenseness I had felt was eased. All was at peace in my world.

But there is more to the story about the little piece of paper with two words of advice and the hand-drawn smiley face. When I graduated and moved out, that little piece of paper moved with me. I displayed it on my refrigerator, secured in place by a magnet. For many years that piece of paper moved with me and served as a constant reminder. Whenever I had to deal with a difficult person or situation, I could always look at that paper and find a solution to my problems.

Today that paper no longer adorns the refrigerator my husband and I share. Rather, it is tucked safely away in a box of other cherished mementos, which one day will be put into a scrapbook or shadow box.

Whenever I feel stressed or impatient in the presence of a challenging person, I visualize my mom handing me that piece of paper and I act accordingly. Who would have ever guessed the timeless value of two little words and smiley face on a simple little scrap of paper?

~Michelle A. Watkins

Never Too Busy

Kids spell love T-I-M-E.
~John Crudele

My mom's life was a busy one. Raising four kids on her own was a full-time job in itself, but she also worked outside the home. Remarkably, she always seemed to find a little bit of extra time for us despite her schedule.

She would bundle us up and take us over to my aunt's in the evening when she worked as a waitress in a small diner. We would just be finished with school and have to hurry so my mom would be on time for work. I thought when this began that she would pass us over to our aunt and hurry off as soon as we made it through the front gate, but that didn't happen. Instead we would sit on the porch, my mom in her waitress uniform, and we would rock in my aunt's big wooden swing and talk about what happened that day.

"I learned how to add numbers up to the hundreds," my sister Sandy would say.

"That's wonderful," my mom would reply, hugging her tight.

"I learned how to write my name!" Larry, my younger brother, would shout.

My mom would get a piece of paper and a pencil out of her purse and hand it to my brother. "Show me how you do it," she'd ask softly.

"Do you have enough time to hear what I did today?" I'd ask her.

Mom would smile at me and nod. "I'm never too busy for something important like that!"

She'd sit and listen as I described whatever wonderful adventure I'd had at school that day. Then she'd give us all a hug, wish us good night, and hurry off down the street. No matter how much of a hurry she must have been in, she always treated what we had to share with her as if it were the most important thing in the world.

There always seemed to be time for us. If my mom came home after a very long day from her two office jobs, I knew we would open the door to her smiling face. She would take just a few minutes to catch her breath, and then we'd gather in the kitchen and talk to her about everything under the sun while we helped her make dinner. She never seemed too tired to ask us questions and she was really interested in what was important to us, even though I know she must have been exhausted from work.

She gave us the gift of time again and again throughout the years. She would appear at the school play in which I had a part, even though I knew she would have to make up the time at work. She would smile at us when we came down during the summer to the office where she worked and asked if she had time to have lunch with us.

"I can't think of anyone I'd rather have lunch with," she'd say, and then we'd take the sandwiches we'd brought along with us down to the river that flowed through the city, sit on the grass and have a wonderful lunch. I never thought about all the things she could have done for herself, the break from activity she might have enjoyed, because she actually did love to give us any time she could.

Later on in her life, when she came to live with us following her retirement, my mom gave the gift of time to my children too. They would run around excitedly, asking their grandma if she would play with them, or read them a story, or go for a walk with them. By then my mom had health problems but she would always nod and sit down and read to them or tell them stories about when she was a little girl.

Those moments were a tremendous gift that my children still talk about and treasure.

In the last few years of her life, I would take her to lunch or sit with her on the porch, and we would talk, reminisce about the past, dream of the future, and just enjoy being with each other. My mom would listen as I shared all of my hopes, my fears, and my dreams for my family, and she would always hang on every word. I would look at her and ask her if she minded me taking up so much of her free time.

"Nonsense," she'd tell me. Then she'd give me a wink and say, "I'm never too busy to spend time with you. It's one of the greatest joys of my life."

I will always remember those wonderful words, and the loving heart behind them. It is a gift my mom gave to me for which I will forever be grateful. In this oh-so-busy world of ours, and in a life filled with challenges, she always had time to share her joy with me.

~John P. Buentello

Gotcha!

There is a wisdom of the head, and...
a wisdom of the heart.
~Charles Dickens

"Please tell me I'm seeing things," I said to myself as I drove into the driveway. On my front porch was Mother, waving her arms frantically and yelling in my direction. With her were two policemen. She was a sight in her multicolored muumuu with her hair in bulky rollers. The policemen appeared to be consoling her, with amused expressions on their faces.

"Where you been? Whatsa matter, you never heard of telephones?" she shrieked at me in her heavy European accent. I climbed out of my car and wished I could disappear! My new romantic interest was pulling into the driveway behind me.

That afternoon she had called me at work to ask when I was coming home. I had told her I would be there soon. But as I was leaving, the attractive new guy, Larry, asked me to have a drink and a sandwich. "Sure," I replied nonchalantly. I had noticed him before, but it was the first time he had given me a second glance. I was excited and nervous. We went to the bistro next door, had a couple of glasses of wine, a bite to eat and a few laughs. We seemed to hit it off as we chatted. I found him delightful. Minutes turned into hours. You know how it goes. I didn't want the evening to end so I invited him home for coffee. Since we were in separate cars, he followed me in his.

That's when he had the pleasure of meeting my mother on the porch!

"You scared me half to death! I called the hospitals. I called the police!" Her ranting continued! I shuddered as I noticed that Larry was witnessing this fiasco. I questioned my decision to invite him home. It wasn't the first time she had embarrassed me in front of my friends.

"You don't care how worried you make your mother? You said you'd be home hours ago!" she went on.

Mom was a drama queen before drama queens were invented.

It's not as if I were a teenager. I was already in my thirties and previously married. A grown woman living with an overprotective mother was not exactly the image I wanted to portray to my new beau.

Mom had come to stay with me for a few months. She was an old-school Eastern European matriarch who had a heart of gold but who could be tough as nails. Living with her was a challenge. But I reminded myself that the situation was temporary.

I introduced Mother to Larry and she led him into the house. I remained outside briefly, thanking the officers for their courtesy and apologized for inconveniencing them. Satisfied that no one had been hurt, missing or kidnapped, they left. I let myself inside quickly, not wanting to give Mom a chance to scare Larry away. It wouldn't be the first time she had ruined a relationship. She could be downright rude to my friends, calling one a jerk to his face. Another was a bum. She was not one to mince words.

I found the two of them in the kitchen. Larry was sitting at the kitchen table. She had already served him a piece of her "famous" Czech pastry. She stood over him until she heard the word she had been expecting. "Delicious!"

She beamed. "I made it from scratch!"

I sat down silently at the opposite end and observed their relaxed conversation. They huddled together over his napkin, on which she had sketched a map of the "old country." Larry said he had always admired people who spoke more than one language.

Larry took my mom in stride. Without trying, he had won her over.

To my surprise, he kept returning. Months later, Mom moved into her own place. But whenever she heard Larry was coming, she'd bring a special home-cooked meal she knew he'd like, to "put some fat on his bones." As she patted her belly, she would proudly announce to anyone who'd listen, "I gained seven pounds since I met my Larry."

I had resisted and resented her past advice about my love life. Although I didn't agree with her meddling, I admit when it came to men, Mother did know best.

Actually, when I think of it, some of those other men really were "bums" or "jerks."

Mom, if you can hear me, thank you!

Larry and I have been married twenty-eight years. Mom is gone now. But if I close my eyes, I can hear her loud sigh of relief, coming from the front pew, when the preacher pronounced us man and wife. Then she snapped her fingers and brazenly proclaimed, "Gotcha!"

~Eva Carter

65

The Absence of Fear

*I am not afraid of tomorrow, for I have seen yesterday
and I love today.*
~William Allen White

My elbow hit the call button. Again. Oops. It was the second time I'd accidentally summoned the nurse to my mother's room. Her hospital bed was not designed for two people, but I snuggled my thirty-three-year-old self beside her anyway. We lay in her bed and giggled like schoolgirls waiting to be admonished.

Soon the door swung open and Trevor, the night nurse, filled the doorway. His thick tattooed arm held open the door and he peered at me from behind his black-framed glasses.

"Yes?" he asked, with arched eyebrows.

"Sorry." I winced. It wasn't my first apology for the evening.

He crossed his arms dramatically and leaned against the door. A smile tugged at his lips. We'd built a strong rapport over the past four months and he was one of my favorite nurses.

"You do know the story about the little boy who cried wolf, right?" he asked.

"Really, I am very sorry. I'll be more careful."

"Mm-hmm," he replied, clearly unconvinced. He gave me a wink before his eyes traveled to my mother.

"Do you need anything, Mrs. Stiving?" he asked.

"No, Trevor. I'm fine." She smiled. "How are your exams going?"

Trevor worked nights so he could attend classes during the day. He groaned at the question and closed his eyes.

"Torture, pure torture."

It was an odd word choice considering our situation. Tubes and wires snaked out of my mother's arms while dark ugly bruises covered her veins. The skin around the port in her chest was red and swollen. This was where the chemo was administered—the poison designed to kill the cancer that was trying to kill her.

"I know you will do great," she said with a smile. "Your skills and talents are a blessing to those you care for."

Trevor's face softened and his arms dropped to his side. I lay there quietly while my mother's words reached his heart.

"Thank you," he said in a voice much smaller than before.

I was accustomed to my mother having this effect on people. Though her situation was dire she found joy in those around her and believed in the power of encouraging words. While my family and I were guilty of seeing her caregivers as service providers, she saw them as people with their own hopes, dreams and disappointments. She knew the name of the cleaning lady that mopped the floors at night and asked her often about the grandchildren she was raising. She listened intently to the morning nurse Angie who was struggling with a troubled teen. She held the young orderly with the broken heart in her arms. Her compassion brought relief to the weary soldiers of medicine, and like a beacon of light, they were drawn to her.

Trevor recovered and cleared his throat.

"You call me if you need anything," he said to her, then turned to me with mock annoyance. "That doesn't mean you."

"It won't happen again." I made an apologetic face. "Cross my heart…" I used two fingers to draw an invisible X across my heart but stopped before completing the rest of the phrase. *And hope to die.*

The silence fell heavy and I wondered if my mother finished the thought. We had been told the chemotherapy was not working. Her body had rejected it violently, resulting in fluid around her heart that required emergency surgery. Afterwards, the doctor gently told us that she had ATRA syndrome, meaning she was severely allergic to the only treatment that could save her. He said the decision to try it again would be up to her but he warned us that if the cancer didn't kill her, the ATRA might.

Trevor closed the door, leaving us alone. We lay there quietly listening to the rhythmic beeps of the machines beside her.

"Mom," I finally whispered. "Are you afraid…" I paused, unable to complete the question. The words I left unspoken lurked like shadows in the room but she saw them.

"To die?" she asked.

I nodded, our heads closely touching on her pillow. We stared at the ceiling while I waited for her reply.

"Well," she sighed, "I figure if I know how to live then I know how to die."

It took a moment to absorb the words. I had never thought about knowing how to do either. She squeezed my hand and continued.

"So no, I am not afraid. And I don't want you to be either."

And for the first time, I wasn't. Her steadiness strengthened me. Perhaps it was the absence of fear that gave her peace. With peace there is no room for despair. I reached to wipe away the renegade tear that slipped down my cheek and my elbow hit the call button. Again.

Oops.

~Brenda Watterson

66

Mom's Old, Useless Bible

Real treasure lies not in what can be seen,
but what cannot be seen.
~Author Unknown

To tell the truth, I don't remember seeing Mom actually read her old Bible. As far as I could tell, it just sat on the nightstand next to her bed.

And that was the best place for it, since it probably wouldn't have survived any meaningful use anywhere else. The black cloth cover was ragged and time-worn, its dog-eared pages yellowed. Once I accidentally knocked it off the nightstand, launching loose pages all over Mom and Dad's bedroom. I expected a tongue-lashing for my carelessness, but Mom was so busy gathering the pages, gently smoothing them and returning them to their place in the book that she paid no attention to me.

Soon after I moved away from home, my sister Kathy and I combined our funds to buy a new Bible for Mom for her birthday. It was a black leather volume, twice as big as her old Bible. The pages were trimmed in gold, and there were maps, references and a complete Bible dictionary included within its pages. We even had her name engraved on the front with gold-leaf lettering.

It was a beautiful book, and Mom was touched and pleased. I remember watching her thumb carefully through the pages, admiring the quality of the paper and the clarity of the printing. From that day on, that was the Bible she took with her to church, and the one from which she read during the family Nativity pageant. But for some reason, it never displaced the old Bible from its position of honor on her nightstand.

And that kind of bothered me.

"I don't know why you keep that ratty old thing," I told her as we prepared to pack it among her most precious belongings for what would turn out to be the last of many relocations in her life—this time to the warm, heavy air of Southern California. "That new Bible we got for you is the best that money can buy. You can't even use this old one anymore."

Mom smiled at me weakly and sat on the edge of her bed, carefully wrapping the old Bible in an equally old, equally shabby white shawl.

"Just because a thing isn't useful anymore, that doesn't mean it isn't valuable," she said softly and deliberately. "You look at this and see an old, worn-out book. But I see the gift your father gave me on our wedding day. I see the friend that was always there to provide strength and comfort when your father was sent to Pearl Harbor during the war. I see the storybook from which I read to all of my children, and the primer from which you all read your first Bible verses.

"This Bible has been in the family as long as we've been a family," she continued, caressing it through the tattered shawl. "It's part of us, part of our history, part of who we are. So even though it isn't especially useful anymore, there is still value in what it represents. At least, there is to me."

Suddenly it occurred to me that she wasn't just talking about her old Bible. We live in an age of fanatically obsessive utilitarianism. Everything is disposable—even people. If it's old or odd-looking or not particularly useful, we toss it—or him, or her—out. We forget that there is value beyond utility, and worth beyond "what's in it for me right now."

When Mom died, Dad gave me her "new" Bible. It's among my most cherished possessions. It's the Bible I read and take to church. It means a lot to me, and it really is beautiful and incredibly useful. But I'd trade it in a minute for Mom's old, useless Bible.

I even have the perfect place for it: on the nightstand next to my bed.

~Joseph B. Walker

On Solid Ground

Reality is merely an illusion, albeit a very persistent one.
~Albert Einstein

I scrunched my face at Mom. How could she not think this was the best idea ever? I wanted to marry Kermit the Frog more than anything in the whole wide world!

As a child I dreamed big and believed in the impossible, even when nobody else did. I made plans to adopt a baby elephant as a pet. Mom shook her head.

"But Mo-om!" I'd moaned.

As always, she gave me the look. "Be realistic," she said.

Soon after this, I decided to sell my little brother to raise money for a new bicycle. Mom's stare spoke volumes as she droned her mantra.

One summer I started digging a hole for a swimming pool in our yard. "Put that shovel down this instant!" she shouted through an open window. "Be realistic!"

And so things went until, at the age of ten, I was diagnosed with diabetes. My perception of myself and the world around me changed. Life wasn't all Muppets and childish schemes. But after a while, my tendency for embracing grandiose dreams did come back to life.

By sixteen, I'd matured just enough to reach for more attainable goals. I wanted to learn how to drive and get my license. My health situation made Mom nervous, but by then I'd learned to find ways around her. Dad was the perfect ally, although when I asked him to help me buy my first car, the clunker he found in a used car lot wasn't the dream vehicle I'd imagined. It only lasted long enough to get me back and forth to work that summer.

The spring before I graduated high school, I lost the battle to go to university in another country, as far away from Mom as possible. I wanted to prove my independence.

Even Dad wouldn't stand by me on this one. "Too expensive," he'd said, which I understood but didn't want to accept.

Of course Mom had chimed in with her mantra, again. If only I had a nickel for all the times she said it. I hated her for stating the obvious.

As I neared the completion of my bachelor's degree, I considered the idea of teaching abroad, and made what at the time felt like the mistake of talking about it with Mom. Before the words came out of her mouth, I heard the drone of her mantra in my head. Of course, then she said it.

I had the rest of my life mapped out. I'd get a full-time job as a teacher, get married and have children—a boy and a girl. And maybe a dog. But with failing kidneys and a new husband unwilling to deal with my health issues, it looked as though my plan was falling apart, one detail at a time. Of course, I talked about it all with Mom.

My marriage ended quickly, as did my teaching career, due to my medical issues. Instead, I had to move to another city for a chance to receive a kidney-pancreas transplant. Mom declared that she was going with me.

My first thought was, "Oh, God. No!" But I did want her help. I certainly didn't want to go through scary, unknown territory alone. I just didn't want to admit it to her out loud.

As we sat in our little apartment one day, the discussion turned to the last dream I held onto—having children. Mom touched my arm, her voice oddly quiet. "You know, Susan. You're going to have to be… " She hesitated and gave me that look.

Together we chimed, "Realistic!"

I tried hard to make a face at her, but laughed instead. She had a point, but there was no way I was going to tell her that.

I'd be sugarcoating it to say our time together was without conflict, but we did make it work. We even shared lovely moments and a great deal of laughter, especially after I received a gift from a friend during my stay in hospital when I first went on dialysis—a golden-haired puppet with blue eyes and a twinkle of attitude. A mini me! I gave her my middle name, Elizabeth.

Mom didn't like my Elizabeth puppet right from the start, which of course made it all the more tantalizing for me to bring her to life. And that I did. I gave her a medic alert bracelet and attached a dialysis catheter to her stomach. I bought us matching jean jumpers, shirts and sneakers, in part to have fun with Mom, but also because the teacher in me wasn't ready to quit. Elizabeth and I became a traveling team of entertainers. Together we gave presentations on diabetes, dialysis and transplants to a variety of audiences.

But the most entertaining audience of all was Mom. She would actually engage in serious, sometimes heated "discussions," not with me, but with Elizabeth—the puppet! It was hilarious to watch Mom become infuriated, stare into Elizabeth's eyes and oh-so-seriously tell the puppet to "Be realistic!" The irony of it all brought me immeasurable delight. No doubt the memory of it always will.

It might have taken me decades, but I finally figured out that resistance to Mom's mantra was futile. It's difficult to admit, but Mom really did have a point.

Because of her tenacity, encouragement and love, these days my reality shines bright. I've discovered a heartfelt passion for writing. I am married to the love of my life—an incredible, funny and considerate man named Henry who has stood by me and supports me in all I do. Mom loves him too, and because I do not have my own offspring, I am free to love all children, which I do. Henry and I even have two dogs.

And thanks to Mom—and the years spent trying to prove her mantra to "be realistic" wrong—my feet are planted securely on solid ground with my head still well within reach of the stars.

~Susan Blakeney

68

I'll Be Right There

There is no instinct like that of the heart.
~Lord Byron

It was nearing midnight. The late-night news was over and it was certainly far too late for a social call. I picked up the phone anyway, my hand shaking uncontrollably as I dialed the number I knew by heart.

"Mom, I need you," I said when she answered. No hesitation, no excuses. Concern echoing in her voice, she simply stated, "I'll be right there."

There was so much blood... every expectant mother's worst fear. When she arrived, she simply took over. That was exactly what I needed her to do. She packed me up and sent me to the hospital with my husband. "I love you," she said as I was leaving. "It's going to be okay. The baby is going to be okay."

She got this same call at several points during each one of my three complicated pregnancies. Her response was always the same: "I'll be right there." Emergency room visits, specialists, bed rest... this woman who had held my hand, worried and prayed for a miracle was there to welcome each of her three grandchildren into this world.

With a brother years older and a sister who never depended on anyone, I have always been the one who called my mom. What do you think, help me decide, just want to say hi—that was me. As we grew up, I could tell my mom never minded someone still needing her.

In college, I was in a relationship that had wrecked havoc with my heart. Nearly falling apart, I called to hear her comforting voice. "I miss home," I said. A few hours later I had a plane ticket in my hands as I boarded a last-minute flight. The entire weekend we never even talked about "the boy." I just relaxed, ate homemade meals and was mothered. Somehow by the end of that weekend everything made sense again.

A few years later I met a wonderful man. Shortly before I got married I called my mom in a frenzy. The dress. After seeing an unflattering picture, I was certain I had not picked the right one. I'll admit this was not one of my finer moments, certainly making me look a bit like a bridezilla. "I'll be right there," she said. My mom got in her car, drove across the state, and brought the wedding dress to me. When I tried it on this time, it was evident that this lovely, white concoction was perfect. "See," she said, glowing, "it's the one and you are beautiful!" Somehow she knew the exact right thing to do.

Three years ago, I woke up one morning and half my face was paralyzed. Panicked and confused, I picked up the phone again: "Mom, I need you." "I'll be right there," she said. I cannot imagine how helpless she must have felt in this situation as she walked in on a daughter who no longer looked like her own. She had no cure to offer to make this one better, just herself. She was there for months, cooking up a storm, doing dishes, taking care of children, and filling in for me while I rested and focused on getting better. My husband nicknamed her the "cleaning fairy" and asked if she might be willing to stay forever.

For each important event in my life, my mom was simply there. Sometimes because I asked her to be, other times because she knew I needed her.

As I look down at my own sleeping little one, my heart is so full of love it takes my breath away. I would move mountains for this child. I will be there for her, I will tell her I love her, sing her endless lullabies, and read her countless stories. I will pick her up and kiss her boo-boos. As she grows, I will braid her hair, watch her school events, and be her biggest fan. If a boy ever breaks her heart I will tell her I never really liked him anyway. I will listen and not say a word when she needs to talk and complain.

There may be times that I question how to be the mother she needs, but I am confident I have learned from the very best there is. In those moments I will think about what my mom would have done. One day I may even get a call from her telling me she needs me, and I already know what my answer will be: "I'll be right there."

~Katie Bangert

69

The Memory Box

Leftovers in their less visible form are called memories.
Stored in the refrigerator of the mind
and the cupboard of the heart.
~Thomas Fuller

We were planning a celebration for my mother's ninety-fourth birthday. After getting my ticket to fly from Arizona to Michigan, the next task was to figure out a present. Since my father's passing, my mother had been making a concentrated effort to downsize. She loved her Hummel and teacup collection, but she had made it clear—no new ones! Jewelry was out. A gift certificate, maybe. But that didn't seem quite right. I couldn't think of anything appropriate to celebrate ninety-four years!

A few days before my departure, as I sorted through clothes for travel, I found a silver dollar my mother had given me when I got my first car. My mother always gave us silver dollars to place in our car's glove box for good luck. I smiled as I held the silver dollar, remembering the joy of my first car, a Volkswagen Beetle. How perfect that I had the coin to remind me of those good times.

Then it struck me—perhaps what we could give Mom was not a thing, but a feeling. A gift that would say she mattered, that she made a loving impression in our lives. We could each relate a treasured memory about her, and then place a dollar coin in a box to represent that memory.

I floated the idea by one of my sisters, and she loved it. She volunteered to go to the bank and get twenty one-dollar coins. By the time I arrived in Michigan, she had selected a small teakwood box that had belonged to my mother—a perfect choice to hold the memory coins.

The night before the party, I sat on my sister's porch with my daughter, who also flew in for the celebration, trying to decide which memories to share. My mother, a first-generation Greek immigrant, had passed on food traditions that we all continue today. Every Christmas, the Greek pasta dish, *pastitsio*, is a central part of the evening celebration meal. And there isn't a dinner guest who comes to my home who isn't served Kalamata olives and feta cheese as an appetizer. On special occasions, guests are treated to a Greek tradition that we like to call the "Opa cheese." It is a dish, actually called *saganaki*, where cheese is melted in a pan, then covered in brandy and set aflame. The flames are celebrated with rousing cheers of "Opa," then doused with a squeeze of lemon juice.

"It's the *koulourakias* that are my favorite memory," my daughter said.

"Oh yes," I said, remembering back to the times when my children and I would spend hours with my mother, carefully forming the traditional Easter Greek cookies into circles or small braids. My children loved to pry open the small cans and add the sesame seeds and anise, bringing to life the unique Greek flavors in the shortbread dessert.

My mother's recipe had been passed on to her by her mother, and included such vague directions as "combine five handfuls of flour with enough liquid to make the mixture pliable." After I moved to Colorado, it took my mother and me a bit of trial and error to adapt my grandmother's recipe to high altitudes.

Our early attempts looked like extremely fat fingers, still tasting good, but missing the delicate form of the true *koulourakias*. Eventually we got the modifications right, and the making of *koulouakias* became a tradition during her visits.

My daughter and I were still digging out old memories even as we drove to pick up my mother for the drive to the restaurant. As other members of the family came, some took me aside asking how this memory thing was going to work.

"We'll figure it out as we go along," I told them, sounding more confident than I felt. In fact, I wasn't sure how it would go or even how she would react to this idea. My mother has always had a hard time accepting kind words. I was still unsure of what memory to share and worried all of us might end up repeating the same stories. Above all, I hoped we could all get into the spirit of it to make the celebration special.

Family members began to gather at the table. A corsage was pinned to my mother's new dress and she seemed pleased with it. Once the food was ordered, I nodded to my sister as a sign that it was time to quietly pass out the coins, hopefully without our mom catching on. I presented the teakwood box to my mother and told her this was going to be her birthday gift. I opened it and showed her it was empty.

"An empty box?" she questioned, looking around at the family to see if this was a joke.

"Empty now, Mom, but each of us is going to tell a story, a memory that we've carried with us, from our lives growing up. And with each memory, there will be a coin added to the box," I carefully explained.

My sister Mary Ann started, telling how she found a dress she really wanted when we were vacationing in our favorite spot, Myrtle Beach. "That dress made me feel so special, but I knew it was expensive."

My sister continued, adding that when my mom brought my father back to see the dress, Mary Ann knew my mom had already talked my dad into buying it. She placed her coin in the box, thanking Mom.

After the first story, the ball started rolling. By the third memory, everybody was in full swing, laughing about trips to the World's Fair in New York, camping trips to the lake, and our first attempts to make special Greek dishes. Once the twenty coins we brought had been added to the box, family members were searching purse bottoms for additional coins to add. It was amazing to hear what memories had stayed with us and what was special for each person. One good memory led to another.

The evening ended with laughter and silly photos. There were lots of hugs. On the drive back, my mother added a few of her own memories, telling my daughter and me stories we had never heard before.

"What a great life," my daughter reflected.

"Yes, such a good life," my mother quietly expressed.

Catching her tone of voice, I wasn't sure if she was speaking to us, or perhaps to the spirit of my father who was so present in many of our stories. We all sat in silence for the remainder of the drive home, not wanting the moment to end.

My daughter's time with us was short, her departure scheduled for the next day. On the way to the airport, we stopped at the independent living facility where my mother lives so they could have a few more minutes together. I tried hard to hold back my tears, knowing this could be their last visit.

Taking my daughter's hand, my mother said, "At ninety-four, my time is short." She pressed one of the coins from the memory box into my daughter's palm. No words were necessary; we knew her intention. Remember that I mattered in your life.

The rest of my visit seemed to fly by. On the afternoon of my departure, I brought my mother a few items she had asked me to pick up for her. Entering the apartment, I noticed her sitting in my dad's old chair, close to the window, looking out at the woods. In her lap sat the memory box.

"You know," she started, still not looking at me, "I have been thinking about all the wonderful memories we shared at dinner the other night. This box, these memory coins are very special."

"They were wonderful memories, weren't they?" I added, agreeing with her.

Looking down at her box, it was a few moments before she spoke again.

Then she quietly said, "I've decided what I am going to do with the coins."

Expecting her to say a trip to Macy's or a luncheon out, I was surprised at what followed.

"I'm going to give them away," she said, rocking the memory box in her lap.

At first I wanted to protest, confused by why she would choose to give away those coins that represented our memories, our lives together. Then she explained further.

"There are many people here who help me when you girls and my grandchildren can't be here. These coins carry such special feelings, and I'm going to give them to people here who go out of their way to make my life better. I want to pass them on and keep those positive feelings moving forward."

There was quiet between us for a few moments. I was stunned at first by her plan.

"What do you think?" she asked, looking at me.

I closed my eyes, felt the tears form and love deepen in my heart. Then, I rose and hugged my mother. "Perfect," I told her. "Just perfect."

~Diana Creel Elarde

A Heart Like Hers

Alas! there is no instinct like the heart...
~Lord Byron

"Mom, how much salt should I put in this cookie dough?" I shook my flour-dusted hands, and a plume of white shot into the air. Baking wasn't one of my innate gifts, but I had volunteered to help my mom make some treats for a church event. On the other side of the kitchen, she frosted a pan of brownies in a few expert swipes.

"Oh, a couple of shakes." Dishes clattered into the sink.

"Is that an official measurement? Is there a "shake sized" scoop in the baking drawer?" A smile betrayed my sarcasm.

"Oh Logan, I've been your mom for twenty-two years; you should know better than to ask for exact measurements."

My mom was notorious for her inexact measurements. She was an amazing cook, but nothing she made turned out exactly the same way twice. Her units of measurement were scoops, splashes, shakes, and handfuls. When my mom did laundry, she didn't use the cap to see how much detergent to use, she poured it straight in. When she painted a room, she didn't figure square inches and feet, she just guessed and scraped the very bottom of the bucket when we ran low.

That's not how my mind worked. I needed to know precisely the amount of supplies required to get the job done. Which meant I needed to know exactly how much salt was in three "shakes."

"So like a half-teaspoon maybe?" I asked. Mom chuckled.

"I don't even know if I have a half-teaspoon measuring scoop anymore. Just give it three strong shakes. Good enough."

I held the flip-spout Morton container over the bowl of dough. It went against my deepest convictions to follow my mom's ambiguous instructions, but I grimaced and gave in. One. Two. Three.

"See, told you it would be okay," Mom told me.

"I still don't see how you married an engineer," I said. "This must drive Dad crazy."

"Oh, it did." She wiped my stray flour off the counter with a wet cloth. "But he's gotten used to it."

I finished mixing the dough and scooped it onto an empty baking sheet.

"Thanks for helping in the kitchen, Logan," Mom said. "I have so much to do. I don't know how your dad and I are going to be ready for our trip to Jamaica on time."

My parents were preparing to celebrate their twenty-fifth anniversary in Jamaica. They had talked about taking this trip for years. My brothers would spend the first day with me, then the rest of the week with my grandparents while I worked my summer job.

"Don't worry, we'll get everything done on time," I said. "Is there room for me to slide these cookies into the oven?"

My mom nodded and lowered the oven door.

A few days later, my dad hefted suitcases into the minivan as he and Mom scrambled to make their flight. Three barefoot boys shuffled around on the warm pavement as they said goodbye.

"Grandma and Grandpa aren't expecting the kids until tomorrow morning," Dad told me. "But I know you'll be fine watching the kids until then."

"Of course. I'll keep them busy," I said.

"Dinner for tonight is in the Crock-Pot," Mom said. "I went grocery shopping yesterday so you would have food in the house, and there's a list of meals with instructions on the fridge. I love you." She gave me a tight hug.

"Thanks so much. You guys have a good time," I said. The boys and I waved goodbye as the car pulled out of the drive and took off down the hill.

"Okay kids, what should we do?" I asked. Five-year-old Isaiah grinned.

"Trampoline?" he questioned.

I underestimated the amount of work it would take to watch three boys for a day.

First, Gabe skinned a knee on the trampoline. I found a box of superhero Band-Aids in the medicine cabinet, patched up the battle scar, and we moved into the family room to play board games.

Then, Isaiah accidentally dropped the *Monopoly* box when he pulled it out of the cupboard, which meant a mushroom-cloud of pastel money needed to be sorted and put back into the box.

I washed sticky peanut-butter hands, helped build a pillow fort, and played catch in the yard. By bedtime, I was more than exhausted. I tucked the boys in bed, then slipped into my own.

The next morning, I poured Cheerios for the boys and helped them pack. We loaded their overnight bags into my tiny orange car and I strapped the kids in back.

When we arrived at my grandparents' house, I rapped on their door. My grandma answered it, gently smiling.

"Hi boys, it's so good to see you." She leaned in and gave me a peck on the cheek. "Why don't you guys come on in?"

When we shuffled into the living room, my grandpa gave us big bear hugs. We visited with each other for the rest of the morning, and I stayed until after lunch. When it was time to leave, I ran through my list of instructions for the kids.

"Isaiah's blanket is in his bag. He won't be able to sleep without it. You'll probably need to remind Sam to take his allergy medication. He usually forgets. I made sure all of them took baths this morning, so you won't have to worry about that at bedtime. And if you have any questions, feel free to call me."

I said goodbye, walked out to my car, and began backing out of the driveway. Then I saw my grandma running down the front walkway. I rolled down my window.

"Before you leave, I just wanted to tell you how amazing you are with the boys. They think the world of you, and I can tell how much you love them. I've never seen a young man take care of his brothers the way you do."

I smiled. "Thanks Grandma, that means a lot to me." I gave her a hug through the window.

There was a lot to clean up when I got home. The sink was full of dirty dishes. The table was messy with crumbs. Dirty laundry was in a pile in the bathroom. I grabbed an armload of towels, dumped them into the washing machine, then poured some Tide on top. As soon as the drizzle of blue detergent hit the mess of laundry, I realized what I had done. In the rush of cleaning up after a busy day taking care of the kids, I had gauged the right amount with my heart instead of measuring with the cap.

Just like my mom.

I had unknowingly inherited her habit of imprecise measurement, even after I swore a hundred times I never would. I jerked the bottle up and cringed. Then I thought about my grandma's words, and realized I had inherited something else from my mom as well. Her loving servant's heart. That's really what my grandma had seen, a reflection of my mom. My mom who selflessly took care of others. Who constantly applied Band-Aids and wiped down messy tables and conquered mountains of dirty laundry.

Nothing could make me prouder than to have a heart that showed even a glint of my mom's.

Precise measurements or not.

So I shrugged and poured another splash of detergent into the machine.

~Logan Eliasen

*Thanks
to My
Mom*

Mom Was Right

A 100 Percent Chance of Mom

To describe my mother would be to
write about a hurricane in its perfect power.
~Maya Angelou

The clouds were already gathering that morning, hanging low and moody in the South Texas sky. As we sat around the breakfast table before school, we listened to the San Antonio weather forecaster. He was predicting sleet overnight—a rare thing in our part of the state, even for January.

A possibility of sleet or a bona fide ice storm was exciting, I had to admit. But even more so was the fact that the first game of our junior high girls' basketball tournament was set to begin that evening in a town about fifty miles from ours.

The tournament was a big deal. We were dominating this season, and if we could win this first game against our toughest competitor, we'd likely win the whole tournament. We'd solidify our rank as the best in the region. There was even a pep rally planned for us that afternoon. (A pep rally for any type of girls' sport in Texas in the 1980s was a reason to check to make sure you hadn't been abducted by aliens and relocated to an alternate universe.)

Basketball, though, hadn't always been important to me. In fact, this was only the first year I'd played.

Let's just say I wasn't known for my athleticism. I was not lean and mean. I fell more into the chubby and uncoordinated camp. I was a full-on straight-A, teacher's pet nerd. Spelling bee champ, science competition winner. Trying out for the basketball team had been my way of trying to break out of that mold. I wanted to fit in with the cool kids for once. I wanted to wear those sweet uniforms and high-top sneakers.

And it was working. I not only made the team, I was a starter on defense. (Turns out, you really only need height and brains to play some positions in life.) The cheerleaders even knew my nickname: "Special K."

I was living the dream, as much as you can when you're thirteen.

And then came that game day.

The predicted cold front slipped through the county, dropping temperatures into the mid-30s by noon. It was raining buckets when I reported to the gym after school to meet up with the rest of the team. As we waited for the school bus that would take us to the game, we huddled together, giggling like cool, athletic girls do, excited about the game, jumping up and down to stay warm in our official team sweatshirts.

That's when I saw her. She was marching toward us, small red umbrella overhead. Dark, thick hair to her shoulders. Sunglasses on, even in the gray. Her camel-colored long coat pulled tightly around her curves and whipping around her knees. Her car keys still in one hand. Her lips pressed into a painted-on don't-mess-with-me smile. She looked like a force even a fifty-mile-per-hour northern wind couldn't reckon with.

My stomach dropped. I knew that look well. She was determined to do battle of some kind, and I understood by then it had everything to do with me.

She walked up to our coach, who was looking down, checking things off on a clipboard. Poor innocent soul.

My mother began to explain, politely at first, that under no condition would her daughter—the one trying desperately to shrink into the shadows—go anywhere on a rundown, hick-town, bald-tired, rattrap of a school bus when the backcountry roads we'd be traveling would most certainly be a sheet of ice within an hour or two.

We heard the coach attempt to reassure her that all would be well. That the school district and the tournament managers agreed there was no reason to cancel the game. That she was, perhaps, overreacting.

She took that coach down with just a few quick choice words. Then she walked over and pointed me in the direction of her faded maroon Lincoln Town Car, parked right where the aforementioned bus would soon be.

The unfairness of it all was incomprehensible to me. Everyone else was getting to go!

As we drove away, I saw my teammates nudging each other. I was sure they now considered me an overprotected baby, not cut out for the tough life of an athlete. With a mother who was quite possibly a hair shy of crazy.

That evening, I ate Mom's warm grilled cheese sandwiches and beef stew in silence. And then I watched the sleet begin to come down. I watched the county road in front of our house turn into a skating rink. Conditions got treacherous in a hurry.

Luckily, my team made it home safely, although it had taken three hours to go those fifty miles home after the game. We'd won, and we would end up advancing and winning the tournament. I played in the rest of the tournament, but not as a starter. The coach made me run additional laps in practice on Monday for letting down my team, as if I'd had a choice in the matter. My teammates made fun of me for the rest of the season.

Back then, I'd wished she could just be like all the other moms who didn't seem to mind that their kids were heading out onto slick roads. I'd wished that she hadn't made a scene. But now, I'm a mama myself.

Now I see I was the lucky one.

Some parents might have simply taken the school district's word for it and bowed down to authorities who were perceived to know more than the parents. But my mother has never been one to let others make decisions for her or to automatically assume people in positions of power can't be challenged. She'd done her own research that day. She knew she was right, and nothing was going to stand in her way when it came to keeping me safe.

That day and so many times since, she has taught me that sometimes it takes courage to be a parent in ways no one tells you about. That it's not okay for someone else to put my son in danger, and that I have every right to step in and protect him. It's something one particular school administrator has already learned about me after seeing no reason to keep the back door to the afterschool care classroom locked in the evenings before parent pickup.

Even though I'm at the age she was when I was in junior high, I remain so thankful that I still have my mom on my side. Because I know, even though she's in her early seventies now, she'll fight for me, always willing to hand out another dose of her take-charge-now, ask-for-forgiveness-later attitude if I need it.

And besides, I'm pretty sure there may still be some icy roads in my forecast.

~Kathy Lynn Harris

Reclaiming My Sparkle

You yourself, as much as anyone in the entire universe,
deserve your love and affection.
~Buddha

Eighth grade is the year your mom might curl your hair for a school dance, take you shopping for cool clothes, or help you navigate the awkward changes of puberty. It's not the year you expect your mom to save your life. But that's what happened to me.

At the start of seventh grade track season, I weighed 110 pounds. My coach called me "beefy" and my brother made mooing sounds whenever I walked by his room. So I began counting every calorie that entered my mouth. By the start of eighth grade, I'd dropped thirty pounds.

Only I still felt fat.

One evening after dinner, Mom followed me outside. "I'm worried about you," she said softly.

I sighed and rolled my eyes as we took a seat on the wooden swing.

"You don't really eat anymore," Mom said. "You just slide food around your plate."

I looked down at the ground, my eyes fixated on dozens of tiny black ants zipping around.

"They're so lucky," I thought. "They don't have anybody telling them their thighs are chubby."

"Christy, have you heard of anorexia nervosa?"

"What? You think I have it?"

"Your clothes hang on you. You sleep all the time. Your hair is thinning."

Mom scooted closer and gently laid her hand on mine. "I love you," she said. "I'm going to do what's best for you, even if you don't like it."

"What's that supposed to mean?" I asked defensively.

"How do you feel?" Mom asked.

This sounded like a trick question. Was she expecting me to admit to feeling weak, agitated, freezing, and irritable? That my stomach was raw from constant hunger?

"I feel fine," I said flatly, pulling my hand from Mom's grasp.

"You've always had a sparkle about you... " Mom's voice trailed off. "That sparkle's gone."

The following morning, our family doctor suggested that I go to an in-treatment hospital sixty miles away. My length of stay could be weeks or months, depending on my progress. I felt angry, blindsided, and ambushed.

That evening, I laid into Mom at the dinner table.

"Why do you have to send me away?"

"We're just trying to get you healthy," Mom said.

She set down a glass of milk in front of me. I pushed it away. She scooped a heaping mound of noodles onto my plate.

"That's enough!" I shrieked. I felt like my mom was trying to fatten me up before sending me away to further fatten me up. As I stared at the steaming spaghetti sauce, my blood boiled.

"I don't want to be fat!" I yelled.

"You're not fat," Mom said. "You never were."

"Just eat something," Dad said, offering me a slice of garlic toast.

"Eat! Eat! Eat! That's all you ever say anymore!" I cried.

I covered my ears and zoned in on the negative self-talk that played like a looping tape in my mind.

"At least drink your milk," Mom said.

"Gross, no!"

"Please!" Mom pleaded. "Do this for me."

Pre-anorexia, there was nothing I wouldn't do for my mom. Certainly drinking something simply because she asked me to would have been a no-brainer. But now, my paranoid mind couldn't stand the thought of ingesting even one calorie, let alone 110.

"Get that away from me!" I said, standing up and backing away from the glass as if I were staring at a tube of poison.

Mom continued to patiently hold the drink out in front of her.

My senses were on overload. Every hair on my body stood on end. I imagine that's how it might feel to be robbed at gunpoint. Only this wasn't a bad guy; it was my mom. And she wasn't threatening me with a weapon; she was offering me dairy.

Mom shifted her body weight slightly, and it set something off inside me. Like a cornered jungle cat, I swatted at the drink, sending it crashing to the floor. Milk exploded all over the area rug. Mom gasped and jumped backwards. I darted down the hallway to my bedroom, where I slammed the door shut and started sobbing.

Mom cried too, for different reasons.

The next morning, I went to the hospital wearing my thickest sweatshirt and clunkiest pair of hiking boots. Bangle bracelets and beaded necklaces hung on me to add weight to my frame. Despite looking like a blinged-out rodeo clown, I felt confident I could outsmart the doctors. If Mom and Dad saw that I'd put on pounds, they might reconsider admitting me.

My plan was foiled, however, when the nurse explained hospital protocol for weigh-ins. She instructed me to remove my jewelry, shoes, even my hair barrette. I also had to take off my clothes and put on one of those hideous striped polyester gowns that tie in back. But that wasn't the worst part.

"Turn and face the other way before you step onto the scale," she said. "We don't let our patients see their weight."

Though the number was at my back, it read seventy-seven pounds.

"Say goodbye to your folks," the nurse said.

Panic washed over me. I lost my breath the way you do at the crest of a steep roller coaster. I was twelve years old. I didn't want to be left alone in this strange place that reeked of bleach. I didn't want to wear this frayed pink polyester gown. And I certainly didn't want to spend my every waking moment being lectured about how I needed to gain weight.

Mom laid her soft hands on my sunken cheeks.

"I adore you," she said as she wrapped her arms around my skeletal frame.

I was angry, but mostly I was scared. I clung to Mom; I didn't want to let go.

While at the hospital, I befriended a sixteen-year-old patient named Beth. She'd been in and out of the hospital seven times in the past four years.

"I see your mom in here almost every day," Beth said. "My mom stopped visiting after the third time she admitted me. I'm a huge embarrassment to her."

"Because you're sick?" I asked.

Beth nodded.

"That's awful," I said. "I'm so sorry."

"So, it's not like that with your mom?"

"No," I said. "Not at all." Although I'd had my fair share of arguments with my parents in recent months over my food issues and weight loss, their love never wavered.

The next time Mom came to the hospital, I shared Beth's story.

"Would you keep visiting me — even after the seventh time?"

"I'd be here even if you were hospitalized seventy times," Mom said.

"I'm sorry I let you down, Mom," I said quietly.

"You've never let me down," Mom said. "It takes tremendous strength to battle this illness, and you're doing it all on your own."

I shook my head and grabbed her hand. That's where she was wrong. I was not alone.

At that moment, something inside me clicked, and for the first time I wanted help. I wanted to get healthy. I wanted to reclaim my sparkle. And thanks to my mom's fierce, unfailing love, I did.

~Christy Heitger-Ewing

73

Stand Tall and Proud

That which seems the height of absurdity in one generation often becomes the height of wisdom in another.
~Adlai Stevenson

Mother encouraged me to stand straight and use good posture. She found a way to do it without nagging or embarrassing me. I was thirteen and as tall as she was—five feet, seven inches. A head taller than my girlfriends. A head and half taller than the boys. I didn't want to be tall. I didn't want to be different.

Mom often placed her hand on the small of my back and ran it up my spine. "Stand tall and proud," she'd whisper.

Dad's large, rough hands rubbed my shoulders. "No slumping. You're beautiful—just like your mother," he'd say.

I didn't feel proud or beautiful. Just tall.

One hot June day the mailman delivered a package. I'd dog-eared several catalogue pages marking clothes I wanted for my birthday. But it was a month until I'd be fourteen. Mom was pulling weeds from her flowerbed and told me to put the package on the kitchen table.

That night she carried the package into my room while I lay in bed reading. "Susan," she said, "this is for you. It's something you'll probably never wear. But you'll have it if you need it."

Why would she have ordered something that I wouldn't wear? I eagerly opened the thick brown paper envelope. It was something stiff. Made from ugly white material—like the drop cloth we'd used when painting my bedroom. This thing had hooks and laces.

"What's this?" I asked.

"A back brace," Mom answered. "I know it's hard to stand up straight. I remember when I was in high school. I was taller than everyone."

"A back brace? For what?"

"It's to help you have good posture. You don't need this brace now. We'll just put it in your closet and if you ever think it's too hard to hold your shoulders up and stand straight, you can wear it."

Mom put the hideous brace, hidden in its brown package, on the shelf in my closet. Front and center, right at eye level.

I threw that package onto the closet floor and kicked it to a back corner. I wanted to throw it in the trash, but I knew I couldn't. Throughout my high school years, the brown package stayed in my closet.

Mom continued to rub her hand up my spine. Dad still patted my shoulders. But they didn't tell me to stand tall or not slump. They didn't have to. I didn't ever want to look at that back brace again, and I sure wasn't wearing it. And I continued to grow taller.

I survived my high school nickname, "Six-foot Susie." I even accepted my next to last place in our high school graduation line of only fifty-five seniors. We lined up shortest to tallest, and all my girlfriends were in the front. Only one boy, Randy, was taller than me.

When Mom and I packed my clothes for my first quarter at college, she found the wrinkled and worn package on the closet floor. "I don't think you need to take this," she said.

Years passed. The summer after I married, Mom and I cleaned out my closet so she could turn my room into her quilting and sewing room.

"Where's the brown package?" I asked when the closet was completely empty.

"It's gone," Mom said.

"Where? Did you find someone who needed to wear that awful brace?"

"No. I threw it away when you left for college. It did its job. I'm glad it was never used."

"So you bought it thinking I'd never wear it?"

"I hoped not. That might have been the best money we ever spent when you were in high school. You learned to stand tall and straight with wonderful posture."

Mother never took a child psychology class or a parenting class. But she knew. Even now, decades later, whenever I feel my shoulders slump, I think of that ugly back brace that I never ever wanted to put on.

~Susan R. Ray

74

Grumbling in the Garden

Many things grow in the garden that were never sown there.
~Thomas Fuller

I hated every minute of it. Digging in the smelly dirt in spring, planting the tiny seeds in meticulous rows, weeding the plants while sweat poured down my face. Picking, canning and freezing vegetables, only to find them on your plate, staring at you on a bleak winter day.

I wanted to spend the summer with my friends—lying in my back yard tanning and listening to the radio with a cool glass of iced tea. But instead I spent every Saturday and my summer vacations working in my mom's large vegetable garden.

My parents both grew up on farms before moving to town so they wanted to keep gardening. They used a large plot of land at my grandparents' house to grow enough food to feed our family and fill the freezer for winter. My mom was determined that I would learn how to plant and harvest a proper garden.

"Gardening is such a waste of time!" I would complain. "Why bother spending months working on planting peas and beans when you can just buy a bag of frozen vegetables for $1.99 at the grocery store?"

"Just keep picking," my mom would say, smiling and handing me another basket to fill with beans.

I grew up and left home, happy to leave that old vegetable garden behind.

But a few years later, living in a little house with my new husband, I looked out the back window and saw a big sunny spot. "That might be a good place for a vegetable garden," I thought, surprising even myself.

Not much came out of that garden that year but I could hear Mom's voice in my head—"Put the peas in rows, the lettuce in bunches. Leave room between the tomatoes and cucumbers so they can spread. Pulling weeds right after it rains is easier."

Over the years, with each new house I've moved to, the first thing I've looked for is room for a garden in the back yard. My vegetable garden has become my happy place. There is nothing like standing barefoot in the dirt, excitedly seeing the first tiny green sprouts. Or watching the tiny flowers bud into peas, beans and cucumbers. And especially the taste of that first ripe tomato, a sweet carrot still sprinkled with dirt, or an ear of fresh corn, raw off the stalk.

As a teenager I would groan, sitting down to a table full of garden fresh vegetables, but now I exclaim to my own three teens, "Look at all this food—you will never eat something so good as fresh picked from your own back yard!"

My mom now chuckles at my gardening passion, remembering a daughter who would stomp angrily through the dirt, complaining her mother was ruining her summer.

Now a third of my small back yard is a vegetable garden, and every year it grows just a bit bigger.

When my son Simon was five, his eyes grew wide as he helped me pick peas and beans one morning. "Wow Mom, we have so much FREE food!"

So, thanks, Mom, for making me learn what I thought I would never need to know. For knowing more than I did, just how much I would love digging in the dirt. Thank you for teaching me when I was unteachable—for somehow sparking an interest that would lead to a lifetime joy.

~Lori Zenker

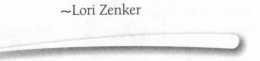

75

Tough Love

Don't handicap your children by making their lives easy.
~Robert A. Heinlein

A t some point during my adolescence, her name changed. "Momma" was much too babyish, so I decided to simply call her "Mom." It made me feel more grown up.

I was the fourth daughter born to my parents. One would think Mom would have been used to teenage girls, but each one of us presented her with a different challenge. My three older sisters were eager to gain their independence and move away from home at age eighteen. I was the most scholarly and had ambitions to go to college. Unlike my mother and sisters, I wanted a career.

I considered myself lucky to be an ordinary girl growing up in a traditional family. My dad worked hard to provide for his family while Mom was ever-present in all things home. My relationship with my mother was as good as most teenage girls. She was lenient with me because I had never caused her any problems. She approved of most of my friends, but she didn't quite understand the Mohawk haircut on one of the boys I brought home. "And I thought the Beatles haircuts with the bangs hanging in their faces were bad," she exclaimed. I was surprised at her reaction. If she had given him a chance, she would have recognized his fondness and respect for me.

It was when I began dating one of the "Beatles haircut" boys that Mom started to worry. She commented, "You don't seem to spend much time with your girlfriends anymore since you have this new boyfriend." It was like she had a sixth sense because, of course, her concerns were valid. Halfway through my junior year in high school, I shocked my family when I revealed that I was probably pregnant. After an examination by an obstetrician confirmed my fears, Mom and I left his office and drove home in silence. My father awaited our return. Mom broke the news and Daddy's eyes glistened with tears. I gloomily asked them, "What am I going to do?"

Daddy's voice cracked when he spoke up, "Pam," he said, "This is a very serious situation. I don't think you understand what you have gotten yourself into. Having a baby is a lifetime commitment."

Mom interrupted. "How do you plan to take care of a baby?"

"I don't know," I murmured.

"Well, you will have to take full responsibility for your own baby. I have already raised you four girls and I still have your brother to take care of." She left the room before I could talk back.

Daddy's head hung low when I looked up at him. He didn't say anything more to me. Stunned by my mother's desertion, I retreated to my bedroom. I needed my momma.

The day after my seventeenth birthday, I married my boyfriend. I gave birth to a beautiful, healthy baby girl six months later. It was love at first sight as she lay in my arms, occasionally looking into my eyes as if to ask, "How do you plan to take care of me?"

"I will do my best, baby girl," I whispered to myself.

We brought our newborn baby home to my parents' house because we didn't have a home of our own. The plan was to live with my parents until my husband graduated from high school and found a job. Then we would start looking for our own place.

And true to her word, Mom was hands-off when it came to baby duties. She slept through the 2 a.m. feedings, was busy with other household chores during diaper changes, and was too tired in the evening when it was time to prepare the baby formula and bottles. She was a doting Grandma while I was Momma to my child.

After a few months, my husband and I found a small one-bedroom apartment for our young family. We furnished it with hand-me-down pieces and shared our bedroom with our infant child. My duties multiplied to include household chores. And I still didn't know how to take care of my baby.

My sister gave me a book written by a man with a strange name. Dr. Spock seemed to know everything about caring for babies, so he and I became very good friends as I attempted to make sense of it all.

I survived. I took my dirty laundry, including pails of wet diapers, to Mom's house because I didn't have a washing machine in my apartment. Grandma played with her newest grandchild while I did the dirty work. I learned the hard way that a momma's work was never done.

My second daughter was born nearly three years later. My momma duties doubled, but somehow it seemed easier. It was then that the light bulb went off.

Mom had given me a gift! Her tough love forced me to take charge of my own life and to be a responsible mother. She knew what she was doing all along.

And my little girls grew up to be teenagers, too. I embraced those years nervously. As typical girls do, they twirled before a mirror and asked me, "How do I look, Mom?"

I answered, "Honey, if you act as nice as you look, you will be fine." The first time I heard those words leave my mouth, I couldn't believe it. How many times did I get annoyed when Mom responded with silly statements like that instead of giving a straight answer? I think my daughters growled under their breath the same way I did so many years ago. And when had my name changed from Momma to Mom? Had I been too busy to notice?

Years passed and the time came to say a final goodbye to my mother. I crawled into bed beside her as she lay dying. We reminisced about our lives together. "I'm proud of you," she said.

I was grateful for those last three days we had together. I finally had a chance to say, "Thank you, Mom, for allowing me to grow up. You knew exactly what you were doing."

~Pam Carter

76

Advice Worth Trying

*Vitality shows in not only the ability to persist
but the ability to start over.*
~F. Scott Fitzgerald

My palms sweated, and my hands shook. Whose idea was it to be here, anyway? Well, in truth, it was my mom's. "Take ballroom dancing lessons," she had said.

So here I was, standing outside the door of Studio Two. All I had to do was walk through the door. It sounded easy, but it wasn't. I knew I would be walking into a room filled with experienced dancers, graceful, controlled people who had been practicing a long time. Many had won contests. I didn't even know the names of the dance steps.

I was sure they were appropriately dressed. I had no idea what someone wore to dance lessons. Sweats and a T-shirt, or a fancy dress with stiletto heels? Heck, I didn't know. So, I compromised. I wore a dress and medium heels. It was a fun dress, kind of swishy when I moved, and it matched my shoes. It would look fantastic while I danced. After thinking about it, I wasn't sure the dress was right for practicing. I wondered if I should have worn the sweats.

I didn't have to go through the door. I could have turned around and gone home, back to my empty apartment and all the memories it held. I could have sat on the sofa where we cuddled, watched TV, and talked about our future. I could have gone into the kitchen where we practiced making gourmet meals, and fixed late night peanut butter and cracker snacks. I could have climb into the bed where we made love, and where I'd awoken each morning with the haunting memory of his final goodbye. No, I couldn't go back where all those memories waited for me. I couldn't go back without making an effort to go forward, since it was, as Mom sternly told me, time to move forward with my life. I opened the door and walked inside the studio.

I immediately saw what one should wear to dance lessons and what I had on wasn't it. I looked at all the curious faces staring back at me. Jeans, shorts, casual dresses and leotards were what people wore to dance classes. I couldn't have made myself stand out more had I planned it. Okay, people, I made a mistake, but you don't have to gawk, I thought to myself.

"Hold your head up and smile." Mom always said. "That will get you through anything." I began to doubt her wisdom. I was definitely not feeling the love in the room. I knew what they were thinking. "What is she doing here? She has two left feet. She'll never learn to dance. She doesn't even know how to dress for dance class."

"Are you here for lessons?" a tall, willowy lady asked as she came toward me in a pink leotard with a filmy skirt over it. A faint scent of lilacs tickled my nose. She seemed like a nice lady. She might save me.

"Yes, um, yes, I'm here for lessons." My hands shook again and my feet acted like they could leave any minute and take me with them.

I wasn't sure exactly what kind of look I was getting from the pink lady, but I was pretty sure it wasn't approval. "Come with me," she said. I could tell from the way she said it, she wasn't happy I came to her class for lessons. She was probably thinking how little I looked like a dancer. I followed her past several couples standing on the dance floor and ended up on the other side of the room, where folding metal chairs lined the wall.

"We have three other new students this evening. You can join them and watch as some of our more experienced dancers demonstrate a few steps." Pink lady abandoned me to return to the dance floor... so much for help from the nice lady.

A couple of guys and another woman occupied chairs and, as they had made the sweats choice, I figured they were inwardly laughing at my stupidity. Maybe not, but I was pretty sure they were. It didn't matter. I'd made the commitment. I came to learn to dance so I was going to dance. I sat and looked at the couples on the floor, pointedly ignoring the other newbies.

The lady in pink turned on a waltz. Sensuous music filled every corner of the room. We watched for a short time as the dancers effortlessly glided around the floor. It was beautiful to watch. I began to think my mom might have been on to something after all.

Unexpectedly the lady in pink motioned for those of us sitting to join the other dancers. I didn't move. One of the men and the other lady got up and eased out on the floor. That left two of us, and we both knew what that meant. I figured he was really embarrassed to be stuck with the only female in the room dressed for church instead of dance. Too bad, my friend, you'll get over it, I thought, still not moving. I looked at the other couple as they took their place with the experienced dancers.

"Come. We must practice, practice, and practice. That's the only way you will learn," insisted the lady in pink. She was hovering over us, motioning for the two of us to get up and come to the dance floor.

My attention was drawn back to the lone male. He had moved to stand in front of me, hand extended, a smile on his face.

"I think that means we're up. We can't get out of this," he said.

I smiled back and took his hand. It was firm, yet gentle. He let go as I stood, and placed his now free hand on my back as he guided me to the dance floor. I liked the comforting feel.

Nerves took over and my feet wouldn't move. He put a hand around my waist and extended the other, taking one of mine in his. We posed in the same position as we had seen the others doing. The music faintly began and built to a strong beat. He took a step forward. I was forced to follow his lead. Another, and then another and… we were dancing! I was elated. He looked into my eyes and, with a twinkle in his, said, "This is so easy I could do this for the rest of my life."

Yes, Mom gave me great advice. That dance was the beginning of a beautiful marriage. Two children later, my husband and I still attend dance classes every Thursday evening.

~Rita Durrett

77

Dorothy and Sophia

My mother always used to say,
"The older you get, the better you get, unless you're a banana."
~Rose, in The Golden Girls

"That's going to be us someday," I said to my mom the morning of my grandmother's funeral. We were standing outside the funeral home watching a friend of the family spin her own mother around the parking lot in a wheelchair. The mother, who had to be well into her nineties, was squealing with delight. With her dementia, she honestly had no idea she was even at a funeral and she was having a grand old time. Her daughter made sure of that. It was nice to see, especially given the day's circumstances.

My mom narrowed her eyes at me. "I don't think so."

"Oh, we totally are. We'll be just like Dorothy and Sophia."

It was a running joke in my family that I was going to end up like Dorothy Zbornak from *The Golden Girls* when I reached the menopausal years, and my mom would slowly morph into little, sassy Sophia. She already had the short stature; all she needed was a gray fro, some massive glasses, and a whole lot of attitude, and she'd be good to go.

Mom shook her head at me like she does whenever she thinks I'm being a weirdo. She went to check on my dad. "Don't deny your future," I called after her.

But she knew I was right. We were going to be like those two someday: a daughter taking care of her mother—a daughter who made sure her mom had a blast in her golden years.

You see, Mumsie (my endearing nickname for my mom) and I are best friends. We tell each other everything. Okay, so I tell her everything, and she tells me most things. I'm pretty sure she leaves out stuff about her and my dad that would set off my gag reflex. But we truly are that close.

"It was you and me in the beginning, and it will be you and me in the end," she admitted to me during my annual holiday visit last year after I had gotten her drunk with a bottle of cheap Chardonnay (she doesn't have my wino tolerance). My dad was off visiting his own mom, so it was just us girls, drinking and watching a marathon of what else but *The Golden Girls*.

Our unique bond began before I was even born, the moment she found out she was pregnant with me to be exact. She and my dad had broken up just weeks before, and she decided not to tell him about me. She decided the instant that little stick turned pink that I was hers and she was mine, and she would give me the best life she possibly could, no matter what it threw at us. We would be a team. We would be best friends.

"Why did you keep me?" I asked that same drunken night. "You were young and single. If it had been me, I probably would've gotten rid of me."

"But I loved you," she replied.

"But you didn't even know me."

"But I loved you," she repeated.

I stared at her in awe, and while I was a little tipsy myself during this conversation, the impact of those words sobered me right up. Mumsie was the bravest woman... ever. Had our roles been reversed, I'm not so sure I would've been so courageous.

And while things did eventually pan out for my parents (my dad worked hard to win her back, and they're still the happiest couple I know, but that's a story for another Chicken Soup for the Soul book), I will never discount her integrity. I will never discount her courage. I will never discount the love she had for her unborn child.

Thirty-four years ago, my mother made a vow to be the best mother she could, even though she was young, scared, and alone. And someday, I'll do the same for her. We'll be just like Dorothy and Sophia. And don't worry, my dad will be there too.

~Kyle Therese Cranston

78

The Meanest Mother in Town

If you have never been hated by your child,
you have never been a parent.
~Bette Davis

I had the meanest mother in the entire world. She gave me ridiculous rules to follow, curfews, and long talks about morals and values. Her constant nagging to turn down my music and to know where I was at all times was a hard pill to swallow at times. I had a bedtime and was never allowed to have my own television or a phone in my room. I couldn't date until I was sixteen.

For a measly allowance, I had chores from an early age. Expectations were high. I had to keep my room clean and make my bed every day. Setting the table, helping out in the kitchen, and doing the dinner dishes were mandatory. I was also expected to iron my dad's handkerchiefs and everyone's pillowcases. Feeding the dog was on my list as well. When school was out for summer, my duty list grew.

She was so mean that when I asked for extra cash or something special, she would tell me to get a job. I had to start working at age fifteen. She obviously had no idea about child labor laws.

If I had a date, she would insist he come inside to meet her and my dad. They would then interrogate him about where we were going and give him the curfew speech. Even after I had dated the same boy for quite some time and she knew him, he was made to come inside and escort me to the car. She refused to let me to go out when he honked his horn to pick me up for a date. She not only was mean, but embarrassing to boot.

I wasn't allowed to watch certain movies or go to a drive-in theater with a boy. She watched me like a hawk when it came to applying make-up. I was sent back to my room on numerous occasions to remove heavy layers. She balked if my skirts were too short. I couldn't get my ears pierced until I was sixteen years old, and then that had to be my gift. She insisted my ears be pierced by a doctor when my friends could have done it at home for free.

If I did something wrong or got a bad grade, I would be punished. Her explanation was always the same. "This hurts me more than it does you" or "I do this because I love you."

I wasn't allowed to receive telephone calls past 9:00 p.m. and the calls could not last more than one hour. If I had not done my homework, there would be no socializing at all.

One of her silliest rules was I couldn't have boys over if she was not home and even if she was, we had to stay in the kitchen or living room. No doors could be closed at any time when a boy came to visit.

I was expected to be home for dinner every night and eat at the table with the family.

She signed me up for sewing and ceramics classes in the summer, explaining I needed to do something productive. I was enrolled in a charm school when I reached the ripe old age of fifteen. I was forced to learn about fashion, etiquette, and how to become a lady.

I was sent to my room for an hour if I misbehaved in church.

She had the audacity to make me write prompt thank you notes for any gifts I received.

When I got my own car she actually expected me to help out with insurance and I was responsible for buying my own gas. When I started working she made me open a savings account. Half my paycheck and any cash gifts had to put into the account, then I could spend the rest as I saw fit. She was adamant about teaching me the value of a dollar and responsibility.

I was forced to call all adults Mr. and Mrs. No first names allowed.

I also had to have good manners; it was drilled into my head from day one.

I was forced to eat breakfast because she thought it was the most important meal of the day. I personally saw nothing wrong with grabbing a doughnut or two and eating them on the run. She saw to it that I sat at the kitchen table and forced me to eat bacon and eggs. Sometimes she made me eat stewed prunes, cereal or homemade pancakes.

If I got into trouble at school, it would be worse when I arrived home.

Several times I would pretend to be sick so I wouldn't have to go to school at all. Each time she could tell I was faking, and gave me castor oil by the tablespoon. I had to go to school every single day. No relaxing in bed for me. I saw no reason I couldn't take a day off, but she seemed to have a problem with that.

She used to threaten me too. I can still hear her saying, "Just wait until your father gets home." Daddy wasn't the type to use violence in any way; however having to listen to one of his lectures was a fate worse than death. There were times I felt I'd rather have been whipped.

I vowed that when I had children of my own, I would be one of the cool moms. I wasn't going to be anything like her; she was cruel and controlling. She was the meanest mom in town.

Years later my first child was born, then twelve months later my second one came along, and finally my third. It didn't take long before I became the new winner of the moniker "The Meanest Mom in Town." I'm proud to say I still hold that title today, thanks to my mom, a great role model.

~Carol Commons-Brosowske

In Gratitude

We often take for granted the very things that most deserve our gratitude.
~Cynthia Ozick

Dear Mom,

I've blamed you for many things throughout my life. I blamed you for leaving my father when I was five. I blamed you for taking me away from Hong Kong, the city where I was born. I blamed you for marrying my stepfather, a man who could never accept me. And I blamed you for being more devoted to your work than to being my mother.

I've hurt you, Mom, just as you've hurt me. You see me as stubborn, resentful, and vindictive. I have to have my way, and anything you do for me isn't good enough. Your gifts are never what I need. The food you bring is not what I want. Even the money you send at Christmas isn't right because it can never take the place of the love I didn't feel in your home. I've resented you because it's easier than accepting responsibility for my own life, even at the age of fifty-one.

I've blamed you, Mom, for what's wrong in my life, but I haven't given you credit for what's right. Despite my protests, you took me back to Hong Kong to see my father when I was thirty-three. If you had not insisted, I never would have realized how much it meant to him to have a son, even one he couldn't talk to because we spoke different languages.

I connected with my father, my family, and my past on that trip. I learned about him and about you — the pain you endured as a twelve-year-old when you lost your parents to Communist soldiers in China and the naked desperation of a child who was forced to flee in order to survive. How you met my father in Mainland China and again in Hong Kong when you could no longer bear to stay in the country that took your parents away. I never would have known my father or his family if you hadn't pushed me to go back to Hong Kong in 1996, and I might never have appreciated the courage it took for you to leave everything you knew to come to America.

When you brought me to the U.S., you gave me the opportunity for an education, the chance to help people by becoming a counselor. If I had remained in Hong Kong, I would not have met my wife, Quyen, and I would never have known the joy of being a father to our children, Kevin and Kristie. In America, I have found a passion for writing stories, a vehicle of self-discovery, and a path to make a difference with words.

You married my stepfather, Roger, and though he and I have never been close, he took care of me when I was a child. He provided a home and made sure I had enough to eat. There are many children in the world who have neither. Roger taught me how to ride my first bike when I was eight. He ran behind me on Cisco Street in China Lake, California and he steadied me on that green, Huffy Sting-Ray until I could stay up on my own.

You have supported our family by waiting tables, providing childcare to neighborhood kids, refinishing old furniture, opening a restaurant, and scrimping and saving to buy a house. You have shown that it is possible for a woman with a grade-school education to enter a country in which she could barely speak the language and fashion a life for her family through hard work and determination. When I think of how much you've lost, how much you've sacrificed, and how much you've achieved, all I can say is thank you, Mom.

~Raymond M. Wong

Birthday Blues

The heart of a mother is a deep abyss
at the bottom of which you will always find forgiveness.
~Honoré de Balzac

"I hate you! I'm not going and I don't know why anyone else would want to go either!" The words spewed out of my mouth with such venom and rage that I knew I'd never be able to take them back.

It was another teenage temper tantrum, one that Mom had become accustomed to during my tumultuous adolescence. But this one stung a little bit more. It was September 6th—Mom's birthday—and it should have been a time for celebration with friends and family. Rather than joining in the festivities at my grandparents' house, I had just unleashed a verbal assault on my mom, and the words left a trail of destruction in their wake.

"Fine, stay home then," Mom said, as she left the house to go to her birthday dinner. "You're so selfish. You can't even behave just this once, on my birthday."

As the car pulled out of the driveway I began to think about the significance of my actions. I sat at the kitchen table, by myself, while the rest of my family was celebrating a pretty fantastic woman's birthday. I wondered why I spewed such hatred toward my own mother, and I wondered how she could still love me when all I did was misbehave and create conflict.

"I need to be a better person," I thought, as I recalled so many similar incidents that had occurred in the weeks, months and years leading up to this.

My self-reflection was interrupted as I heard a car door slam shut in the driveway. Seconds later, Mom walked into the house in tears. Despite the hurtful words I had uttered less than half an hour earlier, she came back because she wanted me to come to her birthday party.

Looking at her eyes welling up with tears, I realized how incredibly selfish I had been. Mom was right. This woman, who attended every one of my athletic events, shuttled me to friends' houses, and bought me the latest fashions, simply wanted me to show up. That was the least I could do, but in my infinite stubbornness and teenage wisdom, I had taken Mom for granted and hurt the one person who I could always depend on.

That birthday was memorable for all the wrong reasons.

For me and Mom, it wasn't our first conflict and it certainly wasn't our last, but it was a turning point in our relationship. Today, as a nearly thirty-year-old woman, I make sure I spend the day with Mom on her birthday. And even though I know my presence is all she wants, I find myself taking extra time and effort to make sure I get the perfect gift. After all, my best friend deserves the best.

~Sarah McCrobie

81

Always Show Up

Commitment means staying loyal to what you said you were going
to do, long after the mood you said it in has left you.
~Author Unknown

I rolled over in bed to look at the clock. I needed to get up if I was going to be on time for work. I'd pulled what the resort called a double shift the day before—5:30 a.m. until 9 p.m., until everything was washed, wiped down, swept up and stored away for the next morning's crew at the summer vacation resort where I served as an event waitress.

I worked there during their two big months—June and July—and we'd served over 400 people the day before. The soles of my feet felt sore and puffy and my back was stiff, but I was due back for a single shift and I needed to get up. I put my head back down on the pillow and considered my options, and produced the most obvious one a self-centered, pampered sixteen-year-old girl was likely to choose.

I would simply call in sick. I would apologize for not making it to work today, but I figured they'd be fine without my services just this one day.

My mother walked into my room.

"You have to work today, don't you, Bec? You better be getting up or you're going to be late." She stood there watching me, not showing any sign of leaving me to my state of exhaustion from all my hard work the prior day.

"I don't think I'll go in today. I'm too tired," I said. "I'm going to call in sick."

I felt a slight tinge of guilt, maybe even a bit of premonition because as soon as the words were out of my mouth, the expression on her face changed, and it wasn't in my favor.

"What do you mean you're calling in?" she demanded, her eyes hard and glaring. And I knew this whole scene was far from over. It's funny how even a sixteen-year-old does know deep down she's botched this one.

She didn't miss a beat. "When you accepted that job, you were telling those people you wanted that job," she said. "You were telling them you would show up and work for them when they asked you to. You were telling them you would respect their giving you that position and that they could count on you."

My mother didn't yell at me to make her point, nor did she swear or threaten me with some bogus form of punishment should I not hoist myself out of that bed. She should have been a lawyer because she used the best weapon there is: shame mixed in with a healthy dose of blunt honesty.

But she wasn't done with me yet, this woman who produced three homemade meals a day for her family of six, and who did all of the laundry and ironing, made the beds, baked and canned, cleaned the house and washed the windows; this woman who walked wherever she needed to go in our small town because she didn't drive a car. The same woman who went to business school to become a legal secretary, but instead fell in love, got married and ended up with four children to feed, clean up after and raise, but who never got to call in sick when she was tired.

"You know, Bec," she continued, "there are so many times I wish all I had to do was get up, splash a little cold water on my face and head into class or to a job." Her wistful expression drove her point to the center of the bulls-eye, and I saw her in a different light, and I knew I had no right to call in sick simply because I was a little on the tired side that morning.

My mother considered a job outside the home something to be appreciated, even if it was just a summer waitressing job.

"Now, get yourself out of bed and into work."

I did, and I survived.

She taught me many things through the years, either by example, or by silence at the right time, or through our late-night girl chats over hot cups of tea that we shared so many, many late evenings when I'd come home to visit as a married woman with children of my own.

The scene presented itself full circle years later. There I was, a mother of two preteen daughters and your typical working wife and mom. We'd finished dinner and I was cleaning up in the kitchen when I commented to the family that I wished I could take tomorrow off from work because I was feeling extra tired that particular evening.

As if on cue from Providence, my younger daughter offered what I'm sure seemed the most logical response to such a request.

"Why don't you just call in sick tomorrow then, Mom?"

And I had to wonder if my mother was just around the corner, listening to see how I would respond to that one.

I think she would have approved.

"I can't do that, honey," I told her. "When you tell someone you're going to work for them, you need to show up, even if you're a little tired."

To this day, both of my daughters remember and honor that tenet my mother drilled into my head so long ago.

~R'becca Groff

Chapter 8

Thanks to My Mom

My Mother the Teacher

82

My First Teacher

The worth of a book is to be measured by
what you can carry away from it.
~James Bryce

In 1960, the schools in rural Minnesota were not required to provide kindergarten, and so began the most memorable year of my school career. Each morning as my brother and sister prepared for school, I too would follow the morning routine. When my siblings boarded the bus, I would kiss my mother goodbye and walk to the back door of our small home. There I was greeted by my "teacher," Mrs. Jager, who graciously welcomed me to our small service porch, which housed a potbelly stove and my own small school desk.

The antique iron and oak desk became an island of paradise for me. I learned the wonders of letters, sounds, numbers and the Golden Rule. My favorite time was just after lunch when my "teacher" read to me of Winnie-the-Pooh and Toby Tyler and taught me it was okay to cry when Toby's monkey died, because indeed, the joy of reading was to make you "feel things in your heart."

My most memorable day was when we took a "field trip" to the city. My "teacher" told me it was a special surprise. After the neighbor gave us a ride to a bus stop and we completed many transfers, I gaped in wonder at the great stone building amidst the hustle and bustle of the city traffic. I will never forget holding my mother's hand as the large oak doors opened and I saw the shiny marble floors and smelled the aroma of books. Rows and rows of books stood before me. I was astounded by the immensity of the whole experience. I whispered to my mom, "Can we afford this?" My mother's beautiful laugh and smile filled the quiet hall. "No sweetheart, we get to borrow as many as fifteen books, for free." My heart raced. I couldn't believe it; we could take any one of these books back to our little schoolroom?

My own children learned the joy of reading as my wife and I cuddled with them and read bedtime stories. As a school principal, I get to observe the mysteries of the printed word come to life for students every single day. I get to watch as the eyes of struggling readers flash with realization as knowledgeable and dedicated teachers inculcate them with the joy of reading. But, I most look forward to reading to my kindergartners about Curious George and *Thomas's Snowsuit* because it reminds me of a cold bus ride with my mother, my first teacher, from a small farmhouse to the Saint Paul Public Library.

~Bill Jager

Back to the Bank

To bring up a child in the way he should go—
travel that way yourself.
~Josh Billings

"Why are we going back to the bank?" I asked my mother. The five of us—my mother, three brothers, and I—had just returned home from a morning of running errands. Packages were mailed, utility bills were paid and cash withdrawn from the bank. Trapped in the car with my younger brothers all morning was torture anyway, and besides that, it was a hot, humid day and the car's torn seats were itchy and uncomfortable. Our little house, with the white bed linens hanging from the clothesline in the back yard, was a welcomed sight.

As a reward for good behavior all morning, my mother had promised to take us to our aunt's pool for an afternoon of swimming. My brothers and I had bolted from the old black station wagon toward the house when we were brought to a halt by our mother's voice. "Everyone back in the car," she said. "We are going back to the bank."

I had only two things on my twelve-year-old mind—lunch and swimming. Although my aunt and uncle lived down the street, it was rare that we were invited over for a swim. Since pools in this part of the country were a novelty, this was an opportunity not to be missed. I couldn't wait to get in the water to work on what I called my water ballet moves and maybe get up some courage to dive off the diving board. All we had to do was eat a quick sandwich, wrestle on our bathing suits, grab our beach towels and go. And now, we had to get back in the car?

We lived in a small, rural town in New England. We drove nearly an hour on narrow, curved roads and routes to the services and businesses we had visited in the morning. I calculated the timeline in my head. This could take at least two hours, not counting the time in the bank. I pleaded with my mother. "Can't we go back tomorrow? We can't go today. Please? We want to go swim. Please?" My mother replied calmly, "We are going back to the bank."

My mother herded us back into the hot, stuffy car. She brought some snacks—apples, cheese, and a rare treat—chilled bottles of Coca-Cola. I would have none of it. I sat in the back seat with my arms crossed tightly against my chest. I stared out the window, seeing nothing. I resisted the urge to physically communicate to my tired, noisy brothers how much their whining irritated me. My mother was driving and singing along to a Chet Atkins song, as if on a leisurely Sunday drive on a spring day.

My mother parked the station wagon in front of the bank. The bank was a grand two-story building constructed of granite blocks. Four tall columns flanked the brass-framed, glass door entrance. The brood tumbled out of the car and up the granite stairs. The polished stone floors and vaulted, painted and gilded ceiling echoed our noisy entrance into the bank. I stayed close to my mother's side as we approached the tellers' windows and then my mother paused. She looked from one teller to the next, and then with assurance she approached a teller standing behind the window at the end of the long, marble and mahogany counter.

The teller was a pretty and petite woman who looked nervous and tense. My mother told the young woman that she was the customer who had come to the bank in the morning and this woman had given my mother the cash she had withdrawn. Talking to this young woman in a kind, soft voice, my mother explained that she had returned to the bank to correct an error that had occurred earlier.

A worried look quickly replaced the teller's smile. My mother reached into her purse with the broken clasp and pulled something out. Then, I saw my mother slide a one-hundred-dollar bill over the marble countertop to the teller. "You gave me one hundred dollars too much," my mother said.

Trying to hold back the tears, the teller leaned forward and whispered, "I'm so sorry. I'm worried and upset and I have made several errors. I was told this morning that if I made one more error, I would lose my job. You see, my husband left me this week. I have two small children to support. Thank you so much for returning this money. I can't thank you enough. Not many people would have returned this money. Thank you so much." My mother simply said, "You're welcome." And gently patting the teller's hand, she said, "Good luck to you."

We filed out of the grandiose bank and into our dirty, rundown station wagon. It was raining now. Any hope of swimming today, or for the rest of the summer for that matter, was lost. As my mother drove the country roads for the second time that day, she said little. She treated this event as business as usual, nothing special. But I knew that something important had happened on that disappointing, swim-less day, though I could not have told you what it was at the time.

But fifty years later, I can tell you what happened on that one summer day. I had been taught, by my mother's humble act, the lessons of honesty, integrity and kindness. Throughout my life, whenever I have been faced with the inevitable what-is-the-right-thing-to-do dilemma, the choice has been made easy thanks to my mother. I simply recall my mother's voice and hear her say, "We are going back to the bank."

~Elizabeth Greenhill

84

Modeling Change

If you don't like something change it;
if you can't change it, change the way you think about it.
~Mary Engelbreit

y mother sat crumpled on the floor, phone to her ear, the cord coiling around her like a snake. It was dinnertime, but she wore the same housecoat she had pulled over her nightgown that morning. She was sobbing. I was eight and I stood there watching, eyes flitting between her and my five-year-old brother. His eyes were wide, his fingers tight around his raggedy blankie. "Who will make dinner?" I thought.

That was the year my dad commuted between Long Island and Holland, Michigan. Every Friday right after school, my mom would pack us into the powder blue Chevy and make the trip to the airport. She was afraid to drive after dark, so we could always count on a long boring wait inside the terminal. My brother and I passed the time by checking the phone booths and vending machines for change left behind. Early evening we would watch as Daddy emerged from the jetway amongst a crowd of business travelers. Grinning and wriggling, we would run to greet him.

Daddy's return each weekend meant I could be a kid again, not worry about dinner or shielding myself and my brother from Mommy's angry outbursts. In my memories of that time, my mom was either moping and weeping or screaming and swinging at us. Daddy was my hero. When Mommy was in one of her moods, he would swoop down, scoop us up, and scurry out of the house. What I didn't know at the time was that my dad drank too much, too often. He was not a mean drunk; he was a sleeping drunk. "Daddy's tired," Mommy would say. It would be some time before even she realized he was a problem drinker.

And then, a couple of years later, she did. Mom started going to Al-Anon and that was when her life, and mine, began to change. Mom worked the program—taking the principles she learned there off the blackboard and applying them to herself. The woman she became bore little resemblance to the mother I knew as a young child. The things she learned in Al-Anon empowered her to change the things she could and accept with grace the things she had no control over. She took responsibility for her life and taught me how to take responsibility for my own.

The Al-Anon liturgy is rife with prayers, pithy little sayings, and acronyms. She recited them to me often, seeming to know just what to say, which slogan for which occasion. They were words I could hold onto, remember, and use as a guide. Moving from childhood to adolescence, Mom was there to help me grow up. She was more than a sympathetic ear; she offered me real tools to fix real problems. Mom was my model. In her I saw how a change of attitude could change a life. Mom taught me to believe in my potential.

"Lorri, how important is it?" she asked, as I sat trembling over my algebra textbook, anticipating the test scheduled for sixth period the next day. "A or F, ten years from now do you think your grade will matter to you or anyone else?" She said, "It's just one test. In life, there will be many. Study hard and then let go and let God."

Of course, Mom was right. Life had tested me in many ways, and the echo of her words always helped to get me through with a measure of peace. They grounded me, pulling me out of senseless worry, reminding me what mattered. She gave me the gift of perspective, showing me how to see the big picture and to value myself apart from my accomplishments and failures.

Another favorite saying of Mom's was "Feelings are not facts." "But Mom I just don't feel like I can," I said, listing all the reasons why.

Mom heard me out and gave me a hug. "I know that's how you feel right now, but feelings aren't facts. Let's talk about what you know to be true."

Mom taught me to take a step back and question my feelings with objectivity. She got me to see for myself that my feelings changed from moment to moment and day to day. They did not make for a firm foundation upon which to base decisions. When I had a difficult choice to make, she told me to list the pros and cons in order of significance. She didn't solve my problems for me. She taught me how to find solutions myself.

At twenty-one I was back living with my parents, finishing up school at a local commuter college. I had no campus life, few friends, and no boyfriend. As was the case most weekend mornings I was dragging around the house, bored and lonely.

"Look at this," Mom said, pointing to a calendar listing in *The Roslyn News*. "A square dance tonight. You should go."

"Not happening," I said. "I can't go alone."

"Sure you can. It's a square dance and besides," she said, fixing me with her gaze. "No one's going to come knocking at your door."

Mom was always pushing me to take charge of my life, to get out, to move my muscles (another one of her maxims), and to change the things I could. "Aw, PLUM, Poor Little Unhappy Me," she mimicked. "If you're miserable being alone, then YOU do something about it. Self-pity will get you nowhere," she said.

So I went to that square dance and somewhere between swing your partner and do-si-do I came face to face with the man who would be my one love for many years.

Two decades later Mom's words still resonated at the most unpredictable times. I was living alone in a new city and I knew only a handful of people—all barely acquaintances. When Barb called and invited me to a small dinner party, I was ready to say "thank you, but no thank you" when I heard my mother's voice: "No one's going to come knocking at your door."

I was in Chattanooga and as far as I knew, she was in New York. Yet there were those words again, inside my head, but coming through loud and clear. I looked around my apartment. All was still save for the hum of the refrigerator and the chirp of crickets through open windows. Not once in the four months I'd lived there had there been a knock at my door. So with my mom's words ringing in my ears, I swallowed my "no thank you" and took down the address for the party.

The evening was uneventful in every way but one: I met the man who remains my beloved life partner.

Today Mom is eighty-eight and I am sixty. She is a wellspring of wisdom and though I don't often turn to her for guidance anymore, it isn't because she has nothing to offer. It's because over the years, she has taught me so well.

~Lorri Danzig

85

Honest Love

Honesty is the first chapter of the book of wisdom.
~Thomas Jefferson

If there were a "Worst Mother of the Year" award, my mom would have won it, hands down. At least that's what I was thinking one afternoon as I stood out in the barn, mucking horse stalls. I mean, clearly, the woman did not love me—not as much as mothers were supposed to love their daughters, anyway. That fact was evident from her review of my recently completed novel. Tears stung my eyes as Mom's scathing words replayed themselves: "I don't think anybody's going to want to read this."

What did she know, anyway? She hadn't even finished reading it, so how could she already judge it so harshly? My book was great, and if she couldn't appreciate it, I would simply find someone else who could. There were plenty of people who'd be eager for a sneak peek at my much-anticipated first draft, people who'd delight in all the laugh-out-loud humor, subtle metaphors, and thrilling action sequences. People who would say the words my own mother so cruelly withheld: "Good job. I'm proud of you. Your book is wonderful."

Anyone else's mom would've said those things. If Mom truly loved me, she would have said them, too.

My tears blurred my vision. The pitchfork missed the wheelbarrow, dribbling manure onto the concrete floor. It was the perfect complement to my mood: crappy.

With a sigh, I scooped up the mess and carried on. Despite my angry bravado from a few moments before, I had no real intention of showing the book to anyone other than Mom. I mean, if your own mother thinks your novel is unreadable, then it's probably not fit for public consumption, right? Enduring her comments had been brutal enough. Hearing them echoed by a friend or another family member would be more than I could handle. No matter how much I resented it, Mom was all I had.

A few days later, when the worst of the ache had subsided, I heaved another sigh and started leafing through my manuscript, digesting Mom's handwritten notes. Most pages had so much red ink they looked like evidence from the Texas Chainsaw Massacre.

Making all of her corrections would take months, if not years. Trekking up Mount Everest would probably be easier. Nonetheless, I got climbing. Er, typing. And, slowly but surely, the novel's new, sleeker shape began to emerge. Even I had to grudgingly admit that Draft Two outshined its predecessor. But that still didn't erase the sting of Mom's initial criticism, or the fact that for every positive comment she made on the most recent draft, there were still at least ten negative ones.

Just as I feared, months turned into years. As I continued to plow through draft after draft, the notion of ever writing another novel was laughable. I would be lucky if I lived long enough to finish revisions on the first one. My passion for writing was still burning, though, so I channeled my creativity into something less daunting: short stories.

Whenever I finished one, I'd bite my lip and hand it over to my nitpicky editor. Each time, some deep, never-voiced part of my soul hoped that, just this once, Mom wouldn't take the cap off her marker as she read. That Sharpie fumes wouldn't permeate the living room. That she would set down the stack of clean white pages without ever having made a single mark, and say, "Perfect!"

They say the definition of insanity is repeating the same action over and over again, expecting different results. Mom's comments usually ranged from single words like "Confusing" or "Repetitive" to entire paragraphs detailing how I should rewrite a particular scene. I ground my teeth as I made the corrections. When every last comment was addressed—even the ones I really, really disagreed with—I'd hand the story back to her. Surely, now she would be satisfied... right?

Wrong.

Off popped the red cap:

"Poor word choice." "Unclear." "Typo?"

Eventually, I could no longer stay in the room while she edited—I barely had any tooth enamel left. One night, after finishing my latest story, I had an idea. Mom was heading off to the flea market in the morning to sell some of her antiques. Instead of giving her the story to read right away, I hid it under the flap of her big brown purse with a red marker (I know—masochist) and a note asking for feedback.

All the next day, as I dumped horse feed into bins and refilled water buckets, my mind was at the flea market with my unfortunate manuscript. Was she reading it right now, that familiar frown of discontent on her face? Had she unsheathed the Sharpie yet? Would she tell me, as she sometimes did, that this particular story was not worthy of publication?

When Mom's Jeep crackled into the driveway that evening, I ran outside. The dogs frolicked around me as Mom handed me some groceries over the fence. She told me which knick-knacks she'd sold, and how she'd bought some cantaloupes from the fruit guy because he hadn't sold anything all day. Then she said the words I'd been waiting—and dreading—to hear:

"Oh, I read your story."

My heart stuttered. "And...?"

Mom scowled, irritation darkening her face. "Why did you give me that thing to read in public?"

I blinked, totally taken aback. That "thing?" And why the heck wouldn't she want to read my story in public?

"What do you mean?" I asked. "Is this because it's fan fiction and not 'real' fiction?"

She fixed me with a strange look. "It made me cry."

I stared at her, forgetting the heavy grocery bags dangling from my fingers. "You cried?"

"Yes! It was awful. I was sitting there at my table with tears running down my face. Everyone was looking at me. It was completely humiliating...."

A warm, beautiful flame sprang to life inside me. She had cried. My mom, who didn't even sniffle when a beloved character died in the fifth Harry Potter book, had been moved to tears by something I wrote.

Once we got inside, I flipped through the manuscript. "You didn't make any notes," I said, oddly disappointed. "There must at least be some typos."

"I couldn't look at it anymore," she admitted.

"Take it back to the flea market with you tomorrow," I instructed. "And write all over it."

My editor glared at me. "Fine."

And sure enough, when she handed my baby back to me the next evening, there were plenty of notes on it. There would always be notes. But somehow, this didn't seem like a bad thing anymore. As I started making corrections, my mind drifted back to that day several years before, when I'd stood out in the barn, seething over Mom's comments. The memory almost made me smile. Turns out, I was actually right about something that day:

My mom didn't love me as much as other mothers loved their daughters.

She loved me more.

She loved me enough to tell me the truth.

~Gretchen Bassier

The Love of Cooking

*Our most treasured family heirlooms are
our sweet family memories.*
~Author Unknown

As I run my fingers gently along the rim of the small chipped wooden box, sweet nostalgia comes flooding back to me. This tiny box holds so many warm memories from many years ago. When I was a child, the box hung on the kitchen wall in the Brooklyn apartment that I shared with my parents and older sister. My mom, an avid cook and baker, filled this treasure box with recipes that she accumulated through the years.

By the time I was a teen, the box was stuffed with my mom's handwritten recipes on index cards, pieces of scrap paper or pages torn from magazines. Mom was notorious for scrawling her helpful hints on some of the recipes. "Be careful not to overcook", "I add less salt than what the recipe calls for" or "Make a double batch, and freeze half for later" she'd write. Her little notations would be of great help in the years to come.

I loved going through the recipes with my mom. "Let's see," my mom would say. "What do you think we should whip up for tonight's dinner?" We would spread out the recipes on the kitchen table and together decide what we should make or bake for dessert. No matter what I chose, Mom would always smile, and say, "Good choice!" I felt so special that I got to choose what our family meal would be for that night.

As the sweet aroma from the kitchen drifted through our apartment, warm cozy feelings of love and comfort always filled my heart. Cooking together had become a big part of my early years. We laughed through disastrous cakes that collapsed into a lopsided mess and rejoiced when the chicken cacciatore turned out deliciously perfect.

Years later, after I got married, I'd often call my mom for one of the recipes that I wanted to try for my new husband. We'd chat on the phone, talking about the times we tried a new recipe and laugh when we reminisced about our disasters. There were times I'd frantically call my mom when a dish I prepared came out awful and dinner guests were about to arrive. She knew just what to do to save the dish. "Just add a little garlic," she'd say, or "Put a potato in the stew to absorb some of the excess salt." Sometimes, when my meal was beyond repair, Mom would say, "Just order pizza!"

My mom has since passed away, and I am now the proud owner of the recipe box. There are more chips and nicks in the aged wood. The recipes are yellowed, fragile, and stained.

When I ask my kids, "What do want for dinner tonight?" I take out my box, and we spread the recipes on our kitchen table. One will say, "Let's make Grandma NaNa's meatballs!" I say "Good choice!" just as my mom did.

As the wonderful aroma of dinner fills my home, I still feel the same comfort as I did many years ago, as if Mom is right there cooking for us. I whisper, "Thank you, Mom, for giving me the love of cooking and passing the love down to my children."

~Dorann Weber

For the Love of Learning

That best academy, a mother's knee.
~James Russell Lowell

"I can't do this, Mom! She just can't make us memorize all fifty state capitals!" My teacher was being so unfair.

My mother was a great one for learning. Growing up on an isolated farm during the Depression, books were her best friends. She read to me and then taught me to read before I was old enough to attend school. I loved to read. I also loved history and science, but this—this was memorizing a bunch of stupid facts! My nine-year-old brain just didn't want to do it. To top it off, there was no pattern. I needed something to hang the names on, any little peg that would give me something to relate them to.

Did I mention that Mom only went to school through eighth grade? Her old-school father believed only boys needed education beyond that level. Besides, the secondary school was in town—she'd have to move away from the farm to attend. World War II had begun and the young teenager was needed at home.

"You know what? I'll bet you can memorize them. Let's think about this."

She always said she wasn't creative, but the things she came up with to help me in school were absolutely ingenious. And they were just crazy enough to stick in my brain, even many years later.

I watched Mom put on her thinking face. You could always tell when she was approaching the intersection of "problem" and "idea."

"Okay, sweetie, think about this. What's the lady's name in Louise-iana?" I thought about that for a bit before I replied, "Louise."

"Uh-huh. And what does Louise do when she puts on her make-up?" She pantomimed brushing some powder onto her cheeks.

"Rouge!"

"And maybe she uses a little baton to do it?"

Baton Rouge. The capital of Louise-iana. Of course.

I wrote it down, giggling at the mental picture of a fancy lady putting on make-up. She must be a Southern belle! After all, she was from one of those places.

The next one was Kansas. Hard as I tried, I couldn't come up with the capital of that state.

Mom bailed me out. The farmer in her must have remembered the old outhouse because she told me again about visiting the "out-in-the-back" facility. It was a two-holer and the Monkey Ward catalog often sufficed for toilet paper. They had to check for snakes and other critters before taking a seat. No lights in there!

Change of subject. "We need the capital of Kansas. So, why do you go to the can?"

"Huh?"

She stuck out her lip. "Think about it. Why would you go to the can?"

"To pee." Eeewwww.

Once I got past the ick factor, it hit me. To-pee-ka. Topeka, Kansas. Man, she nailed it again. And that disgusting image stuck. Forever.

Some mothers were more like the *Leave It to Beaver* mom—always in dresses, with perfectly coiffed hair. (Imagine vacuuming in that getup!) City-born and bred.

My mom was a country girl. The Depression and then the War bred a certain toughness and can-do spirit in her. And she passed that on to me, even though I grew up in the suburbs. She never insisted I fit into a mold. I shouldn't hide my smarts. I should be whoever I wanted to be. Me.

I don't know how the other kids tackled that assignment, but Mom and I laughed a lot over it. She came up with plays on words, mental images, lots of really strange hooks for me to hang the capitals on. Some of the western states were a slam-dunk, because I heard those names on a regular basis. The more distant ones were a different story.

"Alaska?" I whined. "Who even cares about Alaska?"

"Well, your Uncle LeRoy does. He was stationed at Elmendorf Air Base after the war and he did some work on Ladd. Drove a big old dump truck for the construction corps. He loves Alaska."

"Bet he never had to memorize capitals."

"Bet he did. Besides," she paused to summon an accent. "Ju know what theees one ees."

I just stared.

"Come on, ju know."

That one called for an eye roll. But I obliged. "Juneau, Alaska?"

She laughed and nodded. "Like I said."

I passed that test with flying colors. It was only one of many that Mom helped me prepare for. And later, I was able to repay the favor. The lady who only graduated from the eighth grade went on to get her GED and then an associate's degree. She became one of the first medical coders in Denver to utilize a computer.

My mom is now my friend. We still discover new ways to learn things. And it's still fun.

~CF Sherrow

A Teachable Moment

Books can be dangerous. The best ones should be labeled
"This could change your life."
~Helen Exley

The dog days of summer in Central Texas are hot and humid, and our modest home didn't have air conditioning. Momma and I were just trying to get through this August afternoon the best we could. Reading helped take our minds off the heat.

Momma was stretched across the sofa, a pillow under her head, reading. The skirt of her thin housedress rippled in the portable fan's breeze. I sat on the floor, leaning back against the sofa, a curious nine-year-old in shorts sharing the fan's flow. My book rested on the floor.

I looked at the thin hardcover my mom was reading, *Ed Nichols Rode a Horse*. A small silhouette of a cowboy on his horse graced the front cover, but otherwise the book appeared plain and unimpressive.

Before I settled, I asked, "Momma, what's your book about?"

Momma looked over the top of her book, taking a long moment before she answered.

"It's a story about a man, his horse and the hardships he encountered in Texas. Some of it takes place in Bosque County. Some along the Brazos."

With that, my mother returned to her story. I knew Bosque County was near where Momma had grown up. And I also knew it was best if I didn't ask any more questions. My mom took her reading seriously.

We'd been reading for the better part of an hour—the only sounds were the hum coming from the whirling fan and an occasional turn of a page—when I heard something unfamiliar. The sniffling back of tears. Then a sob escaped.

I turned in her direction and saw something I'd never seen before: my mother crying. Tears rolled down her cheeks. She seemed overcome by sadness. Something big—really big must have happened. My mom did not cry. My own face contorted and tears filled my eyes.

"Momma, what's wrong?" I got up on my knees and leaned over the sofa, staring directly into her face. "Are you all right?"

"Jennifer, I'm fine." Momma struggled for composure. She sat up and wiped her eyes. "You don't need to be concerned."

I wasn't buying it. This was not normal behavior.

"Why were you crying?" I asked in a whisper. The situation seemed to merit a whisper.

She looked at me hard. "The book made me cry," she replied.

I was trying to figure out how that plain looking book could make my mostly no-nonsense momma cry when she said the most amazing thing.

"The story made me sad when the horse got hurt."

That's when I learned a profound truth: stories affect us. A reader can be transformed and feel strong emotion over something printed on a page. Words had just become very powerful.

I looked into my mom's eyes. "Momma, could I read your book?"

I held my breath, afraid she'd deny me the right to read such a sad, adult tale. But my mom was a wise woman. She studied me for what seemed a long time.

Finally, she said, "I think you're old enough to handle it." Momma handed me her book.

I read *Ed Nichols Rode a Horse* from cover to cover, and in places I cried just like my mom. The powerful story told on those pages affected me, just like it had my mom. And, the shared reading of it united us. We were unified that hot Texas day over the power of the written word. And from that moment on, I knew what I wanted to become: I wanted to be a writer of stories capable of evoking such compassion and emotion.

What an amazing gift my mom gave me the day she allowed me to see her cry over a story in a book. The way she handled the experience made it a teachable moment in an impressionable, young girl's life. I wish she were still alive so I could tell her how much that shared lazy summer afternoon has meant to me.

~Jennifer Clark Vihel

Yahtzee Queen

Life is more fun if you play games.
~Roald Dahl

Since my family has never been that interested in watching television, we often play games in the evenings. One Christmas, I received *Parcheesi*, *Scrabble*, *Chinese Checkers*, and *Monopoly*!

When Milton Bradley came out with *Yahtzee*, the family quickly gravitated towards that game. No one loved it as much as my mother. After her four children were grown, she introduced Dad to the game. They spent many afternoons and evenings playing *Yahtzee*.

When her four grandchildren came along, Mother found a new round of challengers. As soon as the grandchildren could sit on their knees and write the numbers, they were introduced to the game. The front of the box read "five years and up" but Mother began with her grandchildren as soon as they could roll the dice. Since all the adults played this game, these tykes believed they were very grown up. They never realized they were actually learning to count, multiply and add. They thought of math as a game taught by their grandmother and played for fun. When they entered school, math was not a difficult subject for them.

This tradition has continued with Mother's great-grandchildren. And again, math skills are not problematic as they advance in school.

Yahtzee score pads are frequently in short supply. We often find them at garage sales or thrift stores, but sometimes we have to pay full price. While other grandmothers get stationery for Christmas, we know that *Yahtzee* pads are the perfect gift!

Ten years ago Dad passed away. Mother continues to live alone, and without a *Yahtzee* opponent in the evening she works word puzzles.

But *Yahtzee* is still Mom's favorite game. Mom is nearing ninety and keeping her mind active is one of the goals. She likes to play marathon sessions of *Yahtzee* when I visit her. Sometimes she even lets me win in order to sucker me into another game. She has truly earned the title of Yahtzee Queen.

And thanks to my mom, all her grandchildren and great-grandchildren have wonderful math skills. All from a family game!

~Linda Lohman

90

The Wisest Woman in the World

There is no psychiatrist in the world like a puppy licking your face.
~Ben Williams

The September I entered first grade, I'd just lost my beloved friend and companion of two years, our neighbor's English Bulldog named Duke. He had died from heat stroke during an extremely hot summer's day. The delightful, new experiences of school helped eased the sting of his passing somewhat.

Then one day not long after school started, I was walking home when a black Cocker Spaniel darted out of a yard near the corner of our street. I stopped and turned to him, and saw a side of dogs I'd never experienced. Growling and barring his teeth, he began to circle me.

Startled but deciding this dog simply didn't want to become my friend, I once more started for home. The moment my back was turned, he seized my ankle. His teeth locked into my flesh.

I screamed and kicked, and he released me. Shrieking, I ran toward home, the black curly ball in hot pursuit. Just before I reached our drive, he gave up and set off at a gallop back up the street.

Bursting into the house, so incoherent that for a few moments my mother couldn't understand what had caused my bloody ankle, I fell into her arms and sobbed.

Later, with my wounds cleaned and bandaged, I told her the story. "He bit me, Mommy. He grabbed me and it hurt." By then my words reflected more my sense of betrayal than pain or fear. One of the creatures I loved most in the world had attacked me, had caused me pain for no reason. "I'll never, never trust another dog as long as I live."

"Never is a long time, sweetie." My mother stroked my braids. "And that was only one dog. You can't judge them all by one that made a mistake."

I presume my mother must have called the Spaniel's owners, because from that day on, the dog, Robin, was tied in their back yard whenever I passed on my way to or from school. I was still afraid though. What if the rope broke? What if he came after me again? I dreaded passing that house.

I must have had nightmares about the incident because I recall my mother gently waking me to tell me it was all right, that Robin was safely tied up at his house.

But the trauma only worsened. I refused to visit my grandfather on his farm because he had a St. Bernard/Collie mix named Buster, whom I'd formerly loved and couldn't wait to see each Sunday afternoon.

My fear grew so debilitating that my mother had to walk with me past the dreaded corner house each morning and meet me before I came to it each afternoon. My days in school were haunted by a black horror named Robin. I couldn't concentrate. My teacher contacted my mother.

"Gail, you have to get over this fear," she said the following afternoon as we walked home from school together. "You remember my friend Emma who lives two houses beyond Robin's?"

I nodded, dread already rising. Where was this conversation going?

"She has a lovely black Lab named Chips." I tightened my grip on her hand. "She's invited us to stop by this afternoon and meet him."

"No, no, Mommy, please no!" I stopped and stared up at her, begging with all my heart and soul. "I hate dogs. They're bad. They want to hurt me!"

"Not Chips." My mother smiled gently down at me. "I promise. Have I ever broken a promise to you?"

"No… "

"Then trust me now. You know I'd never take my darling girl anywhere she might be hurt, don't you?"

I hesitated, then slowly nodded.

"Good. Let's go. Emma said something about baking sugar cookies this afternoon."

Moments later we stood on Emma's front step. My heart was pounding as my mother rang the bell. Footsteps approached, the door opened, and there stood Emma with a big black dog slowly wagging his tail by her side. Sweat broke out over my body.

"Opal, Gail, how lovely. Come in, come in. I'm just taking the last batch of cookies from the oven. Chips, sit."

Obediently, the big dog dropped to his haunches and sat watching us, tongue lolling out of his mouth in what probably was a canine grin but which I only saw as fang baring.

"Hello, Chips," my mother said. To my surprise he raised his right front paw. As my mother laughingly accepted the greeting, my breath caught in my throat. He was going to bite her. I wanted to lunge forward to save her but I was frozen by fear. A moment later we headed down the hall with Chips following at a respectful distance, tail still slowly wagging.

We sat in the kitchen. I had milk and cookies while my mother and her friend drank tea and chatted. Chips lay on the floor leaning against the back door. Our gazes met. His tail beat faster and his mouth opened wider. Could it be he was smiling, the way Duke used to? But Duke's mouth was wider and his teeth were all crooked and funny looking. This dog had big, straight, white fangs. But he did appear to be friendly. Maybe he wasn't such a bad dog after all.

I slid off the chair and stood staring at him. His tail wagged just a notch faster but not too fast. Not like he was getting excited or ready to rush at me. I took a step closer. He remained lying by the door, watching me. I took another step and held out my hand. Chips hesitated, then eased forward to sniff. When I managed to hold fast, he licked it.

My terror melted. I sat down beside him on the floor and offered the last of the cookie I held in my hand. He took it with such gentleness that I've never forgotten the touch of his soft, wet muzzle on my fingers.

Only then did I realize that Emma and my mother had stopped talking and were watching us. "Chips is a good dog, Mommy." I stroked the soft fur. "A really good dog."

"I know, sweetie, I know." She smiled.

My love of canines was restored. At that moment I believed her to be the wisest woman in the world.

These days, with four dog books (two of them award-winners) to my credit and a lifetime of wonderful canine associations behind me and continuing, I give thanks to my mother for her clever insight. She saved me from crippling fear and from losing out on all the wonderful opportunities dogs have given me throughout my life.

~Gail MacMillan

91

Happy Feet

Creative people are curious, flexible, persistent, and
independent with a tremendous spirit of adventure and
a love of play.
~Henri Matisse

Growing up, I didn't know anyone who shopped for Christmas in July, but Mom did because she was creative, clever, crafty and thrifty. I enjoyed tagging along to watch her find bargains galore, which consisted of various craft supplies, fabrics, trinkets and metal tins. Mom's motto was: "Making handmade gifts is giving from your heart." After we finished shopping, Mom treated me to lunch and showed me all the new patterns and craft projects she planned to make for Christmas gifts.

The making of Christmas gifts always began the day after Thanksgiving. Night and day the steady rhythm of Mom's sewing machine echoed through the house. I marveled at her sewing skills. At six, I pleaded with her to teach me to sew, but she insisted I was too young. Finally, when I turned eight she gave in and taught me how to sew a straight seam. By age ten, I'd honed the craft and would help Mom make gifts that'd accompany tins of our homemade brownies and cookies for neighbors, friends and family.

"I made these this morning. I thought they were unique," Mom said as she slipped on a cute pair of bright yellow terry scuffs. "I know you'll have fun sewing these terry washcloth slippers. They're easy to make."

"I love them!" I squealed. "I wondered why you bought so many bundles of wash cloths."

I caught on quickly to folding a thick hunter green washcloth in half and sewing the ends together, keeping in mind there'd have to be a small opening at the top edges to insert strands of elastic and yarn. Then I folded the top edges to the outside and stitch a straight seam all around about half an inch from the top. Once the elastic and yarn were threaded through and secured, I tied on a big silver jingle bell and made the remaining red yarn into a bow. How proud I was of my first creation. "Listen to my feet," I giggled as I twirled around Mom's sewing room. "Jingle bells, jingle bells…"

"There she goes, she has bells on her toes," Mom chuckled. "Adding the jingle bells was a great idea. You should make a pair of slippers for your teacher."

Once Christmas sewing and craft projects were finished, Mom and I baked brownies, bars and assorted Christmas cookies for gift giving.

I chose two Santa tins for my teacher's gifts. I filled one tin with a variety of Christmas cookies and placed the slippers I'd made for her in the other tin. "Let's make them look more festive," Mom said, and put the tins in a wicker basket with a handle and secured the tins with wide red ribbon, topped with a bow.

On the bus ride to school the next morning, several classmates teased me about my gift not being wrapped, but I ignored their remarks and asked what was inside their wrapped gifts. One gift contained a set of Christmas candles and the other gift was a necklace and matching earrings. They laughed when I confided that one of my gifts was a pair of slippers.

When I arrived at school, I went directly to the classroom and placed the basket amongst the other gifts on my teacher's desk. Afterward, a classmate taunted, "Her gifts aren't wrapped." Laughter ensued.

My teacher glared at the class, then reached for the basket and removed the ribbon from the tins. She opened the tin of cookies first, "Thank you, they smell delicious." she said and proceeded to open the tin with the slippers tucked inside. "Now what do we have here?"

"They're jingle bell slippers I made especially for you." I beamed as I watched her put them on her feet. Suddenly, the room was quiet.

She stomped each foot, and swayed back and forth to music only she could hear. "I have happy feet," she said. "What wonderful slippers. I want to order four pairs for gifts."

I was glad that we were dismissed at noon for Christmas vacation. All morning I'd barely been able to contain my excitement, as I wanted to tell Mom how much my teacher liked the cookies and slippers. And I had to get busy and fill her order for jingle bell slippers.

The ride home that afternoon seemed longer than usual. When the school bus finally stopped at my house, I leapt down the steps, ran up the driveway and greeted Mom on the front porch. I was out of breath and gulped for air: "My teacher loved the slippers and wants me to make her four pairs of slippers for gifts."

"I know," Mom said. "Your teacher called a short while ago. I told her she could pick them up tomorrow afternoon. We should put them in small plastic bags, label them and give the slippers a name."

I couldn't help but smile, as I envisioned my teacher dancing in the slippers. "Let's call them Happy Feet," I suggested.

As the saying goes, "She marched to a different drummer." That was my mom. And that was a good thing. I'm grateful she encouraged me to be the creative person I am today.

~Georgia A. Hubley

92

A Love of Words

There are many little ways to enlarge your child's world.
Love of books is the best of all.
~Jacqueline Kennedy Onassis

I can still remember my mother's voice as she read the opening line of Louisa May Alcott's *Little Women*. "Christmas won't be Christmas without any presents." I was nine or ten years old. She, my sister and I were settled comfortably in our den—Mom and my sister on the couch and me sprawled out on the floor with a pillow. As Mom read the cherished story about four sisters, I let my imagination carry me away. I could almost imagine I was there with the March girls, living in Orchard House, acting out plays and wondering if Aunt Josephine was really as mean as she sounded. The memories of that special time are imprinted on my heart and have influenced me throughout my life.

Mom was an elementary school teacher, so books were dear friends to her. I was the youngest of five children so our house was full of books by the time I arrived. Dad and Mom were both voracious readers, devouring books about American history, Christian life, and World War II, in which Dad was particularly interested since he'd been a turret gunner on a B-17 bomber over Europe. We kids had a bookcase practically overflowing with children's books. One of my earliest memories is of visiting a bookstore in downtown Santa Fe, right on the famous Plaza. It must have been during the holiday season because Christmas books lined the children's display area, and I begged Mom to buy me the book *Santa Mouse*. I still have it to this day.

When my siblings and I celebrated a birthday, we could always count on receiving a new book. Books sat under the Christmas tree many years as well, and even a trip to the grocery store might yield the newest Little Golden Book. Garage sale finds included sets of Nancy Drew and Hardy Boys mysteries, which provided hours of imaginary adventures. Being a teacher, Mom was like a kid in a candy store when the new Scholastic catalog arrived. She ordered books for herself, for her classroom, for us, and she always ordered a book to give to each of her students for Christmas.

Mom had always read us bedtime stories, usually letting my sister and me each choose a book, but the summer Mom read *Little Women* to us is a particularly treasured memory. Even though we were both old enough to read the story ourselves, there was nothing like listening to the sound of Mom's voice rising and falling, using different tones for different characters, and laughing at the antics of Jo and the others. When her voice would grow hoarse, she would close the book, much to our disappointment. "We'll read more tomorrow, girls," she'd say, giving us something to look forward to. When we finally came to the end of the book, none of us wanted our special time together to end. So Mom read Ms. Alcott's next book, *Little Men*, and then another and another, until the summer drew to a close and school began again.

Many years later I continued the tradition with my two sons. Some of the very same books that lined my shelves as a child now lined theirs. Every night, I allowed them each to choose a book for me to read aloud. Even after they were old enough to read on their own, we enjoyed sharing some special reading time, including the summer I read them every book in The Littles series, a favorite of their grandma's.

Because my parents taught me from a young age to appreciate the written word and storytelling, it wasn't a big surprise when I found I enjoyed writing stories, too. I'd been a fan of Christian fiction for many years, with bulging bookshelves of my own, but I'd never envisioned myself as an author until one day a story popped into my head and simply would not go away. Characters became real people in my imagination, much like they had back when Mom read aloud to me. When I shared my newfound dream of becoming a writer, Mom was all for it. "I'm proud of you, honey," she said when my first magazine article was published.

Mom passed away in May 2013 after a courageous battle with Alzheimer's disease. The dreaded illness stole her memory of the people she loved and the life she'd enjoyed, but many times I'd find her sitting in her bedroom holding an open book in her lap. The pages rarely got turned and her focus wouldn't remain long enough to understand what she was reading, but the love of the written word was so strong in her that even Alzheimer's couldn't destroy it.

After Mom and Dad were both gone, we had to sell the family home. I kept many of the books that belonged to my parents, finding comfort in their familiar spines and covers. A flash of memory of Dad sitting in his chair reading or Mom surrounded by her grandchildren with an open storybook brings me much joy.

Thank you, Mom, for sharing your love of words with me.

~Michelle Shocklee

Chapter 9

Thanks to My Mom

The Other Moms in Our Lives

Thanks to My Nine Moms

There is nothing to suggest that mothering
cannot be shared by several people.
~H. R. Schaffer

How did I acquire nine moms? This is the first question people ask me when I speak about unconditional motherly love. Before I have a chance to answer, they usually follow up with, "Is it a blessing or a curse?" My answer: It is always a blessing, a tremendous blessing.

I was adopted at birth in Melaka, Malaysia by my mom, Nyah. I spent my first eighteen years learning from her. One of the lessons she taught me was that everyone possesses a seed of greatness. She believed this seed was the key to success in life. The essence of this seed allows our dreams, goals and wishes to develop.

At nineteen, while attending college at Louisiana State University, I received the news of my father's sudden passing. I had just completed my freshman year. The timing of his death produced both emotional trauma and a financial crisis for my mother, my sister and me. The ensuing challenges led me to make decisions setting the course of my life, which caused me to not set foot in Malaysia again for fifteen years.

During this time, while living on my own in Baton Rouge, I began the journey of meeting my eight other moms, one at a time over the next eighteen years. I met my first two moms during my college years. My next three moms came into my life after I had begun working. I met my last three moms during my leisure time in the ballroom dancing community. The timing of these wonderful women appearing in my life was God-sent. These ladies found a way to mold my soul and guide my heart. They were my teachers, coaches, and counselors, always available to listen to my ideas and console me during times of need. Most of my nine moms have since passed away, but each of them left me with timeless recipes for living life that collectively formed the basis of my success.

I remember just before leaving Malaysia for the United States, my mom, Nyah, said to me, "Since you were a child you have been exposed to all kinds of experiences. Your father and I have done our best in raising you. Now you are about to embark on a journey where you will continue to encounter and gain new life experiences. Some of them, good or bad, will stay with you for the rest of your life. Always remember, it is how you manage these experiences that will ultimately determine your idea of success or failure in both your personal and professional lives." I didn't fully understand my mom's advice at the time, but since then, having gone through a divorce, leaving a corporate career of eighteen years to start my own business and surviving a personal financial reorganization, I can attest to the profoundness of her insights.

Coming to America at a young age was a dream come true for me. I was eager to embrace the new culture. My excitement to assimilate myself into the new surroundings and lifestyle led me to engage my Southern belle mom, Eleanora Carter, to teach me what I needed to know in order to blend into the community. She was part of my host family. Thanks to her, I learned proper etiquette and manners, adding to what I already knew from my years growing up in Malaysia. Eleanora taught me that, although a warm and engaging personality may open doors, it is one's character that will keep the doors open.

Youthful and energetic, I was always impatient when it came to getting things done. Quite often, I realized the decisions I made were not the best. If only I had given more thought before acting on my enthusiastic impulses, the outcome would have been better. One of the many memories I treasured about my Italian foster mom, Carol Wisdom, was her wise and logical approach to situations. Carol always reminded me that time is a luxury, and having faith that the right thing will come along at the right time and in the right way is a belief I should make room for in my life. This advice has helped me to pass on opportunities that initially looked perfect, but eventually unraveled after failing to endure the test of time.

A consummate perfectionist, I have been told by others that I radiate an aura of stiffness with my one-track mind always on business. This disposition was also the impression my sanguine Savannah mom, Toni Winters, discovered when we first met. Always happy, with a carefree attitude, she taught me how to live each day with gusto. Her self-assured personality convinced me to try new experiences. Toni made me laugh and lighten up by sharing this wonderful recipe for living: "Live like there is no tomorrow; however, always plan that you will have another day to live. What the caterpillar sees as the end of the world, the butterfly sees as the beginning of a beautiful life."

My pragmatic, part-Native-American Texan mom, Dee Jones, taught me to focus on today. Dee reminded me that what I did yesterday is not as important as what I am going to do today. It is my actions today that will define who I am tomorrow. This advice inspired me to fine-tune my personal mission statement. At the core, my mission statement is in many ways a reflection of the best attributes of my nine moms: a reminder to live with integrity, humility, kindness and a sense of humor; to seek healthy and loving relationships; and prepare to be of service to others. This declaration has guided my life choices as a young man and continues to impact my thoughts and actions every day.

I grew up in a spiritual family. My mom, a Taoism practitioner, prayed twice a day for her loved ones. When I was in high school, I enrolled for two years as a novice at a Buddhist temple in Melaka. I was intrigued by the philosophical way of living. In the United States, I enjoyed attending church with my moms. My spiritual and progressive mom, Elsa Mae Stevens, a Southern Baptist, was always thrilled to have me attend church with her whenever I came for a visit. One Sunday, while eating lunch after a church service, the conversation turned toward religion. She was surprised to learn that I was not a Christian but a Buddhist. Since the time we met, Elsa Mae had seen me as a Christian because of my values and how I lived my life. With a smile on her face, she said, "Regardless of what religion you eventually adopt, happiness is always felt by the heart and is not of the mind. Although you can choose to be happy, ultimately you still need to feel happy." On Easter 2008, I received my confirmation and first communion. Elsa Mae was delighted.

Being single, with time to spare, I possessed the perfect credentials for my friend Vickie. She couldn't wait to have me join her dancing group. Through her, I met my ballroom dance instructor mom, Betty Tamas. A professional instructor for over thirty years, Betty was a gifted communicator. She was a natural at conveying brief motivational messages to her students. One evening, I struggled to focus on my dance steps as I was still distracted by a challenging day. She whispered to me, "Dancing with heart and passion creates a lifetime of bliss in a three-and-a-half-minute song." With a big smile she continued, "Do you remember how you felt when you were dancing with Carrie last Saturday? You two looked great and were pretty much glowing as you danced around the floor." Betty reminded me to be deeply engaged in the moment. Since that evening, I have applied Betty's advice whenever I find myself struggling or distracted by multitasking.

Growing up in a small working-class family was a wonderful experience for me. My father was the breadwinner while my mom kept the Tan family well fed and loved. Although my family didn't have much, my parents taught my sister and me how to be generous with our time and resources whenever an opportunity arose to help others. My German mom, Dianne Hiese, took my understanding of empathy to a new height. I recall the year she spent much of her time caring, cooking and keeping company with a neighbor who was dying of cancer. This neighbor became a close friend. When I asked Dianne how she managed to endure the experience, she said, "Every once in a while a situation occurs that requires us to radiate our energy of positive goodwill, compassion and love for others. Until we try to put ourselves beyond our comfort zone, we will not realize we have what it takes to make a difference in that person's life and in ours."

A beekeeper by day and a ballroom dancer by night, my Cajun mom, Ginger White, is the most lighthearted person I know. She believes humor is essential in our daily lives. She uses humor to respond positively to challenging situations. With a big beautiful smile, she can light up any room and change any difficult situation into an inspiring one. Ginger taught me, "The natural life can always be funny and humorous. The most ordinary events usually end up being the sweetest memories. When we pay attention during the small moments, we will realize and appreciate the happiness when it happens." Incorporating a touch of humor into everything I do has added a new dimension to my life.

It was eight long years after I left Malaysia before Nyah and I were reunited. We kept in touch as often as we could, first through letters and then by phone. When she finally arrived in Baton Rouge to spend six months with me, no words could describe how we felt seeing each other after all those years. In the months and years that followed she had the opportunity to meet my other moms. Nyah was grateful she was able to express her appreciation to these women, my surrogate mothers in a sense, who had contributed generously to my life.

The road to my knowledge and wisdom has been defined by the relationships with my nine moms. The riches I have accumulated from these relationships have helped me to experience the American dream in a unique way. I came to the United States to earn an engineering degree, but instead I received an education about the power of relationships, the nature of love and the meaning of life. Thanks to my nine moms I have learned that real connections, true love and success are the results of authenticity, humility and speaking from the heart.

~Johnny Tan

94

Last Duet

They must often change,
who would be constant in happiness or wisdom.
~Confucius

My stepmother Ruth died recently, leaving an empty ache I would never have predicted based on our early relationship. I didn't welcome her into the family or make an effort to know her until after my father died. Then I grew to love her and regretted the lost years and my initial condescension and aloofness.

I first met Ruth in my twenties when my parents were separated. My mother was in Switzerland and we were told that Mom had "left Dad" and he'd sue for divorce. The marriage had been miserable and I accepted the decision.

My husband and I returned from an overseas trip and stayed with Dad in my parents' home. We came home one evening to find a merry party underway. Dad sat at the piano playing a duet with a short brown-haired woman. Other strangers sang along, waving glasses in the air. We stood awkwardly at the door. Dad leaped up, his face flushed, and introduced us to his friends—and Ruth. She had a big bosom and full mouth and stood straight with her chin held high. She smiled warmly at us. We smiled politely back. Two weeks later Mom returned, the marriage was "patched up" and there was no more mention of Ruth.

Six years later my parents divorced and Dad moved into a flat.

He was lonely and we often had him round for dinner. Soon Ruth flew down to visit her daughter and Dad started seeing her. Within a year they married.

Our family viewed Ruth with suspicion. We thought she'd zoomed in to grab him while he was alone and vulnerable. He opened his arms to her with joy and we resented it and kept a polite distance.

She was so different from Mom, who was tall, elegant and cultured. Ruth was short and curvy, and walked with a slight sway from side to side, like a small but undaunted ship bobbing out of harbour. We assumed she was less intelligent than Mom and looked down our noses at her.

She did things that annoyed us. If Dad boasted about his children, Ruth launched into stories about her own daughters or grandchildren that reduced us to chilled silence. One time, when my brother, sister and I had teamed up to buy Dad a piano accordion, I was annoyed as Ruth prattled on while we waited for him to open his card. I wished she'd shut up; I wanted to watch Dad's face as it dawned on him he was getting this wonderful gift from his children.

Sensing our disapproval, Dad withdrew into Ruth's family. My husband and I lived in the same city, so we maintained contact, having picnics and dinner dates with them. They had jolly piano evenings where Dad and I played duets. With Ruth, Dad became a different person from the quiet, controlled man he'd been with Mom. He smiled and laughed more, cracked corny jokes, and entertained. He was happy. Ruth always welcomed us in, but I never truly opened up to her and she chattered to fill the cool silences.

Then, out of the blue, Dad died of a massive heart attack. One morning on the bowling green he bent to play his ball, rose flushed and gasping, and collapsed on the smoothly clipped grass. Friends said the night before "he'd been in top form" at a party, greeting friends and playing the piano.

All through the funeral service, tears hovered behind my eyes. At the wake, one of Ruth's granddaughters started plinking on the piano. My heart hurt so much I couldn't face all the people standing around, drinking a toast to my father. A wave of dark, oppressive grief rolled over me. I rushed upstairs and locked myself in the bathroom, sobbing. I crouched next to the bathtub, my stomach twisted in an agony of loss.

People tried the door but I ignored them. Eventually, through my wrenching sobs I heard a knock, a gentle voice. "Chris, it's Ruth. Please let me in." How she got in is a blur, but she knelt beside me and held me in her arms, tears pouring down her face. Her warm bosom was immensely comforting. She took me through to the bedroom and kept soothing me. I saw the kind person she was, saw then what my father loved about her.

I got to know Ruth well in the following months. I visited her every evening. We'd talk about Dad, her life, and how she'd lost three husbands, each death devastating. She started to relax with me, becoming her natural self. I enjoyed her sense of humour, her delicious chuckle when she related funny things Dad had done. I realised my aloofness must have made her feel unaccepted and nervous around me.

Ruth had no university degrees, but was intelligent and creative. She worked for years as a bookkeeper, and made her own clothes to fit her short, full-busted figure.

One day she showed me a letter Dad had written when she was in hospital. He wrote how much he loved her, how he couldn't bear to lose her and how at the age of sixty he finally knew what love was all about. As I read the letter, my throat choked up and tears streamed down my cheeks. Poor Dad. His first marriage to Mom had been a battleground. I wished he'd married Ruth earlier. His thirteen years with her were the happiest of his life.

I stayed in touch with Ruth for twenty years, visited her different homes, chatted over tea or lunch, and saw her family occasionally. I grew to love her like a mother. Ruth was always interested in me and my life, appreciated every gift or visit. We laughed a lot. She had a lovely laugh, a rich gurgle that started deep in her throat.

She was positive about everything. When she had to scale down, Ruth accepted her reduced circumstances. She regarded the aches and pains of ageing philosophically. "What else can I do?" she'd say.

My husband and I moved into the country and I saw less of Ruth.

One day we made arrangements to have lunch and I booked a table at a restaurant. A week before our date, the unthinkable happened. A mutual friend phoned to say Ruth had died. She'd gone to lunch, risen from her chair and collapsed of a heart attack. She died instantly. I was stunned, torn with sorrow that we never had that last lunch.

I'll miss her laugh, her generosity of spirit, and her kindness. Since I loved my Dad, I wished I'd extended that love to her before he died, instead of after. She taught me not to judge by appearances, to laugh and be positive about life's changes. She was a healing companion for my father and I was grateful to her for that, and honoured she was my friend all those years after he died.

~Chris Rainer

95

Quadruple Love

*Whether your children are yours through biology
or adoption, they are yours through love.*
~Sadia Rebecca Rodriguez

Most people can't say they've had three mothers throughout their lifetime, but I can. I am lucky because I've had three moms: a biological mom, a foster mom, and an adoptive mom.

My sisters and I are identical quadruplets. From the information I've gathered over the years, ranging from newspaper clippings to an Internet search, our birth mother was in her early twenties when she gave birth to us, her boyfriend wasn't in the picture, and she didn't know she was pregnant with quadruplets until the second trimester. When she found out, she insisted that we be adopted together.

It was our dad's idea to adopt the four of us when he first heard about us. As the story goes, my mom looked at my dad like he was crazy. They had talked to family members, close friends, and even made some pro and con lists to see if they should take us into their family; after all, they already had two young sons (ages six and three) at the time.

My sisters and I were in foster care for about three months after our birth. From the information I found, our foster mother tearfully gave us up after she put "a lot of love and time" into raising us.

When my mom, dad, and brothers traveled to visit family in Tennessee for Christmas, they took a detour down to Louisiana to meet us. That was when they gave me the nickname "The Watcher." I was given this title because whenever people would come to look at my sisters and me in our cribs, I would be the only one awake, watching over my sisters and eyeing the people who were intrigued by us. Apparently, this was the first sign that I would be the mother hen of the four of us.

The news spread that we were the first set of identical African American quadruplets to be adopted in the U.S., and the media wanted to pick up the story. My grandfather has recently told me that the plane we took to our new home was also carrying a famous passenger—a champion boxer. When he disembarked the plane, he expected the news crews to rush over and interview him. Instead, they brushed past him and rushed up to my mom and dad to take pictures my sisters and me!

The adoption was closed, meaning that no information is given to the birth parent over the years, so I don't know anything about my birth mother except for the small bit of information I found. I don't know much about my foster mother either. All I know is that I am grateful for these two strong women. My mom is the strongest of all though. She dealt with four babies throwing tantrums, needing diaper changes, teething and fighting.

Growing up, I never felt like my mom was any different from a biological mom. She made my lunch, helped fix scrapes or bumps, offered up encouragement for new projects and ideas, and supported my endless dreams. Even though I technically have had three moms in my life, I wouldn't change that because I know my biological mom and my foster mom wanted the best for me and my sisters, just like my real mom, the one who raised me.

Adoption was never a secret in our family. I knew about it way before I could comprehend what the word meant. Since my mom loved my sisters and me like her own, I have decided that when I get married and start a family I want to adopt a child as well. I would also like for my future children to do the same. It is my goal for it to become a tradition in my family, because somewhere in the world someone needs a mom. Even if they aren't related by blood, they can be related by love. Generous amounts of love.

~Stephanie Jackson

96

Becoming a Daughter

Call it a clan, call it a network, call it a tribe, call it a family.
Whatever you call it, whoever you are, you need one.
~Jane Howard

My home life was rough. My mother was mentally ill and unable to care for me on a consistent basis. My father was distant at best and abusive at worst. We were extremely poor, lived in substandard housing and rarely had enough food in the house. I suffered from low self-esteem and did not deal well with people. I was a feral child, surviving by instinct.

Then God sent me "My Mae." I was her daughter's friend and I spent a lot of time at her house. They had food, a TV, and the house was appropriately cool in the summer and warm in the winter. I felt safe there, but like many of my friend's houses, I had to view it as just a place. I couldn't allow myself to relax or let my guard down, or expect my welcome there to continue. If I didn't allow myself to feel or to trust, I couldn't be hurt.

That started to change one early winter's day. I had showed up once again just to be somewhere other than my house. I wandered into the family room, and the first thing out of Mae's mouth was, "What is on your feet?" My stoic preteen response was, "Shoes." I had on a pair of canvas tennis shoes that had seen better days. They were soaked through from the cold, slushy snow, and my thin socks were poking through the worn canvas.

Mae was having none of that. "It is freezing outside and there is snow on the ground." She told me in no uncertain terms I needed something better and warmer if I was going to be out in the snow. That's how Mae did things. No sugarcoating, always direct. I didn't have anything else. I had never owned much that was either new or nice; I had always just gotten by.

Within the hour, we were at the store and I had a pair of new fleece-lined, lace-up brown boots. The shoes did so much more than warm my feet; they began to warm my heart. I started to let myself feel—to feel loved, to feel like I deserved better.

As the weeks turned to months, I continued to spend a lot of time at Mae's house. It started to feel like home, or at least what I thought home should feel like. I felt a flood of unfamiliar emotions and I didn't always deal with them well. It didn't matter to Mae; she was consistent and loving. But I continued to test her love and commitment to me, challenging her to see if it was real, preparing myself to be hurt once more.

Then one Saturday it finally clicked. My friend and I were lying around doing nothing, as usual. Mae sat us down, her daughter and me, and explained that if we were there and part of the family, we needed to help out. She stated "our" bathroom was horrible and needed a good cleaning, top to bottom, and we were to do it. After the initial excitement at being "part of the family" wore off, I realized I actually had to get up and do something. We went in, wiped everything down, and deemed the bathroom clean.

A couple of hours later Mae asked if we had finished. "Sure, take a look," we said, feeling quite smug. I laugh now, but not so much that day. Through a combination of her daughter's apathy and letting me do most of the work, along with my general ignorance on cleaning, we had not done a very good job.

"You call this clean?" she hollered from the bathroom.

"Sure," we said. "What's wrong with it?" She went over every inch of that room and explained why it was not clean and how to clean it. Who knew you were supposed to use a cleaning product or clean under the toilet seat? We begrudgingly redid the entire bathroom, scrubbing every nook and cranny per her directions. It really did look clean after our redo. I didn't know the difference beforehand, but I could tell the difference after. No one had ever taken the time before to explain to me how to clean a bathroom or how to do many things that I needed to learn. My Mae did that. She taught me how to clean, how to respect myself, and so much more through the years.

I held onto those boots long after I had outgrown them, and I still clean the bathroom from top to bottom the way she showed me. I owe who I am today to Mae, and I shudder to think who I would have been without her.

Like the bathroom, I didn't see the problem in the beginning. But after spending time with her, I could tell the difference in myself. I spent all the time I could in that home. When I could or needed to, I lived there. I may have been a damaged child, but I was not broken. Mae helped me find a way to fix what was damaged. I learned how to believe in myself.

Mae and I talk often, and I go "home" as often as I can. She is as much of a mother to me as anyone can be—she was then and she is now, over thirty years later. The day she bought me those boots, I knew she loved me. And the day she made me clean the bathroom for the second time, she became my mom and I became her daughter.

~Jenni K. Worley

Just Is a Four-Letter Word

The phrase "working mother" is redundant.
~Jane Sellman

I'm not sure when I first heard it, but now when someone says it, I cringe. Yes, I cringe, but then I quickly send up a prayer of thanks for what my stepmother told me years ago, as I approached my own season of motherhood.

I came of age during the late 1970s, a product and beneficiary of the women's movement. College and career opportunities abounded and every time I turned on the television, I would see a sharply dressed woman telling me that I could bring home the bacon, fry it up in a pan, and never let some mystery man forget that he was a man! When I turned on the radio, I would sing along with Helen Reddy, letting the world know that I was a woman, I let them hear me roar, and, look out people, because I was part of a large number of us that were, apparently, too big to ignore.

It was a powerful, wonderful time of change for women. It was a time of great expectations, because to whom much is given, much is expected. Women were given more opportunities than ever and I felt an unspoken expectation to do it all, to be that superwoman—to get a college degree, have a career, marry Mr. Right, have children, continue the career, be the president of the PTA, and still cook the bacon! I think it was during this time of change in our history that "just" became a four-letter word.

I would hear it come up in casual conversation and it always followed the well-meaning question, "So, what do you do?"

"Oh," the woman would say, somewhat sheepishly. "I'm just a housewife." Back in the day, we called stay-at-home moms "housewives." There would usually be a special emphasis on the word "just" and the woman would often look down or away, as though she had somehow failed her gender, or at least Helen Reddy, by being a housewife.

I often wondered why would someone want to be just a housewife? Especially when there were so many opportunities, so much a woman could accomplish? When I graduated from high school, I had plans. I was going to get my college degree, have a career, and write stories on the side. Then I would marry Mr. Right and have a family. It was all planned out, and in that order—but life had other plans.

In my sophomore year of college, I met Mr. Right. We decided to get married during spring break. Not long after, I decided to reconsider my major and future career and started taking some classes at the local community college. And somewhere in the midst of that change, I got pregnant—without a college degree or career in place.

That wasn't part of the plan, but I liked being pregnant and was excited about being a mom. Unfortunately, the timing of my pregnancy made it too difficult to finish that year in college, so I took a sabbatical. I can still remember the mixed emotions I saw on my father's face when I told him the news—happy to be a grandfather, skeptical that I would ever finish my degree now that I was pregnant.

I, too, struggled with the decision to step off the ladder, as I watched others continue to climb up rungs far above me. But as the birth of our first child approached, I grew more and more excited about being a mother. My nesting instincts were high, my desire to make a loving and nurturing home paramount. I felt conflicted. If only I could get that woman out of my head who kept singing about bringing home bacon and frying it up in a pan!

One day I shared my inner conflict with my stepmother, who had become my surrogate mom after the death of my biological mother years earlier.

"Mom, what if I just want to be a housewife?"

I will never forget, and be forever thankful for, the words she said next.

"Lynne, if all you do with your life is to be a housewife and mother, you will have done a great thing. You will have done enough." That was hard to believe at first. Wasn't it wrong to stay home and spend time with my baby and focus my energy on making a nice home for my little family instead of going back to college and embarking on a career? Even if it was my heart's desire, wasn't it beneath me to just be a housewife?

But my stepmother's words, spoken with such truth and certainty, stayed in my head. "If all you do with your life is to be a housewife and mother, you will have done enough." Maybe she was right. And maybe Helen Reddy and the woman with the bacon were right, too. The problem wasn't in whether I decided to put my energies into being a full-time homemaker or a part-time homemaker and full-time career woman or any combination of the two—the problem was with the word "just." The word "just" devalued the decision to be a housewife, or stay-at-home mom, but my stepmother showed me there was value in being a homemaker and that gave me the emotional permission to make that choice.

During the years of being a wife and mother of two, I was a stay-at-home mom, a part-time career woman, a part-time college student (I did eventually get that college degree) and a full-time career woman. Over the years, I did a little of it all and I appreciate the blessing of having choices and being able to choose what was right for my family at any given time. Now my daughter, a wife and college graduate with a fulfilling career, sees a season of motherhood in front of her. She, too, will be faced with wonderful opportunities and choices about how to live her life as a mother—as well as pressure from others about what that should look like. I have tried hard to encourage her to make the choices that are right for her and her own family, and on many occasions, I have shared the loving words my stepmother shared with me,

"Alicia, if all you do with your life is to be a housewife and mother, you will have done a great thing." And there is no "just" in that.

~Lynne Leite

98

Second Mother

A mother understands what a child does not say.
~Author Unknown

I n my junior year of college, my boyfriend moved to Los Angeles to start his first job at a technology firm. We had gotten serious in the short time we'd been dating, and we were prepared to begin a long-distance relationship.

We were not quite ready, however, when Rajeev's parents announced their impending visit from India. He hadn't yet told them about our relationship. They had no idea that I even existed. Neither one of us was quite sure how they would react. But Rajeev decided it was time to find out.

I arrived at LAX on a late Thursday night flight from Austin, Texas and met Rajeev at baggage claim. As we drove back to his one-bedroom apartment, my heart hammered in my chest.

"Have they said anything about us?" I asked. "About me?"

"My mom is excited to meet you," Rajeev said. "She's going to love you."

I didn't know how he could be so sure. I wasn't. His parents expected him to marry an Indian girl. It wouldn't be unusual for them to arrange his marriage as they had done for his older brother.

When we arrived at the apartment building, Rajeev took my hand and I followed him through the courtyard and up the stairs. He unlocked the door, turned to look at me, and squeezed my hand.

"Ready?" he asked.

I nodded and tried to appear confident. I wasn't.

As we walked into the living room, his mother immediately stood up from the couch.

"This is Annette," Rajeev said, pushing me gently forward.

His mother wore a forest green sari, her black hair pulled back in a low bun, and as she moved toward me, a smile spread across her face. She held out her arms. I paused, then hesitantly embraced her. She gave me a strong, solid hug, a motherly hug, and it took me by surprise.

"Hello," she said, pulling away to peer at me again.

Rajeev's father stretched out his hand to shake mine, his business-like approach a clear contradiction to his wife's.

I was relieved when Rajeev filled the room with his words and laughter. After several minutes of polite conversation, I felt myself relax. Surely the hardest part was over.

The next morning, I realized it had only just begun. Rajeev announced his intent to spend a few hours at the office. Was he crazy? He was leaving me alone with his parents? What would I say to them? What would we do? He assured me everything would be fine.

After he left, my shock quickly turned to anger, then anxiety. I locked myself in the bathroom and took an extraordinarily long time to shower and dress. The tiny amount of confidence I had gained the night before was lost. His parents were strangers to me, and yet I held onto the hope that those strangers would one day become my in-laws.

Over an hour later, Rajeev's mother quietly knocked on the bathroom door, and when I finally emerged, I braced myself for all possibilities: small talk, awkward silence, or outright rejection. I had convinced myself it would be the latter. They would tell me the truth while Rajeev was gone. That they didn't approve of my relationship with their son. That I wasn't welcome in their family.

Instead, Rajeev's mother took my hand in hers. "Come," she said, pulling me into the bedroom. She unzipped her suitcase, rummaged through her clothes, and pulled out what appeared to be a stack of fuchsia fabric.

"You try a sari."

It wasn't a question. It was a motherly command.

"Okay," I blurted, agreeing because it seemed the easiest thing to do.

The California sun seeped through the bedroom window as I stood half undressed in front of an absolute stranger. Yet something comforted me. Was it simply the warmth of the sun-soaked room? Or was it this woman's calm and quiet presence?

I slipped on the underskirt and blouse, and Rajeev's mother began wrapping the silk fabric around my waist. She folded the remaining fabric into narrow pleats. I listened carefully as she explained each step in her simple English.

"It's beautiful," I said, running my hand along the crisp pleats. At the same time, I couldn't quite understand what was happening. What did this all mean?

She smiled at me and continued tucking the pleated section into the underskirt. Finally, she draped the remaining silk across my chest and stood back to examine her effort.

"Very nice." She turned me toward the mirror. As I shuffled forward, my feet catching in the many folds of fabric, she laughed.

Outwardly, I was now an elegant, sari-clad young woman. Yet inside, I was still a shy, naive girl, full of doubt and anxious about my place in this woman's life.

My eyes drifted to her reflection in the mirror. Her smile swelled. Her eyes flickered. I didn't see an ounce of scrutiny or judgment. Instead she looked like a proud new mother. Rajeev's words came back to me, "She'll love you."

"Wait!" she said, returning to her suitcase and pulling out a small red fabric pouch. She adorned me in what felt like pounds of gold. Stacks of bangles for each of my wrists, a pair of dangling, chandelier-like earrings, and an intricately carved pendant.

I was still somewhat in shock when she pulled me into the living room to show Rajeev's father, who briefly glanced up from his newspaper. While she snapped photographs of me standing in front of the fireplace, I couldn't help wonder if this was her seal of approval. Her acknowledgment and blessing of my relationship with her son.

I stayed in the sari long enough for Rajeev to see me when he returned to the apartment just before lunch. His eyes seemed to say I told you so. Although I should've been upset with him for leaving me alone, I knew something important had happened that morning. I had been nurtured, comforted, and accepted. I had acquired a second mother in less than twenty-four hours.

When it was time for me to return to Austin, Rajeev's mother pulled me into her arms again.

"You come to India to visit," she said, nodding her head.

I nodded back. "I will."

Over the next twenty-three years, I would not only visit her at her home in India, I would welcome my second mother into my own home as well, each time remembering the immediate acceptance, unconditional love, and unwavering generosity she showed me the first day we met.

~Annette Gulati

99

Chicken Soup for the Soul

Eva

On the shores of darkness there is light.
~John Keats

y eyes were bandaged, and a silicone "buckle" had been fastened around my left eye to hold my badly detached retina in place. Since this was a second detachment, there was a significant risk I would lose all vision in the eye and a better than fifty-fifty chance my right retina would also detach.

I gripped the hospital bed's cold aluminum safety bars and focused on the vague swishing noises in the hall. I smelled disinfectant. So this is blindness, I thought. This is how Eva lived half her life. How did she do it? How was she so gentle, so comforting? How had she given me so much?

Eva's vision was already weak when she moved into my grandmother's house while Grandma's son (my future father) served in the military. With her bad leg, Grandma needed a housekeeper, and Eva needed a place to live. She moved into the unheated room above our kitchen. My father returned from the war with a broken back and married Mom. I was born, then my brother, and Grandma's bad leg turned out to be bone cancer. My overwhelmed Mom needed Eva to stay on. Even though cooking and outside chores became impossible as her vision worsened, Eva still could wash dishes and floors.

By the time I was born, Eva was completely blind. They say she clung to me and carried me through the house as if I were her own. She had memorized the placement of each chair, the number of stairs and which doors swung dangerously half-shut on their own. Grandma was scared Eva would trip and drop me, but Mom later told me she didn't have the heart to forbid Eva to carry me. "She just loved you so much," Mom said. "And her own son was too 'busy' to see her anymore."

Eva and I needed each other. She had time Mom didn't and tenderness Grandma didn't. Grandma was fighting cancer, but she would never have been a cookies-and-lap grandma anyway. Her idea of a boy's birthday present was a pair of new shoes. As her chores decreased, Eva signed over most of her small Social Security checks for room and board, so she did not give me gifts, except the greatest one — an education.

Before I began kindergarten, she handed me a worn nature book and asked me to describe the birds in the photos so she could tell me their names. She prodded me to study each bird and create word pictures. If I told her I saw a red bird, she'd say, "Well, that's probably a cardinal. But you should mention its black bib and the tuft of feathers on its head too. They call them cardinals because Catholic cardinals wear red robes and hats. That makes me remember what they look like!"

Some days she'd send me to the window to spot a bird chirping outside. She'd ask me to describe its looks and behavior. I learned to see details only that bird would have, the way it would hop and stop and turn its head sideways, and then hop and stop again. "Oh, that's a robin," Eva would say. "That's how they find worms. Next time watch one until it gets a worm — it can be quite a battle. Go out on a wet day when the worms come up to breathe." I asked her how she knew so much about birds.

She laughed. "Once you really look at something, once you really love it, how can you forget? Look at things hard and love them, and your memories will sustain you."

Later in life when I became a teacher and had blind and other handicapped students, I expected as much from them as from other students and I almost always got it. Some teachers, not familiar with the handicapped, encourage them to be passive by letting them slide, but

Eva taught me how desperately they needed to connect to the rest of the world. Each time I drew out a blind or deaf student in class—each time I pushed him or her to be more descriptive or exact—Eva's words echoed in my mind.

Eva had been a hungry reader and in mid-life taught herself to read Braille books from the library. She said, "My library card is the most valuable thing I have. It can take you anywhere, to meet people you'd never encounter and learn their deepest secrets." She told stories so vividly and made them sound so exciting, I begged her to teach me to read. When I was six, we spent hours in her room, piecing words together in basic books and even newspapers, so by the end of first grade I zipped through school reading.

"You're so smart!" Mom beamed at my report card.

"Eva taught me to read," I responded.

Grandma snorted. "No! She's blind. How could she do that?"

"She did! We read every day!" I think Grandma was jealous, because the next Christmas she bought me *Treasure Island*, *The Adventures of Tom Sawyer* and *The Merry Adventures of Robin Hood* instead of shoes. Grandma tried to help me read them, but after five minutes, she decided they were beyond me. And of course they were. But later, I secretly took them to Eva. I can't say I read the books exactly, but she knew enough of the stories that when I got tangled up or exhausted from trudging through a page, she would take up the thread and make Long John Silver growl and wink his pirate eyes and make me hear Robin Hood's men laughing around a campfire in Sherwood Forest.

Now, decades later and Eva long gone, as I lay in my hospital bed in total blackness, I thought of the operations she endured to restore her sight. The tools and techniques for eye operations back then were primitive, and her world remained dark. Eventually, from lack of use, her pupils drifted near the bottom of her eyes like half-sunken boats. That might be my eventual fate as well. I hated the prospect of feeling helpless, becoming a burden to my wife, and groping through a dark existence.

Yet Eva had gone on without despair, never complaining. She was grateful for having seen birds and having read great books and found joy in what she could still experience. Although she must have suffered deeply from her son's apathy toward her, she loved a baby boy and passed on her joys to him. She made herself a second mother. Instead of dwelling on what she had lost, she held onto what she loved and taught me to love nature and books as well. In my adult life I would become a professional writer, particularly about nature, and she started me on that path. And now, I realize, she's still with me, teaching me to look harder for the light in the darkness.

~Garrett Bauman

Joined at the Heart

Step Mom, you entered our family at my father's side with
wisdom and patience. Though of your flesh I was not conceived,
you cared and filled an empty need.
~Author Unknown

I was eleven and she was twenty-two when she became my mom. I had loved her from the day, six months earlier, when Dad brought her home to meet me. She was pretty, with the most gorgeous red hair I'd ever seen, which she wore in a shiny, smooth pageboy. I loved her hair, her Southern accent, how she dressed, and the motherly hugs she gave me. There was nothing I didn't love about her. I was thrilled that my dad had married her.

Soon after the wedding, Dad made it clear that there would be none of this stepmother business in our house. "She is your mom and you are to treat her as such," he said. Then he added one of his favorite proclamations, "And that's all there are to it!" I didn't need any coaching. I'd made up my mind the first time Dad brought her to meet me that she was the one for me. My brother and I had a difficult couple of years after we lost our mother. I was at the age where a girl needed a mother. Our new mom brought joy and laughter back into our lives.

Among the many things she taught me was to always look for the best in people, to respect others, and to be self-confident. I found this difficult to do when I encountered a group of bullies in the new school I was attending when we moved to the Deep South. It started the first day of school when a boy asked what side my ancestors fought on in the Civil War. I laughed because I though he was being funny. When I said that I didn't know, the hurtful remarks began. "Hey, Damn Yankee you talk funny! Don't they teach you how to talk right up north? What do they feed you in Yankee land to make you grow so tall?"

One day a girl grabbed my long straight hair and taunted me about not having curls as the other girls did. When I got home, I stormed into the house, slammed my books on the table and announced that I was not going back to school. It didn't take Mom long to get me to tell her what was going on and to come up with a plan of action. She told me that first of all I wasn't to let them know that what they said bothered me. Then she came up with snappy responses for me to use.

"Now we practice," she said. "Stand up tall. Look the taunter in the eye. Give him a haughty look, stick your nose up in the air and respond with one of the replies I taught you." Then she made me practice until she thought I had it right.

I had the opportunity the next day when one of the boys said, "I bet you even have a blue belly."

I snapped back at him, "That is something you'll never find out!" He blushed and walked away. A few more of Mom's catchy phrases and the teasing stopped.

Though always supportive, she could be strict too, and she had high expectations for my brother and me. Her words, "Once you start something, no matter how difficult it is, you have to finish it," still echo in my memory. Any time I tried to give up, she reminded me not to be a quitter. Her words were so ingrained in my mind that I still live by them as an adult.

Our first spring together, when my brother and I tried to teach her to ride a bicycle, we discovered these weren't just words she expected us to live by. She practiced what she preached. None of us knew what we were getting ourselves into as we started the lessons. For days we held onto the back of the bicycle as she wobbled down the street, only to see her fall over if we let go. One night I overheard my dad suggest she give up and she vehemently replied, "I can't! What would that teach the children if I did?"

Though she suffered some scrapes and bruises and our arms almost gave out, one day, to our surprise, when we let go she kept on pedaling. She had mastered the art of riding a bicycle and had taught us a valuable lesson about not being a quitter.

Even after she and Dad had two boys of their own, nothing changed between Mom and me. I was still her daughter. As I grew up, married and had children of my own, she was not only my mom but my best friend. I found myself passing on the many lessons I'd learned from her to my children, who lovingly called her MawMaw.

For years after my father died she remained a strong independent woman, but as she grew older and her health failed, our roles reversed and I found myself caring for her as she'd cared for me.

Then one night, after a visit, as I started to leave her room in the nursing home, I got as far as the door, and before I could open it, a strong compulsion drew me back to her bedside to sit and stay a while. She was tired, but she wanted to talk. She said, "I've always loved you as a daughter. We are closer than blood." She managed a weak smile before she added, "and we've always been joined at the heart." I held her in my arms and told her I loved her and how much having her as my mom meant to me.

That night, a couple of hours past midnight, I got the dreaded call that she had died peacefully in her sleep. I am eternally grateful for that compulsion, or as I've come to think of it, that gentle nudge from God that drew me back to her bedside.

~June Harman Betts

Just Ask

Sometimes the answer to our prayers is
to become the answer to someone else's prayers.
~Robert Brault

It was late summer and my parents were out of town. They lived next door to my ninety-three-year-old grandmother, so I thought I'd call to check on her. After three hip replacements, both of her hips were, at that time, out of socket. She was too old for the surgery to fix them. Her entire independence and mobility was based on a walker. Macular degeneration had taken her eyesight too, and arthritis had taken most of the use of her hands.

Grandmother was happy for the call. She told me about my aunt and uncle's kayaking trip, my cousin Clark's newest musical debut, my cousin Jordan's latest funny stories from preschool and the new steeple on the church. After catching up on all the latest family happenings, Grandmother told me my mom had been reading her my blog and my devotions. She shared how proud she was.

I had just gotten my start as a writer and was writing devotions for a mommy blog. When she mentioned my writing, I remembered a prayer request I had. I knew my grandmother was a prayer warrior and would pray about anything I asked her.

I wanted to attend a Christian writer's conference in Glorieta, New Mexico. I live in Georgia and had two young children at the time, so I wasn't sure about leaving them. To be honest, I was also afraid to fly, not to mention the cost of the conference, the flight, the hotel and my food.

I told Grandmother I had something I wanted her to pray about and gave her the details of the conference. I knew it would be a great opportunity but wasn't sure about the funds and leaving my family. As soon as I paused, Grandmother said, "I'll pay for you."

Thinking my grandmother must not have heard correctly my request to pray, I said, "No, no, Grandmother. I didn't ask you to pay for it. I want you to pray for it. Now just listen," I explained to her. In a matter of minutes, I detailed the whole story of what God had been doing in my life. Grandmother waited until I was completely finished talking. Then she said, "I heard you the first time. I will pray for you, but I will also pay for you." I tried again telling her no, but her next words stopped me.

"Carol, every morning I get up and say 'Lord, let me be useful to somebody today.' My eyes don't work any more. My legs don't work. My hands only work part of the time. This morning I got up the same as always, and said, 'Use me, Lord,' and then you called. I knew after listening to you talk, that today God had answered both of our prayers. He is doing a good work in you, and by allowing me to pay you are allowing me to be blessed too. I want to have a part in God's plan for you."

By the time she finished, I couldn't speak. My throat closed, my eyes were watery, and my heart was full. Finally, I managed, "I am so overwhelmed, Grandmother. God is so good."

God answered my grandmother's prayer that day. He used a ninety-three-year-old woman close to the end of her life to help me realize my dreams. He used her to pay for my conference and see me get published in many places, but most of all He used her to teach me a valuable lesson. You are never too old to be used by God. No matter what you think you have or don't have to offer, God can use you. You just have to ask.

~Carol Hatcher

Meet Our Contributors

Maggie Anderson lives in the enchanting city of Chicago with her boyfriend and their Goldendoodle puppy. She received her Master of Science degree from Johns Hopkins University. Maggie works as an environmental consultant, but her passion is reading and writing fantasy.

Katie Bangert was published in *Chicken Soup for the Soul: Find Your Inner Strength*. She lives in Texas with her husband, three children and many family pets. Katie's passion is raising awareness for those suffering from facial paralysis. She is currently at work on her second novel. E-mail her at katiebangert@hotmail.com.

Thanks to her mom's notes, **Gretchen Bassier** finally became a published author in 2011. Gretchen holds a B.A. degree in Psychology and works as a home healthcare aide. She loves animals, reading, writing and superheroes. Visit her blog for writing resources, reviews and more at https://astheheroflies.wordpress.com.

Garrett Bauman's essays and stories have been published in *Yankee*, *Sierra*, *The New York Times* and a dozen Chicken Soup for the Soul books. He is a Professor Emeritus from Monroe Community College in Rochester, NY.

Bobby Bermúdas is a native of California currently studying in Minnesota.

He plans to pursue a career in computational linguistics while hopefully writing horror fiction, about science, and about himself on the side. All with an understated, comedic bent, to be sure. E-mail him at Bobby. de.bermuda@gmail.com.

June Harman Betts is the author of the trilogy *Father Was A Caveman*, *We Were Vagabonds*, and *Along Came a Soldier*. June's stories have previously appeared in *Chicken Soup for the Soul: Thanks Dad* and *Chicken Soup for the Soul: Food and Love*. Learn more at www.authorsden.com/junehbetts.

Terrie Lynn Birney lives in North Carolina with her husband Chris. Born with cerebral palsy, she has faced many trials and always finds a way to overcome any challenge. Terrie has the support of a wonderful family and friends. She has always loved to write and is thrilled that her dream of being published has come true.

Susan Blakeney is a writer of fiction for children and young adults with several novels in various stages of development. "On Solid Ground" is Susan's fourth short story published in a Chicken Soup for the Soul anthology. E-mail her at susan@susanblakeney.com.

Suzanne M. Brazil has been writing most of her life and has just completed the first draft of her first novel. She is married to her high school sweetheart and credits him, along with their daughter and son, for supporting her writing dreams. One of her core beliefs is "give a girl a good mom and she can do anything."

Mary Wood Bridgman's work has appeared previously in *Chicken Soup for the Soul: Devotional Stories for Wives* as well as in many other publications. Mary has written two middle-grade books, for which she is seeking a literary agent. She is currently writing an adult mystery novel. E-mail her at marybridgman@msn.com.

Ayanna Bryce is currently studying for her Bachelor of Arts degree in both Psychology and Creative Writing. She loves reading, music, and drawing. She plans to go into social work in the future. E-mail her at ayannabryce@yahoo.com.

John P. Buentello is the author of numerous stories, essays, poems and articles. He is the co-author of the novel *Binary Tales* and several short story collections. E-mail him at jakkhakk@yahoo.com.

This is **Eva Carter's** third story for the Chicken Soup for the Soul anthology. She has always had a desire to write but never had time until now. She and her husband live in Dallas, TX. E-mail her at evacarter@sbcglobal.net.

Pam Carter earned her Bachelor of Arts degree from Bellarmine College in Louisville, KY. She is married to Rick Jeffries and has two grown daughters and two grandchildren. A retired IT professional, she enjoys reading, spending time with family and friends, and traveling with her husband. She is currently writing her memoir.

Jennifer Lynn Clay is twenty-five years old, and has been published close to one hundred times in national and international magazines and in several worldwide-distributed books, including *House Blessings*, *Forever in Love*, and *Gratitude Prayers*. Her work has appeared in seven other Chicken Soup for the Soul anthologies.

Carol Commons-Brosowske is a native Texan. She's been married to her husband Jim for forty years. Together they have three children and a granddaughter. She writes a weekly column for *Frank Talk* magazine, and has been published in Chicken Soup for the Soul and Not Your Mother's anthologies.

Harriet Cooper writes essays, humor, creative nonfiction and health articles for newspapers, newsletters, anthologies and magazines. She's a frequent contributor to the Chicken Soup for the Soul series. She writes about family, relationships, health, food, cats, writing and daily life. E-mail her at shewrites@live.ca.

Maril Crabtree grew up in Memphis and New Orleans, but has made Kansas City her home for many years. A former French teacher and lawyer, she turned to writing as her main midlife-crisis relief. Her poetry, creative nonfiction, and short stories have appeared in numerous journals and anthologies. Contact her at www.marilcrabtree.com.

Kyle Therese Cranston is a Boston-based writer who lives for the written word. Besides trying to get her first novel published, Kyle likes to spend her time dork dancing, drinking wine, and serving as co-editor of the hilarious essay series, *Mug of Woe*. Check it out at www.mugofwoe.com.

Lorri Danzig holds a master's degree in Jewish Studies focused on aging. Her "Let It Shine" programs for elders (www.letitshinejourneys.com) approach aging as a journey of deepening wisdom and expanded possibilities. Lorri's works of nonfiction and poetry are published in journals and anthologies. E-mail her at lbdanzig@lbdanzig.com.

Amy McCoy Dees enjoys reading and reading and writing! She is the proud mother of four. She is a civil servant and advocates for public education. She loves life and Jesus! She is currently putting the final edits on her first young adult novel, *Freedom's Secret*.

Denise Drespling is pursuing an MFA in creative writing from Carlow University. She discusses books and writing in her blog *The Land of What Ifs* (www.denisedrespling.com) and lives in western Pennsylvania with her husband, daughter, cats, and vast book collection. She's been called "more entertaining than cable" and "uniquely unique."

Rita Durrett is a teacher in northern Oklahoma. She is a mother of two sons and grandmother to four young boys. She belongs to a cat named Mousey and has two big attack dogs that might lick an intruder to death but, she admits, wouldn't bite unless someone came between them and their food.

Diana Creel Elarde, BA, MA, teaches psychology for Maricopa Community College. Her husband Vincent encourages her quest to become a successful writer. Amanda and Zdravko, her children, are her great sources of inspiration. She is a featured writer for *Thrive Detroit*. E-mail her at Diana@astarinmyhand.com.

Logan Eliasen graduated from Wheaton College with a Bachelor of Arts degree in biblical and theological studies in 2014. His favorite books are *The Great Gatsby* and *The Fault in Our Stars*. Logan enjoys a good cup of coffee, collecting vinyl records, and spending time with his family and friends.

Linda Fisher lives in Missouri, where she writes short stories and blogs about early-onset Alzheimer's. She became an Alzheimer's volunteer and advocate when her late husband developed dementia at age forty-nine. During her spare time, she can usually be found at her grandchildren's sporting events.

Judith Fitzsimmons is the author of *Not at Your Child's Expense*, due to hit the bookstores in 2015. A previous contributor to several Chicken Soup for the Soul books, Judith is a certified aromatherapist, technical writer, and yoga instructor. She lives in Franklin, TN.

Heidi Gaul lives in Oregon with her husband and four-legged family. She loves travel, be it around the block or the globe. In addition to contributing to Chicken Soup for the Soul anthologies, she is active in American Christian Fiction Writers and Oregon Christian Writers. She is currently completing her third novel.

Marge Gower has two daughters and four grandchildren. Marge enjoys her cockatiel, parakeet, and French Bulldog Bugg. Marge's publishing credits include *Devozine*, *The Third Kingdom*, *Love is a Verb*, Fellowship of Christian Writers' *Express Gratitude 2014 Chapbook*, and other Chicken Soup for the Soul anthologies.

Elizabeth Greenhill enjoys writing essays and articles about her many interests, including travel, pets, business, backpacking and wine. She has two adult children, Jordan and Regan. She owns and operates a consulting firm with her husband Lyn. E-mail her at elizabeth.greenhill@outlook.com.

R'becca Groff attended business school and worked in many interesting office settings before leaving that work arena to join the writing arena. She freelances from her home office in eastern Iowa. R'becca is an avid cook and baker, loves the outdoors and spending time on the biking trails.

Annette Gulati is a freelance writer living with her family in Seattle, WA. She has published more than seventy-five stories, articles, essays, poems, and activities in numerous magazines and newspapers. Visit her at www.annettegulati.com.

Alison Gunn is a writer living in Victoria, BC, Canada. Her work has been featured in *Chicken Soup for the Girl's Soul*, *Chicken Soup for the Soul: Shaping the New You*, and *Chicken Soup for the Soul: The Dating Game*. Contact her through her blog at https://cautiousmum.wordpress.com.

Kathy Lynn Harris is the author of two published novels, the Amazon #1 bestseller *Blue Straggler* and the national award-winning *A Good Kind of Knowing*. Kathy has also published children's books, essays, short stories, newspaper and magazine articles, and poems. Read her blog at kathylynnharris.com.

Carol Hatcher is a Christian author and speaker. She has been published in a variety of books and magazines. Carol is on The Presidential Prayer Team writing staff and writes a column for *Just 18 Summers* parenting blog. This Southern belle works to serve the least of these in Atlanta with her husband and three children.

Jill Haymaker is a family law attorney in Fort Collins, CO. This is her fourth story for Chicken Soup for the Soul. She also writes contemporary romances. Jill has three grown children and three granddaughters. Contact her via e-mail at jillhaymaker@aol.com, through her blog at jillhaymaker.wordpress.com or on Twitter @JillLHaymaker.

Christy Heitger-Ewing is a freelance writer living in Avon, IN with her husband and two sons. She is a columnist for *Cabin Life* magazine and also writes regularly for Christian magazines. Her first book, *Cabin Glory* (www.cabinglory.com), was published in 2014. Visit her website at http://christyheitger-ewing.com.

Carol Henderson received her master's degree in early childhood education in 2008. She is a fifth grade teacher, mother of three, and Gigi to nine wonderful grandchildren. She is currently working on several writing projects.

Darlene Herring received her Bachelor of Arts degree in Education and master's degree in English from University of Texas. She has two daughters and loves sharing her passion for reading and writing with her grandchildren. She is a retired high school English teacher and enjoys traveling with her husband.

Georgia A. Hubley retired after twenty years in financial management to write full-time. Vignettes of her life appear in various anthologies, magazines and newspapers. Once the nest was empty, Georgia and her husband of thirty-six years left Silicon Valley in the rear view and now hang their hats in Henderson, NV. E-mail her at geohub@aol.com.

Dale Jackson is a professional air ambulance pilot and writer. He received his MBA from Heriot-Watt University in 2007. He currently resides in Las Vegas, NV, and can be contacted via e-mail at dgjac@juno.com.

Stephanie Jackson, who prefers to go by Steph, is the youngest in a set of quadruplets. She is a self-described introverted-extrovert, or an extroverted-introvert depending on the day. In her free time she likes to write, read, roller skate, juggle, eat cinnamon candies, and craft.

Jeanie Jacobson is on the leadership team of Wordsowers Christian Writers in Omaha, NE. She's published in five Chicken Soup for the Soul anthologies, and is writing a Christian-slanted young adult fantasy series. Jeanie loves visiting family and friends, reading, hiking, praise dancing, and gardening. E-mail her through JeanieJacobson.com.

Bill Jager lives in Bakersfield, CA with his wife Carrie. Bill is an elementary school principal. He loves surfing, golfing, fishing and writing. His favorite times are those spent with his family, his wife, three daughters and their husbands, and his ten grandchildren. And of course, he loves to read.

Judith Lavori Keiser, founder of The Culture Company, teaches "peace thru play." Her Culture Camp programs guide children toward empathy using world cultures. Her Pearls programs for adults offer inspiration for life's transitions. Judy lives in South Florida. E-mail her at info@peacethruplay.com.

Nancy Julien Kopp is a Kansan originally from Chicago. She writes creative nonfiction, memoirs, inspirational nonfiction, poetry, articles on the writing craft and award-winning children's fiction. She's published in fifteen Chicken Soup for the Soul books, other anthologies, newspapers, e-zines and Internet radio. Read more at www.writergrannysworld.blogspot.com.

M.G. Lane is a Michigan-based writer and teacher who enjoys interesting conversations with witty people, traveling, documentaries and spending time with family and friends. She holds a B.A. degree in English, M.Ed. degree in teaching and is pursuing a doctorate in Reading, Language, and Literature. E-mail her at Readmglane@gmail.com.

A court reporter by day, **Jody Lebel** mainly writes romantic suspense novels. Her book *Playing Dead* was released by The Wild Rose Press in 2012 to excellent reviews. Jody was raised in charming New England and now lives with her two cats in southern Florida.

Mark Leiren-Young is an award-winning Canadian author, journalist, playwright and filmmaker. He has published two comic memoirs: *Free Magic Secrets Revealed* and *Never Shoot a Stampede Queen* (winner of the Stephen Leacock Medal for Humour). His comedy act, *Local Anxiety*, has been featured on CBC (TV and radio), PBS and NPR.

Lynne Leite is a storyteller at heart and believes in the power of story to entertain, heal and give hope. She loves faith, family, friends and fulfilling God's purpose in her life—and sharing stories whenever possible! Learn more about Lynne at www.CurlyGirl4God.com.

Aileen Liang is a grade 11 student who is primarily interested in science and literature. She enjoys baking, writing, snowboarding, and playing with her little sister in her spare time. In the future, she would like to become an optometrist and travel the world with her family.

Rachel Loewen is a survivor of an eating disorder, and she is a fierce advocate for mental health awareness. She is finishing up her high school education and plans on attending university in order to pursue her passions in psychology, medieval history, and film studies. E-mail her at rachel.loewen@sympatico.ca.

Linda Lohman writes nonfiction short stories about her faith, family, Yorkie, and 9/11 experience in New York City. She has stories in fifteen anthologies. A California State University graduate, she belongs to the California Writers Club in Sacramento. Expecting miracles, she would love to hear from you. E-mail her at lindaalohman@yahoo.com.

Lorraine Mace is a children's author and columnist. Writing as Frances di Plino, she is the author of the crime/thriller series featuring D.I.

Paolo Storey: *Bad Moon Rising, Someday Never Comes, Call It Pretending* and *Looking for a Reason.*

A graduate of Queen's University, **Gail MacMillan** is an award-winning author with thirty-four published books, and short stories and articles published across North America and Western Europe. Gail lives in New Brunswick, Canada with her husband and Little River Duck Dog named Fancy.

Mary Beth Magee's faith leads her to explore God's world and write about it. She writes news, reviews and feature articles for print and online publications, short fiction, poetry, and devotions, as well as recollections in several anthologies. A novel, *Death in the Daylilies,* joined her anthology work in 2014.

Dayna Mazzuca has a B.A. degree in Political Philosophy and diploma in Journalism Arts, plus courses in theology. She is currently freelancing, storytelling and leading seminars. She is working on a second book of poems, a workbook for those who feel called to write, and enjoying an outdoor life on the West Coast with her family.

Sarah McCrobie has contributed to multiple Chicken Soup for the Soul books. A native of Oswego, NY, Sarah enjoys photography, writing and making memories with her family in the small port city she calls home. She holds a bachelor's degree in journalism from SUNY Oswego and does public relations work in an academic setting.

Kathy McGovern is a well-known author and speaker in the Denver area. She is a frequent contributor to national publications on scripture and spirituality. Kathy writes a weekly scripture column that appears in parish bulletins around the country. Learn how to subscribe by visiting her website at www.thestoryandyou.com.

Larry Miller is General Assignment Reporter and Sunday Late Edition Editor for *The Philadelphia Tribune.*

Marya Morin is a freelance writer. Her stories and poems have appeared in publications such as *Woman's World* and Hallmark. Marya also penned a weekly humorous column for an online newsletter, and writes custom poetry on request. She lives in the country with her husband. E-mail her at Akushla514@hotmail.com.

When **Gail Molsbee Morris** isn't chasing after God's heart, she chases rare birds across America. She can be reached through her nature blog, godgirlgail.com, or Twitter @godgirlgail.

Irena Nieslony is English, but now lives on the island of Crete in Greece with her husband and her many dogs and cats. She has an honor's degree in Drama and English from the University of London and was previously an actress and puppeteer. Now she loves to write and has had five novels published, all murder mysteries.

Alana Patrick is a graduate student at the University of Minnesota working toward her Doctorate of Physical Therapy degree. She wrote "Safety Arms" in high school as a tribute to her mother, Jana. Alana continues to enjoy writing and was recently published in *Chicken Soup for the Soul: Hooked on Hockey*. E-mail her at patri149@umn.edu.

Connie Pombo is a freelance writer, author and speaker. Her stories have appeared in numerous publications and compilations, including Chicken Soup for the Soul anthologies. Connie enjoys traveling, running and swimming. She is working on her first novel, based in Sicily. Learn more at www.conniepombo.com.

Chris Rainer is a graphic designer with a post-graduate degree in psychology. She has taught calligraphy, bookbinding, paper-making and stress management. She lives in a small South African village with her husband, a Border Collie that herds birds and four calico cats who try to catch them.

Marisa Bardach Ramel is author of the forthcoming memoir, *Sally's Circle*, which was heralded as "beautiful" by *Wild* author Cheryl Strayed after an excerpt was published on xoJane.com. Marisa's work has also been featured on ModernLoss.com, Glamour.com, Seventeen.com, Prevention. com, and more. She lives with her husband in Brooklyn, NY.

Susan R. Ray's weekly newspaper column is entitled "Where We Are" and is available at susanrray.com. A retired teacher, she volunteers in a school and writes columns, memoirs, and stories. She keeps a bag packed for the next trip. Susan loves to play, read and write with her seven grandchildren. E-mail her at srray@charter.net.

Joe Ricker teaches writing at Ithaca College in Ithaca, NY, where he lives with his dog Kamani.

Tyann Sheldon Rouw lives in Iowa with her husband and three sons. She writes poignant and funny stories about her family's adventures with autism. Visit her blog, *Turn Up the V*, at tyannsheldonrouw.weebly. com or follow her on Twitter @TyannRouw.

Maria C. Sandoval received her Master of Education degree from the Azusa Pacific University in California in 2006, and taught K-12 in California and Houston. She is happily married and has four daughters and one son. Maria enjoys traveling, cooking, walking and writing. She plans to publish children's books and memoirs.

Donna Savage is a pastor's wife who loves encouraging women. When she isn't writing or teaching, she's trying to simplify her life, see more joy, and conquer her addiction to chocolate. Her phone contains over 100 photos of her grandchildren. E-mail Donna at donnasavagelv@ cox.net or learn more at www.donnasavage.blogspot.com.

Rick Schafer is a retired Navy Chief Petty Officer whose wife, Sara, has had three stories published in the Chicken Soup for the Soul series. They have two children, one grandson, one dog and three grand-dogs.

Rick enjoys volunteer work, creating gourd birdhouses and spending time with their toddler great-nephew.

Eva Schlesinger is the author of *Remembering the Walker and Wheelchair* (2008) as well as two other poetry collections. She has also contributed to *Changing Harm to Harmony: Bullies & Bystanders Project*, ed. by Joseph Zaccardi (2014), and has completed a young adult novel.

Edie Schmidt received her Bachelor of Science degree from the University of the Cumberlands in beautiful Williamsburg, KY. After thirteen years as an editor and radio host, she left broadcasting to be a stay-at-home wife, mother and freelance writer. She enjoys spending time with her family in Central Florida.

Thomas Schonhardt is soon to be married to his wonderful fiancée and currently lives in Columbia, MO. He works for an ad agency and volunteers for the fire department. You can find his work in additional Chicken Soup for the Soul anthologies. E-mail him at Tschonhardt@gmail.com.

CF Sherrow practiced as a physician assistant for twenty-three years and is now a counselor. She writes novels of supernatural suspense as well as a counseling blog on her website, www.cordsofgrace.com. She lives in Colorado, where she enjoys gardening, music, and hiking.

With both her sons grown, **Michelle Shocklee** and her husband of twenty-eight-plus years work as estate caretakers, living on a gorgeous 400-acre ranch in the Texas Hill Country. With sheep, llamas and chickens, plus wildlife galore, there are always plenty of crazy adventures to write about on her blog, michelleshocklee.blogspot.com.

Alisa Smith grew up in Nigeria, West Africa as the child of missionary doctors. She is a graduate of Duke University who became a freelance writer after a career as an intensive care nurse. She lives in Chapel Hill, NC with her husband, animals, children and grandchildren nearby.

Diane Stark is a wife, mother of five, and freelance writer. She is a frequent contributor to the Chicken Soup for the Soul series. She loves to write about the important things in life: her family and her faith. E-mail Diane at DianeStark19@yahoo.com.

Tyler Stocks is a writer and junior majoring in public relations at East Carolina University. His writing has been published nationwide. He enjoys traveling, reading and spending time with his girlfriend and their blind kitten, Fitzgerald. To learn more, visit www.tylerstocks.com.

After twenty-six years, **Mike Strand** retired from Andersen Windows and went back to school. He earned his B.A. degree in English Literature in 2014. He has been a columnist for the Minnesota Brain Injury Alliance's quarterly newsletter *Mind Matters* since 1999. He and his wife enjoy travelling and rehabbing vintage furniture.

Johnny Tan is a talk show host, inspirational speaker, consultant, author and founder of From My Mama's Kitchen. His Internet FMMK Talk Radio show has amassed over one million listeners. Johnny's bestselling and award-winning book, *From My Mama's Kitchen*, honors his nine moms. He welcomes your comments at www.JohnnyTan.com.

Jennifer Clark Vihel won the *Chicken Soup for the Writer's Soul* nationwide short story contest in 2001. Several other of her inspirational stories have been published by *Guideposts* magazine. From her cabin in the redwoods of Northern California, she also writes novels about second chances. E-mail her at jcv@northcoast.com.

Clarissa Villaverde is a blogger, foodie, traveler, and an artist. She aspires to be all of the things she ever dreamed of becoming when she was little, including to be a published author and a pianist, and she is working on those aspirations every day. She wants to see and experience everything the world has to offer.

Donna Duly Volkenannt fell in love with books when her mother read to her *The Little Engine That Could.* Donna lives in Missouri with her husband, grandchildren, and black Lab. In 2012, her humorous essay won first place in the University of Dayton's Erma Bombeck Global Humor Writing Competition.

Pat Wahler is a grant writer by day and award-winning writer of essays and short stories by night. She is proud to be a contributor to seven previous Chicken Soup for the Soul anthologies. A lifelong animal lover, Pat ponders critters, writing, and life's little mysteries at www.critteralley.blogspot.com.

Joseph B. Walker began his professional writing career in 1980 as a newspaper reporter. Since 1990, he has written a weekly newspaper column that appears mostly in small, community newspapers. He has published three books, including *Christmas on Mill Street.* He and his wife, Anita, have five children and eleven grandchildren.

Zachary Waterman is twenty-one years old and currently enrolled at Auburn University. He is also a combat medic in the Alabama National Guard.

Michelle Watkins, a Midwest native, began her professional career as an architectural designer. Feeling a need to work more closely with people, she left the field to become a part-time paraprofessional. She resides in Omaha, NE with her husband, Gary, and pursues interests in writing, gardening, art, volunteer work and reading.

Brenda Watterson left a career to be a stay-at-home mom. Her work has appeared in several publications, including *Chicken Soup for the Soul: Parenthood, Pooled Ink, Women on Writing,* RainbowTreeKids.com, and Scribes Valley Publishing. She lives in Algonquin, IL with her husband and four children. Contact her at brendah2oson@gmail.com.

Dorann Weber is a freelance photographer for a local newspaper as well as for Getty Images. Her photos and verses have been published on Hallmark greeting cards. Dorann lives in New Jersey with her family and various critters, including dogs, cats and chickens!

Susan DeWitt Wilder is the planner for the Southern Maine Agency on Aging. She and her husband Paul Austin have spent way too much time restoring their old houses in Maine and North Carolina. Twelve years ago, they founded Whole Home Resource, providing architectural design and interior decoration.

Karen Wilson received her Bachelor of Science degree in Nursing in 2014. While she works as a psychiatric nurse, she has had a lifelong love affair with telling stories. She plans to pursue writing more, now that she has completed her education. E-mail her at karlwils@ut.utm. edu.

Raymond M. Wong earned an MFA degree in Creative Writing at Antioch University. His writing has appeared in *USA Today*, *U-T San Diego*, *San Diego Family*, *Small Print Magazine*, and *Segue*. His memoir, *I'm Not Chinese: The Journey from Resentment to Reverence*, was published in 2014. Learn more at www.raymondmwong.com.

Jenni K. Worley is a proud wife, mother of one, and grandmother. She lives in the Ozarks region of Missouri and spends her time doting on her granddaughter, writing, sewing, gardening, and crafts.

Lori Zenker lives in a very old house in a small farming town in Ontario, Canada. She has great hopes of turning her entire back yard into a vegetable garden (a dream her three teenagers do not share). This is the fifth Chicken Soup for the Soul book she's been privileged to be a part of. E-mail her at lori@zenker.ca.

Chicken Soup for the Soul

Meet Amy Newmark

Amy Newmark was a writer, speaker, Wall Street analyst and business executive in the worlds of finance and telecommunications for more than thirty years. Today she is publisher, editor-in-chief and coauthor of the Chicken Soup for the Soul book series. By curating and editing inspirational true stories from ordinary people who have had extraordinary experiences, Amy has kept the twenty-one-year-old Chicken Soup for the Soul brand fresh and relevant, and still part of the social zeitgeist.

Amy graduated *magna cum laude* from Harvard University where she majored in Portuguese and minored in French. She wrote her thesis about popular, spoken-word poetry in Brazil, which involved traveling throughout Brazil and meeting with poets and writers to collect their stories. She is delighted to have come full circle in her writing career—from collecting poetry "from the people" in Brazil as a twenty-year-old to, three decades later, collecting stories and poems "from the people" for Chicken Soup for the Soul.

Amy has a national syndicated newspaper column and is a frequent radio and TV guest, passing along the real-life lessons and useful tips she has picked up from reading and editing thousands of Chicken Soup for the Soul stories.

She and her husband are the proud parents of four grown children and in her limited spare time, Amy enjoys visiting them, hiking, and reading books that she did not have to edit.

Follow her on Twitter @amynewmark and @chickensoupsoul.

Chicken Soup for the Soul

Meet Jo Dee Messina

Jo Dee Messina is an award-winning, multi-platinum recording artist with a string of chart-topping hits. A true performer since the age of six, Jo Dee moved from Holliston, Massachusetts to Nashville at nineteen and later released her self-titled debut, granting her the first of many Top 10 Hits. Her music career is filled with number one hits, including "Bring on the Rain," "Bye Bye" and "That's the Way."

A two-time Grammy nominee, she has won countless awards for her music, including the Academy of Country Music Award for Top New Female Vocalist; Billboard Magazine's Most Played Country Female Artist of the Year Award and a Boston Music Award for Outstanding Country Act.

Her latest album, *Me*, released to rave reviews March 18, 2014. In the spring of 2013, Jo Dee had created a Kickstarter campaign to raise money to make the album instead of following the traditional record label route. Her campaign allowed fans to be extensively involved in the creation of *Me*.

Jo Dee is an avid philanthropist, supporting charities such as the Red Cross, Harvest Hands Community Development Corporation, St. Jude Children's Research Hospital, the Special Olympics, and many others. She also organized a series of benefit concerts that raised $2.3 million for people affected by the Joplin tornado in 2011.

She is married with two young sons and is a dedicated runner, having completed many marathons.

Learn more at www.jodeemessina.com. Follow her on Facebook at www.facebook.com/jodeemessina and on Twitter @jodeemessina.

Thank You

e owe huge thanks to all of our contributors. We know that you poured your hearts and souls into the thousands of stories that you shared with us, and ultimately with each other. As we read these stories, we were moved and inspired by your personal accounts of all the things that your mothers have done for you. You made us laugh, nod our heads in recognition, make note of something we want to try with our own children, and even tear up a few times.

We could only publish a small percentage of the stories that were submitted, but we read every single one and even the ones that do not appear in the book had an influence on us and on the final manuscript. We owe special thanks to assistant publisher D'ette Corona, who read all the stories submitted for this book and helped narrow down the list for us to choose the final 101. She, along with managing editor Kristiana Pastir, helped us shape, edit, and proofread the manuscript, along with senior editor Barbara LoMonaco.

We also owe a very special thanks to our creative director and book producer, Brian Taylor at Pneuma Books, for his brilliant vision for our covers and interiors.

~Amy Newmark and Jo Dee Messina

Share with Us

We all have had Chicken Soup for the Soul moments in our lives. If you would like to share your story or poem with millions of people around the world, go to chickensoup.com and click on "Submit Your Story." You may be able to help another reader, and become a published author at the same time. Some of our past contributors have launched writing and speaking careers from the publication of their stories in our books!

We only accept story submissions via our website. They are no longer accepted via mail or fax.

To contact us regarding other matters, please send us an e-mail through webmaster@chickensoupforthesoul.com, or fax or write us at:

Chicken Soup for the Soul
P.O. Box 700
Cos Cob, CT 06807-0700
Fax: 203-861-7194

One more note from your friends at Chicken Soup for the Soul: Occasionally, we receive an unsolicited book manuscript from one of our readers, and we would like to respectfully inform you that we do not accept unsolicited manuscripts and we must discard the ones that appear.

teleflora®

We want to thank Teleflora for sharing the beautiful floral arrangement on our front cover!

Teleflora's "Sunny Day Pitcher of Daisies" is a perfect gift for Mother's Day or any other occasion. A cheerful bouquet of daisies in a keepsake pitcher that is sure to please for years to come.

Order Yours Today!

www.teleflora.com   800-835-3356

Chicken Soup for the Soul.

The Power *of* Forgiveness

101 Stories about How to Let Go and Change Your Life

Amy Newmark & Anthony Anderson

Forgiveness frees us to get on with our lives and we can all benefit from letting go of our anger. Whether it's forgiving a major wrong or a minor blunder, forgiving someone is healing and freeing. You don't have to forget or condone what happened, but letting go of your anger improves your wellbeing and repairs relationships. You will be inspired to change your life through the power of forgiveness as you read the 101 stories in this book about forgiving others, changing your attitude, healing and compassion.

978-1-61159-942-8

More bestsellers to

Chicken Soup for the Soul

Hope & Miracles

101 Inspirational Stories of Faith, Answered Prayers & Divine Intervention

Amy Newmark
and Natasha Stoynoff
Foreword by John Edward

Good things do happen to good people! These 101 true stories of wondrous connections, divine intervention and answered prayers show miracles and good happen every day, giving hope whenever you need it most. You will be amazed and uplifted as you read these inspiring stories. Great for everyone — religious and not — who seeks enlightenment and inspiration through a good story.

978-1-61159-944-2

brighten your day

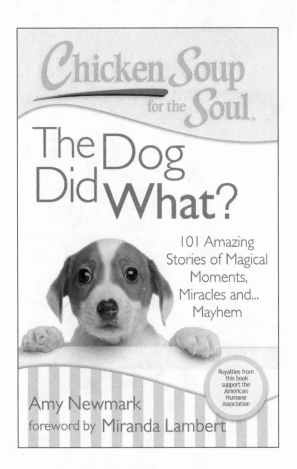

Chicken Soup for the Soul®

The Dog Did What?

101 Amazing Stories of Magical Moments, Miracles and... Mayhem

Royalties from this book support the American Humane Association

Amy Newmark
foreword by Miranda Lambert

Our canine friends make us smile every day with their crazy antics, their loving companionship, and their amazing intuition. You will enjoy reading the 101 heart-warming and often hysterical stories in this book about our canine companions and the magic they bring to our lives. This collection will make you laugh and touch your heart. We know you'll be saying, "The dog did what?"

978-1-61159-937-4

Bestselling stories about

Chicken Soup for the Soul

for the **Soul**

The Cat Did What?

101 Amazing Stories of Magical Moments, Miracles and... Mischief

Royalties from this book support the American Humane Association

Amy Newmark
foreword by Miranda Lambert

Our feline friends constantly surprise and charm us with their silly antics, their loving connections with our family members, and their surprising intelligence. You will enjoy reading all the 101 amazing and humorous stories in this collection about the mischief, miracles, and magic our cats bring to our lives. After reading these stories we know you'll say, "The cat did what?"

978-1-61159-936-7

the rest of the family

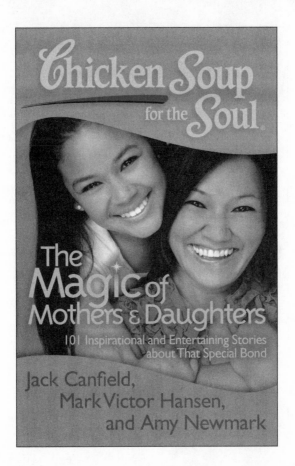

Chicken Soup for the Soul

The Magic of Mothers & Daughters

101 Inspirational and Entertaining Stories about That Special Bond

Jack Canfield, Mark Victor Hansen, and Amy Newmark

Mothers and daughters. They are, at the same time, very similar and completely unique. This relationship — through birth, childhood, teen years, adulthood, grandchildren, aging, and every step in between — can be the best, the hardest, and the sweetest. Mothers and daughters will laugh, cry, and find inspiration in this collection of stories that remind them of their shared love, appreciation and special bond.

978-1-935096-81-8

More love